For
Not to be taken
from the room.
reference

The *Complete*
Footwear Dictionary

The *Complete*
Footwear Dictionary

Compiled and Edited
by
William A. Rossi, D. P. M.

KRIEGER PUBLISHING COMPANY
MALABAR, FLORIDA
1994

Original Edition 1994

Printed and Published by
KRIEGER PUBLISHING COMPANY
KRIEGER DRIVE
MALABAR, FLORIDA 32950

FROM A DECLARATION OF PRINCIPLES JOINTLY ADOPTED BY A COMMITTEE OF THE AMERICAN BAR ASSOCIATION AND A COMMITTEE OF PUBLISHERS:

This publication is designed to provide accurate and authoritative information in regard to the subject matter covered. It is sold with the understanding that the publisher is not engaged in rendering legal, accounting, or other professional service. If legal advice or other expert assistance is required, the services of a competent professional person should be sought.

Library of Congress Cataloging-In-Publication Data

Rossi, William A.
    The complete footwear dictionary / compiled and edited by William
A. Rossi.—Original ed.
        p.   cm.
    ISBN 0-89464-715-6 (acid-free paper)
    1. Footwear-Dictionaries. I. Title.
TS947.R67   1992   91-48230
685′.3′03—dc20   CIP

10 9 8 7 6 5 4 3 2

About the Editor

William A. Rossi is a doctor of podiatric medicine (D.P.M.) and a widely recognized authority on footwear and its related fields. His experience in the footwear industry covers almost a half century. His father started as a custom shoemaker, then operated a family shoe store for more than 50 years. After graduating from podiatry college, Dr. Rossi was involved for several years in podiatry practice, teaching, and research.

But it was footwear and the footwear industry that attracted him. His earlier writings groomed him for the publishing field where he served for twenty years as editor of two footwear industry publications and involved him in all facets of the industry—retailing, manufacturing, tanning, styling, fitting, management, sales, technology, the foot/shoe relationship. He was particularly fascinated by the history of footwear and the shoe industry. In 1972, he launched William A. Rossi Associates, shoe industry management and marketing consultants, in which he is still active.

Dr. Rossi is the author of seven books on footwear and the shoe business, plus four retail sales training manuals and over 600 published articles. He has visited and studied the footwear industry in some 28 different countries, including the former Soviet Union and the East European nations, and has published reports on most of them. He is also the author of the extensive articles on footwear in the *Encyclopedia Britannica* and the *Columbia Encyclopedia*. His monthly articles over the past ten years in *Footwear News Magazine*, a series called "The Selling Floor," have been widely read and followed for their down-to-earth practicality.

He has conducted seminars for retailers, has lectured in England, Canada and Japan, and has given scores of talks before shoe industry groups. As a long-time student of the footwear industry, he is perhaps "the ultimate scholar" in his field. His unique background has given him a panoramic view of the world of footwear, making him eminently qualified to compile and edit THE *COMPLETE* FOOTWEAR DICTIONARY.

PREFACE

Over the years there have been several published dictionaries and lexicons related to footwear. All have two shortcomings: they are either too specialized or too limited in content and scope. They tend to focus mainly on one segment, such as leather or shoe manufacturing. Most are little more than glossaries and there is virtually no dictionary dealing with footwear retailing or footwear fashion. Further, because the language of shoe business is constantly evolving, many recently coined terms cannot be found in existing dictionaries.

Throughout my 20 years as editor of two footwear industry publications, my editorial staffs and I had frequent need for a single, definitive guide to footwear industry terminology to ensure accuracy in preparing editorial copy. But none was available. The editorial process became frustrating because we found ourselves constantly having to reach for different dictionaries or other sources to find the terms we required. It consumed unnecessary time and effort.

Why, I often asked myself, wasn't there one *complete* footwear dictionary—one all-encompassing volume? Why wasn't there a single dictionary that included all the important terms embracing footwear retailing, manufacturing, leather, man-made materials and fabrics, fashion and styling, shoe components, foot anatomy and foot health, lasts, shoe fitting, handbags, history?

I waited many years for such a dictionary to appear. It never has. We have thus continued to have a "language barrier" among shoe manufacturers, retailers, fitters, suppliers, foot and shoe therapists, technicians, etc. We are an industry of specialists, compartmentalized and operating within a fragmented chain of shoe business language communications.

It is my hope that this new dictionary—the first comprehensive footwear dictionary ever published—will finally resolve this long-standing problem. Several years of intensive research have gone into preparing this work. I have deliberately avoided the more technical terms such as those relating to leather tanning, shoe manufacturing, machinery, chemicals, medical, etc. The objective has been to create a practical volume that can provide quick and easy reference on almost any needed footwear-related terminology.

While it is selective in content, our dictionary nevertheless has a very broad scope and substantial depth. It contains nearly 4,000 terms and definitions, an unprecedented range. There are, for example, terms for 81 different kinds of boots, 70 different kinds of leathers, 59 kinds of heels, 38 shoe fabrics, 30 shoe constructions, 26 kinds of slippers, 20 kinds of handbags, 12 different kinds of shoe straps, 18 types of athletic or sports footwear, plus hundreds of shoe retailing terms, scores of shoe fashion terms in addition to numerous foot terms, and so on. Further, the entire dictionary is cross-referenced for easy search.

As a bonus, I have added two unusual appendixes. One deals with the origin of common shoe terms like oxford, pump, boot, sandal, clog, blucher, bal, ghillie, mule, suede, patent, and many more. Also listed are the surprising number of words in the English language that have foot and footwear origins—words like scruple, slipshod, blackguard, buck, cop, bootlegger, pecuniary, flapper, etc. These supplements are informative and entertaining.

Does the industry really need a comprehensive dictionary? After all, it has managed without one for these many years. However, being without a good dictionary is like being in a foreign country without understanding or being able to speak or read the native language. You can still manage. But you also miss a great deal—the pleasure of being able to converse fluently, or to move about with confidence, or to fully absorb and understand what is seen and heard, or to fully enjoy the native land and its customs and people.

Certainly one should be literate in the language of his or her own profession, business or industry. The better one understands and speaks one's "native language"—in this case, the language of shoe business—the better chance of success and the greater the enjoyment of living and functioning within that environment.

William A. Rossi, D.P.M.
1994

A

A. Designation for a narrow shoe width. See also *shoe size* and *width*.

AA to AAAAA. Designations for progressively narrower shoe widths. (See also *shoe size* and *width*.

abduction. To move outwardly or away from. E.g., abduction of the forefoot on weight bearing.

abrasion resistance. The ability of a material or component to resist abrasion or wear.

accent. Emphasis or prominence given to a design feature or decorative color in the costume or shoe.

accessory. An article of apparel that helps to complete the costume, such as shoes, handbag, or neckwear. Selected to harmonize with or accent the costume's design or color.

accounts payable. Debts, bills, or invoices due for payment.

Achilles notch. See *notched collar*.

Achilles tendon. The tendon extending down from the calf muscles and attached to the back of the heel bone. The largest and strongest tendon of the body.

acquatic shoes. Made of materials not affected by water, with casual or sportswear styling. Used for water sports, beachwear, or boatwear.

acrobatic shoe. A lightweight, soft upper shoe with soft, flexible sole, often buckskin. Used by acrobats and circus performers.

active shoe. A somewhat loose designation for footwear designed and used for wear by people in foot-active occupations other than sports. Usually casual in styling.

acupressure. A skilled form of pressure manipulation of particular sites on the body or foot with the hands or fingers to alleviate a disorder or distress of the part. See also *reflexology*.

adduction. To move inwardly. E.g., a turning inward of the forefoot toward the other foot.

adhesive. A sticky substance used to bond two or more pieces of material. In the shoe trade also known as *cement* and used to bond the outsole or linings to the upper.

adjustment. 1) In the store, a correction or settlement with a customer who returns the merchandise for a revised price or credit or replacement. 2) The fastening that holds the shoe in place on the foot, such as a buckle, strap, or button. 3) Any change in the shoe via a modification (insole insert, wedge, cookie) that makes the shoe fit or feel better or accommodates some foot disorder.

advertising. Printed, spoken, or visual display material and information to describe and enhance a product, service, or business via any of various forms of media: newspapers, magazines, radio, television, billboards, direct mail.

advertising allowance. A credit or discount given to the retailer by the vendor to advertise or promote the vendor's merchandise or brand. Also called a promotional allowance. See also *cooperative advertising*.

advertising budget. The sum allocated by a business for advertising, usually as a percentage of sales.

advertising mat. A prepared matrix or printed form, or photo, copy and layout, provided to the retailer by the vendor to advertise the vendor's merchandise in a local newspaper or other print media, with space left for the retailer's imprint or logo.

aerobic. Referring to oxygen intake, or stimulating oxygen and blood flow through the body by some form of physical exercise.

aerobic shoe. A sneaker-type shoe designed for use with aerobic exercises or aerobic dancing.

after market. For certain products, a secondary or follow-up market. E.g.: cushion insoles sold primarily to the shoe manufacturer to be incorporated in the shoe, then also sold separately to consumers via retailers as a packaged product.

age of stock. The length of time that unsold merchandise has been in stock.

Aerobic shoe.

aging of shoe. The process of the shoe wearing out or "growing old" through combinations of abrasion, perspiration, chemical erosion, and thermal conditions.

aglet. The metal or plastic tip of a shoe lace.

air sole. An outsole or midsole containing tubes or compartments holding air, creating a cushioned effect for the foot. Used in some sports or comfort shoes.

a la mode. French term meaning in fashion or according to the current fashion.

Alaska shoe. A heavy overshoe with rubber sole and rubberized upper, usually of vulcanized construction.

Albert. trade term for an A-width shoe.

alcibade. A low, laced military boot similar to the modern hightop sneaker, except made of heavy leather. Worn by Greek soldiers and named after the Greek general Alcibades (540–404 B.C.E.)

allied shoe trades. Businesses which serve as suppliers to footwear manufacturers, such as tanners, makers of shoe components and materials, and related services.

allover. Covering the entire surface with one material, color or pattern design, such as a plain, black patent pump.

alligator leather. See *leather*.

allowance. In fitting children's shoes, the extra length or width allowed for foot growth. In adult shoes, the allowance of size for foot stretch or expansion on weight bearing.

allowance. In a store, the credit or refund given to the customer for return of purchased shoes because of some defect or functional fault.

almond toe. A tapered toe or profile shaped like an almond. Also known as a *petal* or *thumbprint toe*.

alpargata. A sandal-like shoe of Spain and South America, often with rope sole and held on the foot with thongs.

alum tannage. See *tannage*.

ambulatory. Of or for walking; able to walk; not confined to a bed or wheelchair.

American welt. See *shoe construction*.

anatomical last. A last contoured on the bottom to conform to the sole shape of the foot. It may have a cupped heel, an arch contour, or a raised metatarsal.

anatomical shoe. A shoe made over an anatomical last. It may have additional orthotic features for the insole or counter or heel.

aniline dyes. A group of hundreds of synthetic dyes derived from coal tar products. Some are used for dyeing leathers to give the popular aniline finish. See also *finish*.

aniline finish. See *finish*.

animated display. Any display, window or interior, with moving or animated parts.

animal shoes. Special shoes or coverings, usually padded, for paws or hooves of certain animals to protect from extreme cold, rocky, or harsh terrain, or on long treks.

ankle. The joint connecting the lower ends of the two leg bones (tibia and fibula) with the top surface of the talus bone of the foot. It includes the ligaments and other tissues of the joint.

ankle tips. See *malleolus*.

ankle collar. A padded collar around the topline of the quarter to soften the rubbing of the shoe rim against the ankle bone tips and heel tendon. Usually on active sports footwear.

ankle corset. An elasticized band worn around the ankle and instep for support.

ankle sprain. A violent twisting or side bend of the ankle with traumatic stress on the ankle ligaments, followed by swelling and pain.

ankle strap. See *strap shoe*.

ankle stay. Used vertically inside an ankle-high boot, usually children's, between the upper and lining, much like corset stays, for extra support of the ankle. Used in some juvenile orthopedic shoes.

ankle support. Any device or material for support of the ankle or protection against ankle injury, or for reduction of ankle swelling.

anklet. 1) A fabric or knitted cloth worn around the ankle for warmth. 2) An elasticized material worn around the ankle for support. 3) Short hose reaching just over the ankle. 4) An ornament worn around the ankle.

ankylosis. A fixation or fusion of any joint, as in the foot.

antelope leather. See *leather*.

anterior. In front, forward.

anterior heel. A particular kind of metatarsal bar. See also *bar*.

anthropometry. The science and study of measurements of the body or sections of the body. Foot anthropometry (podoanthropometry) is used to determine or establish foot types.

anti-bacterial. Substances that destroy or prohibit the growth of bacteria inside a shoe or on the surface of the foot.

anti-fungal. A substance that destroys or prohibits the growth of fungus on a shoe or foot.

antique finish. See *finish*.

antique leather. Crushed leather with a smooth finish, dyed brown or tan. The dye settles in the hollows of the surface without sinking into the ridges. Thus the deeper portions of the grain are more heavily dyed than the ridges, resulting in a weathered look popular in some kinds of footwear.

antique shoe. Museum-type footwear a century or more old.

antiquing. Applying special finishes to leather or shoes to produce a weathered or burnished or dual-tone effect.

anti-slip socks. A fabric sock with a thin-layered rubber sole with traction design. Used indoors as a slipper sock that prevents slipping.

anti-static shoe. See *conductive shoe*.

aponeurosis. A fibrous membrane that covers certain muscles and connects them to tendons.

appliance. Any orthotic device as a separate unit or incorporated into the shoe, designed for comfort, corrective, or modifying purposes for either the foot or shoe.

appliqué. A decoration, such as a floral design, applied to a surface. Sometimes used for ornamentation of shoe vamps.

apres-ski shoe. A shoe or demi-boot, usually warm-lined, worn for after-ski occasions indoors or outdoors.

apron. An inserted or overlaid part of the vamp in a moccasin. See also *plug*.

apron tongue. See *tongue*.

arch. Any arched structure of the foot. The foot has two "true" arches (the long inner and the transverse). In addition are the long outer and the metatarsal arches which are not considered "true" arches because they normally flatten on weight bearing.

> **inner long arch**. Starts behind the great toe joint and extends to the inner front of the heel. It yields

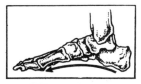

INNER LONGITUDINAL ARCH

OUTER LONGITUDINAL ARCH

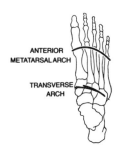

ANTERIOR METATARSAL ARCH

TRANSVERSE ARCH

The foot's four arches.

> a bit on weight bearing but normally returns to its original height when weight is removed.

> **metatarsal arch**. Comprises the heads of the five metatarsal bones forming the ball of the foot. It is slightly arched with the foot at rest, but normally flattens on weightbearing.

> **outer longitudinal arch**. Begins just behind the head of the fifth metatarsal bone and extends rearward to the front of the heel bone. A low arch with the foot at rest, it flattens on weight bearing.

> **transverse arch**. Situated under and across the tarsal bones just behind the instep. It is not visible to the eye but is normally arched at all times.

arch corset. 1) An elasticized band worn around the instep to provide snug support for the long inner arch. 2) Any bandage or tape applied by a medical practitioner to offer temporary relief for arch strain.

arch height. The height of the arch at its center or highest point, measured from the floor. Arches can be high, medium, low or flat, and in each instance be normal. Arch height tends to be generic.

arch length. Measured from start to finish of the arched portion above the floor line.

arch shoe. Any shoe designed to provide added support to the inner long and/or metatarsal arch. Sup-

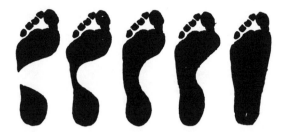

Footprints indicating differences in arch height, from high (left) to flat (right).

port is provided through the design of the shank, an insole orthotic, an arch cushion, or padding.

arctic. A lined overshoe with cloth upper and rubber bottom, fastened in front with buckles.

argyle. Multicolored diamond pattern as an allover or side panel on socks, usually men's. Named after Lord Argyle who introduced the style.

arithmetic grading. A last grading system in which the increments of size and width are on an arithmetic rather than a metric scale. The arithmetic system, used in the United States, Britain, and Canada, is based on 1/3 inch per full shoe size and 1/4 inch between each width. See also *shoe size*.

arithmetic shoe sizing. See *arithmetic grading*.

army shoe. Regulation dress shoes worn by Army personnel. Does not include combat boots or other military footwear for non-dress use.

arrears. Unpaid or overdue debts; any obligation not met on time.

art canvas. An open mesh canvas, usually linen, sometimes used for embroidered shoe uppers. Also called embroidery canvas.

arthritic foot. A rigid foot with all or some of its joints stiffened by arthritis, making walking difficult because of lack of flexibility.

articulation. The abutment of two or more bones to form a joint; the action between two or more bones forming a joint.

artificial grain. A grain appearance given to a flesh split by pigment with or without embossing.

artificial leather. Usually a man-made material processed and finished to imitate the feel and appearance of genuine leather.

artois shoe. A fashion shoe of France for men and women, with large, ornamental buckle. Named for the Count of Artois in the 18th century, later to become Charles X in the 19th century.

artisan. In shoemaking, a skilled craftsman or designer/craftsman.

ashley heel. See *heel*.

assembly. In shoemaking, the sequence of joining the various materials and components by a series of operations to produce the finished shoe.

asset. Anything owned that has exchange or collateral value.

assortment. In any merchandise line, such as footwear, the variety or available selection of merchandise for the customer.

asymmetric. 1) Lack of similarity of form or arrangement of two or more pieces on either side of a dividing line; the opposite of symmetric. 2) In a shoe pattern, the dominant line movement which flows either to the right or left of the instep. E.g.: a shoe with off-center lines such as a strap extending from the vamp to the outer side of the foot with no matching strap on the inner side.

astragulus. An older term for the talus bone. See also *talus*.

astronaut shoes. Shoes designed by NASA exclusively for walking on the moon. Special materials are used for soles, uppers and interior. Other special footwear designed for space flight wear, adapted to the required conditions.

atelier. A workshop or studio; also, a shoe designer's or artisan's shop where custom-made shoes are fitted and sold; a showroom.

athleisure footwear. Footwear with athletic design or styling but used for casual or recreational wear.

athletic shoe. See *sports shoe*.

athlete's foot. A common skin infection of the foot caused by a contagious fungus, resulting in redness and itching, usually between the toes. The medical term is *tinea pedis*.

at-home footwear. Dressy slipper/shoe footwear with a flat or little heel, usually with colorful fabric uppers, worn for at-home entertaining or leisure.

attache handbag. See *handbag*.

attached rib. A rib of fabric or other material attached to the insole by adhesive or stitching and providing a wall for welt sewing.

attrition. In retailing or manufacturing, a gradual loss of customers and sales; a weakening or wearing away of business due to any of several causes.

au courant. French term meaning current, of the present, hence in vogue and fashionable.

audit. An examination of financial records or checking of business accounts to verify accuracy and legitimacy.

automatic bargain basement. Usually found in department stores where discontinued merchandise goes through a serious of automatic markdowns week to week until sold or finally disposed of as distress merchandise.

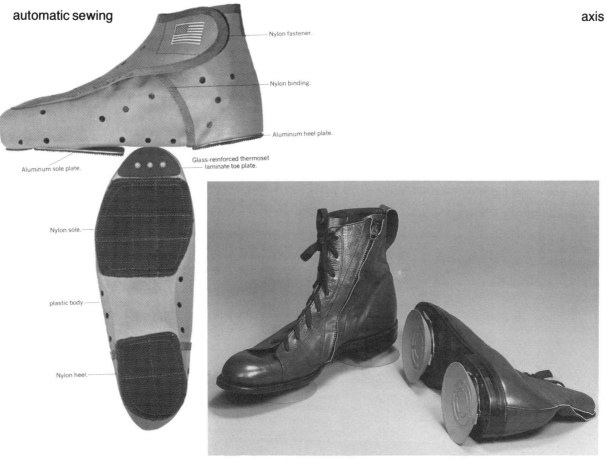

Nylon fastener.

Nylon binding.

Aluminum heel plate.

Glass-reinforced thermoset
laminate toe plate.

Aluminum sole plate.

Nylon sole.

plastic body.

Nylon heel.

Astronaut shoes with special design and materials for space flight and moonwalking.

automatic sewing. In a shoe factory, stitching operations performed with computer-controlled sewing machines.

automation. Not requiring manual direction or handling; machinery or equipment that is computer controlled to perform a sequence of operations.

avante gard. The leaders in new or unconventional movements in fashion or the arts.

average sale. In a store carrying a range of prices, the average of all sales or prices combined.

aviation boot. See *boot*.

awl. A small, pointed tool for making holes in leather; an essential tool of the traditional shoemakers.

axis. A real or imaginary straight line on which an object rotates; a main line of reference for related measurements or movements.

5

B

B. Symbol for a shoe width; narrow for men, average for women. See also *shoe size* and *width*.

babiche. A thong cord made of rawhide or gut. The name is American Indian.

Babinski reflex. Light stroke pressure applied to the outer border of the foot's sole, then across the ball. Normal response causes the toes to point downward and inward. Other responses can indicate a neural abnormality. Used to test the nervous system of the body and foot.

babouche (or baboosh). A slipper with a turned-up toe and no heel, often in bright colors. Native to Turkey.

baby doll last. A wide forepart with a rounded, mildly bump shape to the toe. Popular with young women in the 1920s and occasionally later because it makes the foot look smaller. The shoe usually has a higher heel. Sometimes called a baby doll toe.

baby Louis heel. See *heel*.

baby shoe. An infant's shoe with a soft upper and either a firm or flexible sole; usually a laced hightop or bootee. Sizes range from 0 to 6. See also *cacks*.

Babylonian shoe. A shoe dating back to ancient Babylonia, 800–1000 B.C.E. Well-crafted and made with soft, bright-colored kidskin; sometimes richly embroidered and often perfumed. The fine crafting was later adopted by the shoe artisans of medieval Cordova, Spain.

back. 1) Leather made from the hide that is cut longitudinally along the spine into two sides, with head and belly sections trimmed off. Usually used as soling leather. 2) To reinforce a component such as an insole or upper by cementing a backing material to it. See also *gem insole*.

back cone. On a last, the portion of the cone section between the "V" cut in the center and the back end of the last.

back dating. Dating a purchase order earlier than the actual purchase date, for accounting, invoicing or other reasons.

backing. An extra underlayer of material, such as a lining, that reinforces the upper layer.

backing cloth. Any lightweight, durable fabric undercoated with adhesive and used for backing purposes, chiefly on shoe uppers.

back curve. See *heel curve*.

back interest. A fashion pattern or styling design or treatment for enhanced visual effect at the shoe's backpart.

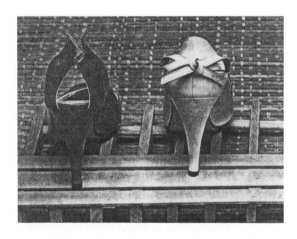

Examples of back interest styling.

backless shoe. See *open-back shoe*.

backline. On a last or shoe, the exact center line at the shoe's backpart, top rim to heel seat.

backpart. The quarter section of the shoe, approximately from heel breast rearward.

backpart width. The width of the heel end measured parallel to the heel featherline plane at a specified distance from the heel point on the last.

back strap. See *strap shoe*.

back-to-school. An important selling period for retailers of juvenile and teen apparel and footwear, usually from about mid-August to early September.

bagged edge. Joining the edges of the upper and lining with a clean inside seam that conceals the stitching.

bait pricing. Advertising low prices on selected items of the store's merchandise to attract customers.

bait and switch. Sales tactic in which unavailable merchandise is advertised at a very low price. The customer is told the advertised merchandise is sold out, and is then switched to higher priced merchandise.

baku (or bakou). Fine, lightweight straw used for shoe uppers.

bal. A laced shoe pattern in which the front of the quarter is stitched to the vamp at the throatline. Bal is short for Balmoral, the Scottish castle of British royalty, where the style was first introduced by Prince Albert in 1853.

BAL

Bal or balmoral style.

balance. A state of equilibrium or stability enabling the foot and/or shoe to tread properly for normal and efficient function.

ball. In the foot, the ball comprises the heads of the five metatarsal bones and the surrounding tissue. On the shoe the ball is the corresponding section or area. Along with the heel, the ball is one of the two primary weight-bearing and tread sections of the foot and shoe.

ball break. On the shoe, the line that creases across the top of the vamp when the foot is flexed in taking a step. See also *flex angle*.

ballet slipper. See *slipper*.

ball girth. A measurement around the ball of the foot or last to determine shoe and last width and volume allowance inside the shoe. A key measurement in lastmaking and custom shoemaking.

ball joint. Usually the big toe joint, but can also include the outside ball joint formed by the head of the fifth metatarsal bone.

ball measurement. See *ball girth*.

ball width. The linear foot measurement taken across the ball at the two widest points, for selection of corresponding shoe width.

balloon toe. A high, full-rounded shoe toe with a bulbous or knobbed look. See also *bulldog toe*.

ball-and-socket device. A scissors-like tool or device with one head a metal ball, the other with a hole. When a material is placed between the two and the handles are squeezed, a cavity is created in the material where the ball and socket are mated. Used as an adjustment device in shoe fitting to accommodate a protrusion on the foot such as a bunion.

BALL AND RING BUNION STRETCHER

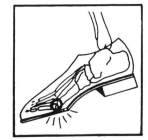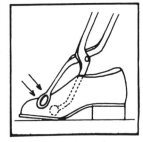

Ball and ring device to create shoe pocket for bunion.

Balmoral. See *bal*.

banded shoe. A women's shoe with leather straps one or more inches in width across the vamp and instep. A popular fashion in the 1940s.

bandy legs. Bowed legs. Medical term is *genu varus*.

bar. 1) British term for a shoe strap. 2) A piece of material of any of various shapes or thicknesses, used for shoe modifications or as an orthotic to alter foot tread or gait, or as an adjustment to accommodate some foot problem. The shape and size is determined by the shoe therapist. Some common types of bars:

comma. A comma-shaped bar wedged laterally toward the heel on the sole or inside of the shoe.

Denver. A metatarsal bar, the apex of which coincides with the rear edge under the proximal half of the metatarsal shafts. Also known as a *Denver heel*.

Hauser. See *comma*.

Jones. A metatarsal bar placed between the insole and outsole.

Mayo. A metatarsal bar with the front edge curved to match the contour of the metatarsal heads.

metatarsal. Any bar of leather, rubber or other material attached to the shoe sole, with the apex just behind the metatarsal heads. Usually heart-shaped.

rocker. A transverse bar with a thick apex rising 1/8 inch behind the metatarsal head to be protected.

Thomas. A narrow metatarsal bar with an abrupt drop front and back.

transverse. See *metatarsal bar*.

bar coding. A grouping of lines of various thickness on a merchandise package that can be electronically scanned to identify and record the merchandise by price, stock number, color and other data. Used for inventory and sales records. Bar codes are assigned by the Universal Product Code (UPC) Council. Each manufacturer or supplier is assigned an individual code.

barefoot sandal. A simple sandal with large cutouts, straps or thongs. Usually worn without socks or hose.

bargain. 1) Something offered, sold or bought at a price favorable to the buyer. 2) A negotiation between buyer and seller to arrive at a mutually agreed price or settlement.

bargain basement. A store department, usually below street level, where clearance merchandise is always on sale at markdown prices; usually associated with a department store.

bark tannage. See *tannage*.

baroque. Grotesque or fantastic in style; exaggerated or over-ornate. Applied to apparel or manner of dress.

barrel heel. See *heel*.

bar shoe. A square-toed shoe with open instep, a wide instep strap buttoned at the side, and a heavy sole. Plain types were worn by European peasants in the 15th and 16th centuries, and more ornate types were worn by the upper classes.

baseball shoe. See *sports shoe*.

basement. A department in a department store, usually where lower priced or clearance merchandise is sold.

base plane. The bottom surface of the heel of the last. With the last positioned for heel height, the plane is used as a reference point for defining certain measurements and placements on the last.

basic shoe. A loose term for any conservatively styled shoe in any footwear category; a staple shoe not subject to fashion cycles or whims.

basic shoe styles. The seven basic shoe styles or designs from which all footwear fashions throughout all history have been derived. The seven are: the moccasin, sandal, mule, clog, boot, pump, and oxford. The moccasin is the oldest, dating back at least 12,000 years. The oxford is the most recent, dating back over 300 years. All footwear fashions, no matter how seemingly new or modern, are variations of these seven basic designs.

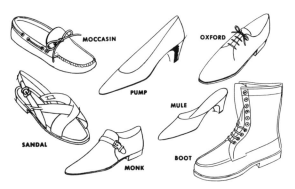

The seven basic shoe styles from which all footwear fashions are derived.

basketball shoe. See *sports shoe*.

basket weave. One of the basic weaves; a plain fabric or other material with two or more warp or filling threads or strips side by side.

bastard. A skin from a crossbreed of goat and sheep which has hair instead of wool.

bastard boot. See *boot, cavalier*.

bat. A retail trade term for a shoe out of style, hence unsalable.

bathing shoe. A heelless, one-piece, stretch-rubber slip-on shoe for beach or water wear.

bating. The process of preparing hides and skins for tanning after they have been limed, unhaired, and washed. The bate material makes the hide or skin soft and pliable and also removes undesirable plumpness in the tanned leather.

batt. A women's heavy laced oxford, originally worn in England, brought to New England by the colonists in 1636.

baxea. A simple, woven straw sandal worn by peasants, poor children, priests, and philosophers of ancient Rome.

beach shoe. A casual flattie shoe with colorful leather or fabric upper, used for beach, recreational or resort wear.

beading. Colored beads applied to a material or shoe for decorative effect.

beamhouse. The tannery department where raw hides and skins are prepared for tanning operations (washing, soaking, fleshing, etc.). The name is derived from the wooden beams over which the hides and skins were placed for these operations.

bear's paw. See *duckbill*.

beating out. The shoemaking operation of leveling the bottom of a turn shoe after the shoe has been turned.

Beatle boot. See *boot*.

beau monde. French term for fashionable society, or the world of fashionable people.

beaver top. A soft shoe or slipper with a warm fabric upper, usually felt.

bed slipper. See *slipper*.

beginning of month. See *BOM*.

bellows tongue. See *tongue*.

belly. The under or belly section of the hide. Belly leather is of lesser quality than leather made from the sides of the hide, and is used for shoe insoles, linings, and slipper soles.

benchmade shoe. Originally a handsewn shoe produced by a single craftsman. Today it means a shoe whose sole has been handsewn to the upper. Also, a shoe made entirely by hand at a shoemaker's bench.

bend. The portion of the hide from the spine and upper-side sections remaining after the shoulders, flanks, belly, and head have been trimmed off. A bend is thick and heavy; leather made from it is usually used for outsoles.

Benny. Trade term designating a B width shoe.

bespangled. A shoe decorated with spangles or other glittering ornaments such as sequins, beads or medallions.

bespoke. British term for a custom-made shoe.

better grade. General designation for a shoe of above-average quality and price.

bevel. The skived or feather-thin edge of a material or shoe component; an edge cut to reduce thickness.

bicycle shoe. See *sports shoe*.

big boys' shoe. A footwear category for older boys' shoe sizes 6 1/2 to 10.

Bigfoot. A legendary, human-like creature of the northwest United States. Named for the huge footprints it has left in its trail. Also known as Sasquatch, an Indian name.

bilateral. Affecting both sides, right and left, as on a foot or shoe.

billing. The sending of bills or invoices to customers for payment due.

bin. 1) In a store, a table with raised edges and containing an assortment of clearance footwear or other merchandise at markdown prices. 2) In a shoe factory bins are used for storage of materials and components.

binding. A reinforcement for the edge of a material, or to give a finished appearance to the edge or protect cut edges from fraying. Originally an old shoemaking term for stitching together the uppers of a shoe by hand.

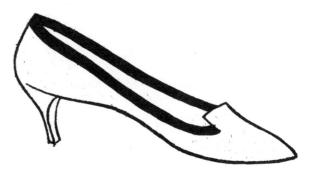

Binding around shoe's topline.

biokinetic sole. See *cantilever sole*.

biomechanics. The science of applying mechanical principles to a living structure, such as stresses and strains, and especially in regard to gait; the study of mechanical forces acting on the body and their effect on body movements.

biomechanist. One trained and skilled in biomechanics.

biped. Any creature that walks on two legs instead of four or more. However, humans are the only creatures who walk erect with a stride.

bitchy pump. A plain sleek pump with pointed toe and spike heel. A perennial classic regarded as a sexy shoe.

blackguard. Young male servants in manors and inns who blacked and shined the boots and shoes of residents and guests in 17th- and 18th-century England. Many were of unsavory character. See also Appendix II.

black pigment. See *carbon black*.

blacking. Outmoded term for black shoe paste or polish.

black shoe navy. A term common around World War II, used in a derogatory manner in reference to navy air pilots. Navy fliers who were not Annapolis graduates were required to wear brown shoes, while black shoes were worn by Annapolis graduates.

Non-Annapolis fliers felt this was a symbol of discrimination and privilege, with Annapolis men receiving faster promotions. Hence the Annapolis men were labeled the *black shoe navy*.

Blake sewing. English term for stitching of shoes by the McKay process. (See *shoe construction, McKay*).

bleed. To run or lose color when wet, due to excessive or improper dyeing.

blind eyelet. A metal or plastic eyelet with a rimless hole on the upper surface. Used in some men's dress shoes and women's oxfords.

blind size code. A size code inside the shoe designed to conceal the actual size from the customer. See also *shoe size code*.

blister. 1) A raised patch of skin filled with watery matter and caused by a burn or friction. 2) A raised area on the surface of leather caused by a tanning fault.

block heel. See *heel*.

blocking. 1) Cutting a shoe sole or upper into roughly the shape of the desired outline. The soles are then rounded by machine into the finished shape. Uppers are usually blocked only when the cutting is to be completed on the cutout machine. 2) The adhesion between layers of material as a result of the moderate pressure applied during storage.

bloom. A light-colored deposit of ellagic acid on the surface of leather that has been treated with certain tannins such as pyragallol or chestnut extract.

blown rubber. See *expanded rubber*.

BLUCHER

Blucher style.

blucher. A shoe with an open quarter at the throat of a circular vamp. The bottom of the lace rows flap out to give more fit allowance at the bottom of the shoe's instep. Designed originally in the 19th century as a half boot pattern by Field Marshall Blucher of the Prussian army.

blucher bal. A modified blucher pattern. The vamp is stitched overlapping the quarter except for a short distance at the throat where the quarter is slit to permit it to overlap.

blue. Hides or skins in the raw state before chrome tanning. Also referred to as "in the blue."

bluestocking. See *Appendix II*.

blushing. A cloudy appearance on finished leather or other material due to the improper evaporation of solvents in the lacquers.

boarded grain. See *grain*.

board-lasted. A lasting method in which the upper is cemented to a stiff piece of leatherboard or fiberboard on the bottom to promote stability. It also reduces underfoot flexibility and resilience.

boarded leather. Smooth leather finished by folding, with the grain side in and rubbing the flesh side with a machine or a cork-surfaced hand board to create an accentuated grain. A similar effect is imitated by embossing. When the close creases run in two different directions it is called a box or willow finish.

boardy. Stiff, inflexible leather.

boat shoe. A two- or three-eyelet shoe with glove-type upper leather and waxy finish, unlined, with rubber sole; for deck or casual wear.

Boat shoe.

bobeline. Rope-sole shoe with canvas upper, popular in 17th-century France. The forerunner of the espadrille shoe.

bobine heel. See *heel*.

bodger. An itinerant craftsman of 16th- to 19th-century Europe who made wood clogs and sabots, hollowing out the wood to house the foot, shaping the sole, then painting or otherwise decorating the shoe.

B.O.M. Beginning of month status of the inventory.

bonding. Joining two parts, such as sole and upper, with adhesives or by vulcanization or other methods.

bones of the foot. The foot is divided into three sections: tarsus (rearfoot), metatarsas (midfoot) and phalanges (toe bones). The tarsus has seven chunky bones closely jointed. They are: calcaneus or heel bone (the largest foot bone); the talus, which forms the ankle joint; the navicular at the roof of the long inner arch; the three cuneiforms at the front-center of the tarsus; and the cuboid at the outer side of the tarsus. The metatarsus consists of five long, slender bones with spaces between; the heads of the metatarsal bones form the metatarsal arch or ball area of the foot. There are 14 toe bones, 3 tiny ones for each of the lesser toes, and two larger ones for the big toe. Altogether there are 26 bones, plus 2 pea-size sesamoid bones under the great toe joint. See also *foot anatomy*.

bonwelt (or bondwelt). See *shoe construction*.

booking. An order given by the retailer, or taken by the shoe traveler, for merchandise from a vendor.

boot. Any footwear extending above the ankle, made of leather, rubber, fabric, man-made, or combinations. There are numerous designs and types for a variety of uses. The boot style itself dates back many centuries and is universal in use. Among the best known, contemporary or historical, are:

Women's button boot, circa. 1900.   Courreges boot.

Alaska. An overshoe 8 to 10 inches high with rubberized cloth top and rubber sole.

ankle. See *demi-boot*.

aviation (or aviator's). A fleece-lined boot with leather upper and a leather or rubber sole. Worn by aviators in the earlier days of air flight.

bastard. See *cavalier boot*.

Beatle. A dressy over-the-ankle boot with 12/8 heel, zipped up the side. Introduced by the British singing group, the Beatles, and popular in the 1960s.

bootee (or bootie). 1) A calf-high men's boot usually with elastic goring over the ankle, or with a laced front. 2) An ankle-high boot with cloth upper and soft sole, made for infants.

bootikin. A small boot with a soft upper and very light sole.

Boston. See *congress boot*.

bottekin. A small boot variously decorated in fancy patterns.

bottine. A low, spat-type boot with combination cloth and leather upper in contrasting colors, buttoned or laced. The bottine, of French origin, is a small, fine quality boot for women.

brodequin (or brodekin). A buskin-like half boot popular with fashionable women in 17th- and 18th-century Europe.

bucket top. A boot with a crushed top of soft leather allowing exaggerated folds. See also *French falls* boot.

buskin. A boot extending calf high, laced with a cord or ribbon. Originated in ancient Greece and continued popular up to the 18th century throughout Europe.

button. Any boot using a series of button fastenings, such as those popular for men and women at the turn of the century.

calceus. An ankle-high boot/sandal, sometimes with high tongue, or with elaborately intertwined strappings around the ankle. It began as a simple boot with the ancient Greeks and Etruscans and became a more elegant style with the Romans, worn mostly by senators, patricians, and other high officials as a status boot in white, black or colors.

carriage. A lined fabric boot with leather sole, often fur-trimmed at the collar. Worn by women in winter over shoes or slippers in horse-driven carriages and in the early open automobiles.

cavalier. A high, soft leather boot that falls in folds, with a wide flared top garishly lined and trimmed with colored lace. Popular with the male dandies of 17th- and 18th-century Europe as part of the cavalier costume. Also known as a *bastard boot*.

Charley. A demi-boot with a high front and either instep or side goring. Popular in the 1960s for both men and women.

chukka. A three-quarter boot with two or three eyelets, or a strap with buckle fastener. Originally worn for polo. The name is derived from *chukker* or *chukkar*, the time periods in which polo is played.

Clarence. Similar to the Wellington boot except that it is laced up the outer side of the shaft. Popular in the 19th century in England and the United States and named for the Duke of Clarence who introduced it.

Cavalier boot with ornate laced top an extreme flare, popular in 17th century France.

Demi-boot.

cloth top. A dressy, over-the-ankle boot with upper of contrasting cloth and leather, usually fastened with buttons. Popular with men and women in the 19th and early 20th centuries, and occasionally appears as a contemporary style.

congress. A low dress or comfort boot with leather upper an elastic gusset at the sides, usually with a pull strap in the back. Popular as a men's boot in the 19th and early 20th centuries. Sometimes known as a *congress gaiter*.

cork. A boot with a thick cork sole with protruding spikes. Worn by loggers who ride logs downstream to the sawmills.

Courréges. Calf-high, straight-shaft women's boot in white calf, kid or patent, with open slots at the top and knotted tie in front. The boot's name is taken from its designer.

cowboy. See *western boot*.

crepida. A half boot with a sandalized bottom portion, popular in ancient Rome.

demi. An ankle-high boot, either slip-on or laced, usually for dress wear.

Men's demi boot.

Doc Marten. A heavy knee-high or calf-high men's boot with wide instep strap and shiny studs, worn for a militant macho look. The name is derived from its designer, Dr. Klaus Maertens of Munich, Germany.

Doc Martens boot.

engineer. A calf-height laced boot with bellows tongue and supporting strap across the instep. An unlaced version has a strap-adjusted gusset on the outer side.

estivan. A boot with an exaggerated pointed toe, for dress wear.

estiveaux. A half boot whose loose upper droops to form creases or folds. Popular in 11th-century Europe.

fashion. A general term for any fashion-oriented boot, usually women's.

finnesco (or finnsko). A boot made with tanned reindeer skins, worn with the fur side out. A native shoe of arctic regions.

fishing. A knee-high rubber boot worn by fishermen.

Women's low-cut fashion boot.

Women's fashion boot.   Hiking boot.

Hunting boot.

flight. A fleece-lined boot with leather upper and usually a zipper closing; sometimes electrically heated. Worn by fighter pilots in World Wars I and II. See also *aviator boot*.

French falls. A leather boot with a high, wide top that crushes down into folds. Popular in 18th-century Europe and America.

gamashes (or gamoshes). A high, firm-shafted boot worn in the late 17th century in Europe and Colonial America.

gum. A high, protective rubber boot.

half. A boot extending halfway between ankle and calf. Also called a "short foot."

half Wellington. See *Wellington boot*.

harness. See *boot, motorcycle*.

Hessian. A knee-high boot, usually decorated at the top with a tassel. Introduced by Hessian soldiers in the 19th century and adopted by the English.

high-low. An ankle-high boot laced to the top.

hiking. An ankle-high laced boot with a lug or traction sole, lightweight leather or leather/mesh upper, firm counter and box toe.

hip. 1) A hip-high rubber boot used for stream fishing; 2) a thigh-high close-fitting leather boot worn by women as a sexy fashion.

hunting. A laced, calf-high leather boot, water-resistant, and with bellows tongue.

hussar. A shiny black leather boot with the top rim

finished with gold or silver braid and a silk tassel at the top of the shaft.

jack. Originally a heavy, knee-high laceless boot with square toe and wide cuff, worn by military officers and upper class men of the 17tti and 18th centuries. Now a military boot of calf height. The name is taken from jacked leather, of which the boots were originally made.

jockey. A knee-high riding boot, often with a tassel dangling from the rim of the shaft. Also known as a *top boot*.

jodhpur. An over-the-ankle riding boot, held in place by a strap around the back of the ankle. Worn with or without leggings.

jungle. A lightweight boot with a combination leather/fabric or mesh/fabric upper and a vulcanized traction sole. Designed as a jungle combat boot.

kamik. A knee-high sealskin boot worn by Arctic natives.

larrigan. A knee-high boot with a moccasin foot, used by lumbermen and trappers.

laced. Any boot laced front, side or back.

leg. Any boot without lacing and reaching between ankle and calf.

lumberman's overs. A rubber arctic boot with thick felt lining which folds over the top of the shaft.

Mongolian. Knee-high boot with leather or cloth upper, felt sole, and turned-up toe; often elaborately embroidered or decorated. Native boot of Mongolia, Tibet, and Korea.

14

Two versions of women's laced boot; left, 1910; right, 1976.

Mongolian boot.

motorcycle. A heavy, over-the-calf, black leather boot with hard raised toe, large heavy heel, and wide strap around instep, ankle and back, and large buckle on the outside. Also known as a "harness boot."

mountain. A sturdy boot of waterproof, insulated leather with eight-inch top and heavy sole, fitted with hobnails for traction and mountain climbing.

mukluk. Originally an Alaskan or Indian boot of soft sealskin with fur inside. Adapted later for military use in cold weather, with the leather from deer, elk, or similar skins. Usually tanned white. Very permeable to moisture vapor and re-

Motorcycle boot

tains its flexibility and suppleness at low temperatures.

Napoleon. A calf-high boot with the top rim higher in front. Worn by Napoleon's officers and later popular with civilians.

outdoor. A general term for any boot worn for rugged outdoor use.

pack (or pac). A moccasin-front half boot worn by lumbermen and hunters.

Pac (or pack) boot.

plow. A heavy, coarse, sturdy work boot seamed at the sides.

polar. See *stadium boot*.

police. A black, semi-dress laced boot with a heavy sole, broad last and full toe. Worn by police as a duty shoe.

Polish. A women's front-laced boot five or more inches in height. Popular in 18th-century Poland.

pull-on. A side-zipped, calf-high boot. Also, any

boot without lacing or other fastening, pulled onto the foot by pull straps at the back rim of the boot shaft; e.g., a western boot.

Russian. A calf-high leather boot with a cuff, and sometimes a tassel, at the top rim.

seamless. A knee-high boot without a visible seam, a seemingly impossible construction. It was achieved by an ingenious French shoe artisan, Charles Lestrange, who carefully removed the whole hide intact without slitting from the leg of a calf. After defleshing and cleaning, the hide was tanned, then the entire unit fashioned into a seamless boot and presented to King Louis XIV, who swore the artisan to secrecy about the process, rewarding him with a handsome stipend.

shooting. A short, sturdy ankle boot for sport shooting. It has minimal pattern pieces to keep the boot water resistant.

short. See *half boot*.

ski. A boot for attachment to skis and worn for skiing. Insulated, with firm upper and rigid sole, ski boots may be of numerous combinations of designs, styles, or materials.

skitty. British term for a heavy half boot with front lacing.

Spanish. Short leather boot with a soft, loose, falling top, in light colors. Popular men's fashion in 17th-century Europe.

spat. A short boot with a cloth upper and leather foot part, in contrasting colors or shades, buttoned at the side. A popular fashion boot for men and women in the 19th and early 20th centuries.

stadium. An ankle-high overshoe, fleece-lined, with water-repellant sole. Worn by spectators at football or other cold-weather sports events.

suwarrow. A form-fitting leather boot with a tassel at the top rim. Named after Russian General Alexander Suvorov, who designed it for his troops during the Seven Years' War, 1857–1863.

thigh. A snug-fitting, soft-leather boot extending to the upper thigh. In the 13th and 14th centuries it was worn by horsemen and cavalry soldiers. Today it is worn by women as a more extreme fashion.

top. A high, solid-legged laced boot of either leather or rubber, used for riding, hunting, fishing, or other sports.

wading. See *hip boot*.

Wellington. A loose, square-toe boot reaching above the knee ill front and lower in back. Introduced by Lord Wellington in the early 19th century and worn by cavalry officers. A half

Wellington is a calf-high version worn today under the trousers as a dress boot.

western. A boot with a creased vamp, tapered toe, 10/8 to 14/8 heel, and the heel shaped in any of various styles. The shaft is notched front and back. The shaft is of plain or fancy leather with decorative stitching or other ornamentation. Boot height varies from below the knee to below the calf. Sometimes known as a *cowboy boot*.

Western boot.

work. A laced utility boot about eight inches in height with heavy, water-repellant upper leather, and a durable traction sole of rubber or polyurethane. Often insulated or cushioned. Used by construction and other outdoor workers.

boot. A novice or raw recruit. The term derives from the 19th-century English men's clubs, assigned to young new members.

bootblack. One whose occupation is shining shoes and boots. See also *blackguard*.

boot camp. A military camp in which raw recruits are trained. Used chiefly in the Navy and Marine Corps.

boot collar. 1) The upper rim of the boot shaft. 2) An added piece of material around the rim, usually for decorative purpose, such as fur.

bootery. A retail store selling footwear, usually children's or women's.

boot hook. A long metal hook with a T-handle at the top which hooks into the boot strap to enable one to pull on a riding or other boot.

boot hose. Long, heavy hose, leggings or spatterdashes, formerly worn in place of boots in the 18th and 19th centuries. Also, hose made to wear with boots.

bootician. A coined term for a store selling footwear or specializing in boots. Sometimes refers to the individual selling footwear.

bootikin. See *boot*.

boot jack. A board or metal frame with a V-shape

opening into which the boot heel is placed to enable the boot to be pulled off.

bootlace. Cloth or leather lacings used to fasten a boot.

bootmaker's finish. See *finish, antique*.

bootman. Archaic term for a servant or stableboy who attended to the cleaning or repair of the boots of residents or guests in English manors or inns. See also *blackguard*.

boot shaft. The leg part of the boot.

boot shoe. One of the early names (17th century) for the oxford or half boot.

bootstrap. A loop attached to the inside top of the boot shaft at the back or sides, to pull the boot onto the foot.

boot stretcher. A device for stretching the shaft of the boot when it is too small to accomodate leg size.

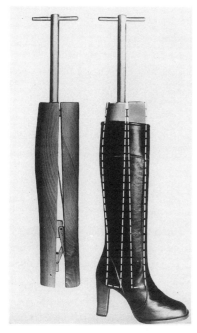

Boot stretcher.

boot tree. A device inserted inside the boot shaft to keep its shape when the boot is not in use. The same principle as a shoe tree.

boroso leather. See *leather*.

Boston boot. See *boot*.

bottekin. See *boot*.

bottier. French word for shoemaker. Also, one who deals in fine quality shoes and boots.

bottom. The bottom parts of a shoe, as distinguished from the upper. The sole, or when made as a unit, the sole and heel.

bottom assembly. In manufacturing, the assembling of the bottom parts of the shoe—insole, welt, midsole, shank, sole, and heel.

bottom filler. The material used to fill the cavity between the insole and outsole to create a level bottom for foot tread. Consists of such materials as granulated cork, latex cork sponge, slab cork, cushion cork, spun fiberglass, felt, granulated leather scrap.

bottoming. The operations of attaching the shoe's bottom parts to the upper.

bottoming room. The factory department in which the bottoming operations are done.

bottoming out. When a cushion insole or midsole becomes permanently compressed or thinned out with wear, losing its shock-absorbing or resilience value.

boudoir slipper. See *slipper*.

built-up heel. See *heel*.

boulevard heel. See *heel*.

bound foot. A foot bound tightly with bandages in childhood to prevent normal growth and to create a doll-size foot in adulthood. The four lesser toes are curled under and the arch and instep are curved sharply into a hump. Common among the women of China and other Asian nations from the 11th to the early 20th centuries, when it was finally prohibited by law. The bound foot was a mark of beauty and sensuality. Also known as *lily foot* and *lotus foot*.

boutique. A small retail shop in which accessory or specialty fashion merchandise is sold. Often attached to a couture house. Sometimes refers to a small fashion shoe store.

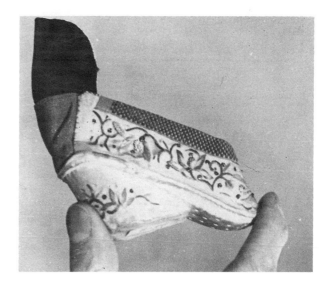

Tiny shoe for Chinese bound foot of an adult.

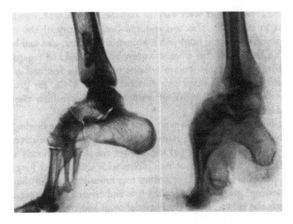

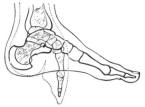

The bound or lotus, foot of an adult Chinese woman, in an X-ray photograph and in the skeletal outline, contrasting it with a normal foot. The bowed effect is identical to the look and position of a foot in a high-heeled shoe.

bow. Any bow-shaped attachment or ornament used for decorative effect on the vamp, instep, side or back of a shoe.

bow legs. See *genu varus*.

bowling shoe. See *sports shoe*.

box calf. Calfskin leather finished with the grain side boarded. Originally a proprietary name for chrome-tanned calfskin leather.

box finish. See *boarded leather*.

box handbag. See *handbag*.

boxing shoe. See *sports shoe*.

box leather. See *boarded leather*.

box toe. The material (plastic, leather, treated fabric, fiberboard, metal, etc.) used to cover the toe portion of the shoe under the upper material. The box toe can be hard to soft, covering the full toe area or only the tip portion. The box toe shape is deter-

Box toe. Bottom, toe shaped by box material. Above, soft box toe pressed down, but quickly returns to original shape.

mined by the toe area of the last. Its purpose is to keep the toe shape with wear. Many work boots use special impact-resistant materials for toe protection. See also *safety shoes*.

boys' shoes. A footwear classification, with sizes 2 1/2 to 6 (extremes 1 to 7).

Boy Scout shoe. A brown leather oxford with round toe and rubber heel. Approved by the Boy Scouts of America for wear with the Boy Scout uniform.

bracelet tie. A pump pattern with an extended back cut from one piece of material, with one or more straps or ribbons around the ankle or leg.

braid. A narrow, cord-like braided strip woven of silk, straw, linen, or leather. Used for trim on a shoe, usually with overlays to decorate the vamp or topline.

branch store. A store other than the main or flagship store of a department or specialty store chain. Branch stores are usually in an outlying or suburban area.

branding. See *marking*.

Brannock device. A patented foot-measuring device used to ascertain shoe size in fitting.

brass tip. A horizontal piece of brass covering the toe tip of the shoe either for protection against abrasion or as an ornament. Used on men's and boys' shoes in the 19th century.

break. 1) The tiny wrinkles formed on the grain side of leather when the leather is squeezed or pressed inward. Generally, the finer the wrinkles or grain break the better the quality of the leather. 2) The creases or folds formed across the top of the vamp when the shoe is flexed.

break-even. The point at which outgo (costs and expenses) are matched by income or revenues.

breaking-in. The process in which the foot and a new shoe adjust and adapt to each other.

breast. The front face or surface of the heel facing the shank.

breastline. An arbitrary line defining the forward boundary of the heel seat, usually matching the point of the heel breast.

breathability. The ability of a shoe material to wick up, absorb and pass off foot moisture to keep the foot reasonably dry and ventilated. More precisely called water vapor transmission. Not to be confused with porosity. The chief breathable parts of the shoe are the linings, insole and upper. See also *permeability*.

bridal shoe. A wedding shoe worn by the bride and bridesmaids, usually of matching style, color and material.

bridge market. The footwear or apparel market between very high price and medium high price—between the salon-type customer and the better grade store customer. Trading down from the top price. An ambiguous term to classify a type of market or customer who likes designer looks but can't or won't pay full designer prices.

brocade. See *fabrics*.

brodequin. See *boot*.

brog. Scottish term for a clog-like shoe with a coarsely tanned leather upper. Worn by Scottish and Irish peasants or farmers.

brogan. A heavy, nailed or pegged work shoe or boot with a coarse but sturdy leather upper, fastened with laces or buckle. Worn by Irish farmers and workmen.

brogue. A sturdy laced oxford with wing tip and perforated toe design, usually of Goodyear welt construction, with firm leather sole. A classic men's style for dress or business wear.

Men's classic wing-tip brogue.

brogue cap. An attached top cap with a central peak and a "C" on either side to simulate a wing-tip effect; sometimes perforated. An imitation cap rather than applied as part of the original pattern.

broken lot. In the store, a style or stock number with missing sizes and widths; an incomplete size selection.

bromidrosis. Excessive foot perspiration giving off offensive odors.

bronzed shoe. A pair of shoes, usually an infant's first shoes, given a special bronzing treatment and saved for posterity.

browse. Casual viewing of merchandise around the store by a customer with no particular article or purchase in mind and not necessarily with serious intent to buy. Browsing not infrequently leads to impulse purchases.

brush coat. A second coat of varnish, lacquer or other substance for finishing patent leather.

brushed leather. A suede finish of deliberately coarser

nap to give a "brushed" effect to the leather's surface. Used mostly for casual or sport footwear.

buckle. A metal or plastic fastening device used on footwear for functional or decorative purpose, or both.

bucket top boot. See *boot*.

buckram. A coarse cloth stiffened with adhesive. Used as a foundation for shoe tips or as a cemented backing for shoe fabrics; e.g., between the outside and lining of a Colonial tongue, bow, or other shoe parts where additional stiffness is needed to retain shape. A reinforcement material.

buckside. Cattlehide upper leather finished to resemble buckskin.

buckskin. Tanned deerskin. Most so-called buckskin is actually suede-finished cowhide or steerhide leather, sometimes calfskin. Nearly always in white, tan or other light colors. Most buckskin is oil-dressed, producing a soft, pliable leather resembling chamois leather.

buddy system. An apprentice system in which a beginner employee is assigned to a more experienced employee who will train and guide the newcomer in the required job knowledge and skills. Commonly used in shoe stores.

budget. 1) A plan or schedule adjusting expenses during a given period in accord with the estimated revenues for that period. 2) A preplanned amount of money devoted to a particular segment of the business (merchandise, advertising, etc.) based on estimated income to balance the outgo.

budget department. A department offering more moderately priced merchandise in a department or large specialty store.

buff. 1) A light, brownish-yellow shade. 2) The color of buffalo leather. 3) to sand or roughen a smooth surface to produce a napped surface.

buffalo calf. See *leather*.

buffalo leather. See *leather*.

buff leather. Skins of deer, elk, oxen, or buffalo dressed with oils to look and feel like chamois.

buffskin. Leather prepared from buffalo hide and dressed with oil to look and feel like chamois.

built-up heel. See *heel*.

bulla. A blister.

bulldog toe. A hard bump toe common on police and service shoes. Popular on men's and women's dress shoes and boots in the 19th and early 20th centuries.

bull hides. Hides from uncastrated male cattle.

bumper. A rubber strip attached over the front toe surface for reinforcement. Common on sneakers and some athletic shoes.

Bulldog toe.

bump toe. An exaggerated high, knobby, full-rounded shoe toe design popular in the early 1970s for men's and women's platform footwear.

bundschuh. Originally, little more than a piece of coarse leather for the upper, roughly attached to a wooden or stiff leather sole, worn by German peasants until the 16th century. In the Middle Ages the bundschuh was a symbol of poverty and oppression, and later became the rallying symbol of the peasant uprising and rebellion in Germany at the beginning of the 16th century.

bunion. A swelling and inflammation of the tissue at the side of the great toe joint, caused by shoe friction and irritation. Usually accompanied by some degree of deformity of the alignment of the bones of the great toe joint. See also *hallux valgus*.

bunionette. A small bunion. Usually situated on the outer border of the foot at the ball or fifth metatarsophalangeal joint. See also *tailor's bunion*.

bunion shoe. A shoe made on a special last with a cavity or "pocket" to accomodate and prevent pressure from the shoe on the bunion.

burial shoe. A cheaply constructed black shoe or

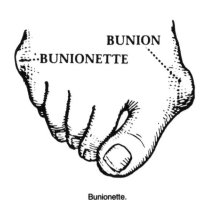

Bunionette.

slipper worn by the deceased in the casket. Often provided by the undertaker.

burned soles. Leather which has become hard and brittle because it has been heated to a temperature of 110 degrees F. or higher, eliminating the fatty tanning oils.

burnishing. Polishing by machine to give the shoe upper a bright, glossy finish. On better grade shoes the sole and heel edges are waxed and burnished.

bursa. A small sac or pouch containing a lubricating fluid that prevents friction or pressure between a tendon and a bone. Bursa sites on the foot are at the side of the great toe joint, under the heel, and beneath the Achilles tendon.

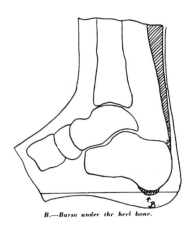

B.—*Bursa under the heel bone.*

Bursa

bursitis. Inflammation and swelling of a bursa.

buskin. 1) A low boot dating back to the pre-Christian era. See also *boot*. 2) Knee-high hose with decorative metallic threads, worn by the clergy during the 13th to 16th centuries. 3) A women's low-cut indoor shoe with a small triangular gore at the instep.

business shoe. A loose designation for a conservatively styled dress shoe worn by either men or women during business hours.

butt. The part of the hide or skin covering the rump of the animal. Used to make sturdy leather.

button fly. A reinforcing strip of leather with button holes which laps over the front of a button shoe or boot.

buttonhook. A metal prong with a hook at the end, pushed through the buttonhole onto the button to draw the button through the hole. An essential instrument in the 19th and early 20th centuries when button shoes and boots were popular.

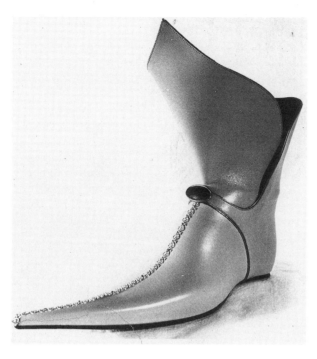

Buskin-type shoe.

Buttonhook.

button shoe. Any shoe or boot in which buttons are the means of fastening.

button strap. See *strap shoe*.

butt seam. See seam.

buy. A lot purchase from a vendor's line, as in "making a buy."

buyer. The individual authorized to make purchases from a vendor. Usually a position in a department or large specialty store or a chain organization. In a broader sense, anyone who buys at wholesale from a vendor, such as an independent retail shoe store.

buying budget. The sum allocated for merchandise for the store.

buying office. The official department of a large volume store or chain where the buying is done for the store or stores.

buying trip. A buyer's trip to a trade snow, or a visit to a vendor's showroom in another city.

by-product. Anything produced from residues in the course of producing something else; a secondary or incidental product. E.g., hides and skins for leather are a by-product of cattle or other animals which are slaughtered primarily for their meat.

C

C. Coded designation for a narrow-medium width for men, a medium-wide for women's shoes.

cable stitch. Embroidered stitch similar to a chain stitch; a knitted stitch producing a raised cord. Used as a decorative feature in some shoes.

cabretta leather. See *leather*.

cacks. A footwear designation for an infants' turn shoe with no heel. Cacks are sized from 1 to 5 (extremes 0 to 6).

CAD. See *computer-aided design*.

cadence. The tempo or rhythm of the steps in marching or walking.

calcaneus. The heel bone. A more modern medical term for *os calcis*.

calceus. See *boot*.

calcei. Latin name for a sandal or shoe.

calendar sole. Sheet soling material that has been pressed between rollers.

calendar. To prepare sheets of material by pressure between counter-rotating rolls. Most coated materials used for shoe uppers, such as PVC-coated fabrics, are prepared by calendaring.

calfskin leather. See *leather*.

California process. See *shoe construction, slip-lasted*.

caliga. A very open, heelless, sandal-like shoe ranging from ankle to below knee in height, with a heavy hobnailed or spiked sole. Made of leather or cloth, with front lacing and covered ankle. Worn by soldiers of ancient Rome, with variations in design according to rank. The soles of officers' caligas were not hobnailed. Named after Emperor Caligula, whose boyhood nickname was Caliga, meaning "little boot," and who as a boy wore hobnailed boots made especially for him.

callosity. See *callus*.

callus. A hard, thickened place on the skin resulting from an over-production of skin cells to protect the skin from repeated friction and irritation.

calzado. Spanish word for footwear.

calzatura. Italian word for footwear.

CAM. See *computer-aided manufacturing*.

Cambridge slipper. See *slipper*.

camp moccasin. A moccasin with a soft or firm sole and oil-tamed leather, used for camp wear.

camp shoe. Any type of footwear designed and used for camp wear.

campagnus. A military campaign boot with laces that anchor on a long leather tongue that protects the front of the foot and leg. Worn by Roman military officers. Heavily tooled and gilded according to rank, with an ornamental insignia, such as a real or ivory head of a small animal such as a fox, over the instep.

campus footwear. Any contemporary style popular with college students and worn on campus.

cancellation. 1) A notice from a vendor to customers that one or more stock numbers have been deleted from the line. 2) Cancellation of an order or shipment from a vendor by a retailer.

cancellation shoe store. A store that sells only or mostly cancelled, discontinued or closeout merchandise—usually vendors' branded merchandise sold at below regular price.

canepin leather. Fine leather, usually kidskin, but sometimes lambskin or chamois, used for gloves. French in origin.

canoe moccasin. A moccasin pattern similar to a deck shoe; usually oil-tanned, water-resistant upper with soft or rubber sole.

cantilever sole. A traction sole for shock absorption, with a raised outer rim. The sole's middle is smooth and the heel raised to direct the foot along the shoe's center line to disperse shock waves to the sides. Used for some running, court, and aerobic footwear. A variation of this is known as a *biokinetic sole*.

canvas. See *fabrics*.

canvas footwear. A sneaker-type shoe with canvas or

part canvas upper and rubber sole, made by the vulcanized process.

canvas mesh. See *fabrics*.

canvassing. See *house-to-house selling*.

caoutchouc. A word of South American Indian tribes meaning "weeping wood" and referring to the milky latex sap of rubber trees. Discovered by Europeans in the 18th century, it was later developed into raw rubber, which led to the development of vulcanized rubber and synthetic rubber.

cap. See *toe cap*.

capeskin. See *leather*.

capital turnover. The rate of return of capital invested. Net sales divided by the average cost of the stock.

caravan show. A local show or exhibit held jointly by a group of shoe travelers in a given city in the same territory represented by all the travelers, for the convenience of local retailers. The objective is to reduce or make unnecessary individual store calls by the travelers.

carbotine (or karbotine). A primitive shoe of the earliest civilization, it was a simple piece of crude leather drawn around the foot and held on with a rawhide thong around the vamp throat and ankle. Later adopted by the peasants and shepherds of ancient Asia, Greece, and Rome. The native American moccasin is a variation of this. The shoe later acquired a separate sole. Today, in France, the term "carbotine" applies to undressed hides.

carnauba wax. A natural wax taken from the carnauba or ceara palm of Brazil. Used for leather dressings and shoe polish. Also known as ceara wax and palm wax.

carbon black. A fluffy white powder obtained from natural gas and used in some rubber soles to impart certain conductive properties to the shoe. See also *conductive shoe*. Also used in making leather with a pigment finish, and called black pigment.

carpincho leather. See *leather*.

carriage boot. See *boot*.

carrying charge. 1) Interest or other extra charge paid on the balance due on an installment purchase. 2) Costs associated with ownership of property, such as taxes, insurance, and upkeep. 3) Carrying costs on the store's merchandise, such as shelf and storage space and depreciation of outdated merchandise.

carryover. Unsold merchandise retained in stock from one season to another.

cartilage. A tough, elastic, whitish, gristle-like tissue between large bone joints, such as the knee joint, serving as a protective buffer layer.

carton. The cardboard box in which a pair of shoes or boots is packed. The carton comes in various standard sizes. The front face of the carton is usually labeled with the brand, size and width, stock number, color, etc.

case. 1) The large container in which the shoes are shipped from the vendor to the retailer. A case contains anywhere from 12 to 36 pairs of shoes. 2) The individual lots of shoes processed through the factory, each carrying a tag and case number.

cash flow. The flow of cash from sales or revenues used either for cash reserve or to pay bills or to invest in improvements. The state or condition of cash reserves relative to current bills and debts.

cashier's desk. The checkout desk where the customer pays for the purchased merchandise.

casino foot. Sore or tired feet caused by standing for long hours at gambling casinos, such as those who play the slot machines for extended periods; or employees who stand for many hours at their jobs.

cast. A plaster mold of the foot used in making orthopedic footwear or foot orthotics. Today, materials other than plaster are also used. See also *color*.

casual shoe. A loose designation for semi-dress, sportive footwear for leisure, recreational, or informal wear, usually with lower heel and in color. The term "casual wear" originated in 1934 when designer Coco Chanel first introduced casual wear clothing.

category. A classification of footwear based on use, style, age group, lifestyle, size range. E.g., infants', boys', men's dress, casual, slippers.

catalog manufacturer. A manufacturer or distributor who sells to consumers through catalogs rather than through a retail store.

catalog store. A store where retail purchases are made through catalogs. Floor space is elevated to display merchandise. Usually affiliated with large chains, such as Sears.

cats and dogs. Leftover odds and ends of merchandise; broken lots or distress merchandise.

cattlehide leather. Leather made from the hides or skins of cattle; e.g., calves, cows, steers, and oxen. See also *leather* and *side*.

cavalier boot. See *boot*.

cavus. A foot with an abnormally high arch or instep. See also *pes cavus*.

cellular. Consisting of or containing cells, or a state of porosity.

cellular plastics. Resins in sponge form. The sponge

may be flexible or rigid, the cells closed or open and interconnected, and of any particular density. Such materials are commonly used for cushion insoles, midsoles or outsoles.

cellulose. The chief substance composing the cell walls or fibers of plant tissue; a synthetic material with the same structure. Used for making the paperlike materials used in shoe insoles.

cement. See *adhesive*.

cement process. See *shoe construction*.

cemented welt. See *shoe construction*: *silhouwelt* and *namrog welt*.

center-depressed outsole. An outsole with edges higher than the center to create a cupped footbed.

certified pedorthist (C. Ped.). See *pedorthist*.

chain stitch. A sewing method for attaching the sole to the upper with a single-thread stitch using a loop design.

chain store. Relative to footwear, a retail organization with eleven or more stores. The number eleven, an arbitrary figure, was originally specified by the U.S. Census Bureau for compiling shoe business statistics to differentiate between chains and other types of footwear outlets (independents, department stores, discount stores, etc.). However, there are many independents with eleven or more stores that do not classify or regard themselves as chains.

chamois leather. See *leather*.

channel. A slanting cut made around the rim of the insole to provide a groove for the stitching and to keep the line of thread below the surface of the material in the construction of a Goodyear welt shoe. The cutting of the channel is called "channeling."

chaparejos. Spanish name for chaps. See also *chaps*.

chape. The metal framework of a shoe buckle.

chaps. The leather leggings worn by cowboys to protect legs and pants.

Charlie. Trade term for a C width shoe.

Charley boot. See *boot*.

chauffeur's foot. A vocational disorder of the forefoot sometimes occurring among professional car drivers (taxis, trucks, etc.) who are constantly using foot pedals. Symptoms include foot soreness, cramps and burning.

chaussure. French word for footwear.

cheater. Trade term for an insole or slipsole insert used to make an oversized shoe fit more snugly.

checking. 1) The separation of layers on a built-up leather heel resulting from faulty adhesion, exposure to dry heat, etc. 2) Very fine cracks appearing on the surface of leather, usually after short wear,

caused by temperature changes, perspiration, or poor finish.

checkout counter. See *cash desk*.

chemistry. See *leather chemistry, leather chemist*.

cherry picking. In buying by the retailer, the selective choosing the best-selling items in the vendor's line rather than buying a large share of the line.

chestnut. A tanning extract from the bark of the chestnut tree, once commonly used in vegetable tanning.

chevrettes. Skins from goats that have been weaned but are less than a year old. An immature goatskin.

chic. French word meaning a knack, style or discerning good taste, as in clothing or fashion.

chilblains. A painful swelling and soreness of the foot or hand caused by overexposure to cold.

children's shoes. Juvenile footwear category in the 81/2 to 11 size range (8 to 12 extremes). Also, a loose term for all juvenile footwear.

chiropodist. Outmoded term for a podiatrist. See also *podiatrist*.

chiropody. See *podiatry*.

chisel toe. A narrow, flat, tapered toe shape on a last or shoe.

choked-up vamp. See *vamp*.

chondromalacia. Severe knee strain and pain from injury or stress, common among distance runners, football players, and other athletes.

chopine. An extremely high (up to 30 inches) platform shoe, popular with upper class European women of the 16th century. The wood platforms were ornately painted or otherwise decorated. Maids usually walked on either side of the wearer to help maintain the precarious balance.

chromium. A silvery metal whose salts, when compounded with other chemicals, are the basic ingredient for making chrome-tanned leather.

chrome tannage. See *tannage*.

chrome retan. Leather first tanned with chromium salts, then retanned with vegetable extracts.

chromo. A customer who tries on many shoes before buying. Origin unknown.

chukka boot. See *boot*.

CIM. See *computer-integrated manufacturing*.

Cinderella sizes. Women's small shoe sizes in about the 1-to-4 range.

circlet. A small metal tube with a flat head like a nail, driven into the rear edge of the heel for extended heel wear.

circular vamp. See *vamp*.

classic. Any apparel of such good taste or perennial popularity that it continues in style despite chang-

CHOPINE
Venetian chopine or
zoccolo.
Wood, about 2 feet high
xixteenth century

Velvet brocade chopine,
Spanis, sixteenth cen-
tury

German chopine.
Leather with
lace and fringe, c. 1610

White leather chopine,
English,
seventeenth century

ing times or fashions; e.g., a men's wing-tip brogue or a women's plain black pump.

classification. A category of footwear given an assigned designation; e.g., fashion boots, work boots, casuals, etc.

classification merchandising. A system of buying, selling, and promoting footwear by use, wants or needs; e.g., fashion shoes, duty shoes, athletic footwear, etc. It focuses the customer's attention on making selections from particular categories and encourages multiple-pair purchases.

clavis. See *heloma.*

claw foot. A foot deformity wherein the toes are in a permanently clawed position, usually with heavy calluses under the ball, and abnormally high arch and instep. See also *pes cavus.*

claw toes. See *claw foot.*

clearance. A sale of slow-moving, post-season or broken-lot merchandise at reduced prices.

clear vinyl. A transparent polyvinylchloride (PVC) upper material used on women's fashion shoes. Also known as clear vinyl.

cleat. A knob or spike on the sole of a shoe for increased traction; arranged in groups or patterns. Used on golf, football, soccer, and other sports footwear.

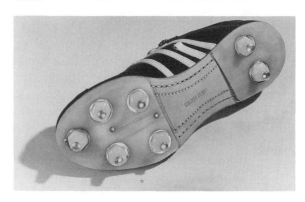

Cleats on athletic shoe.

clicking. The cutting of shoe upper parts by hand or machine in accord with the required pattern shapes.

clicking knife. A knife or blade used in hand or machine clicking.

clicking machine. An automatic cutting machine used for clicking.

climate. The thermal conditions inside the shoe created by the combination of heat, friction, humidity, and perspiration. Climate has much influence on foot and shoe comfort.

clientele. Customers, patrons or clients.

clip. The tightness of shoe fit on the last around the topline; to fit tightly or snugly on the last.

clipon ornament. Any ornament clipped onto a shoe for decorative effect. Usually sold as a supplementary item.

clock. A decorative, vertical side panel in contrasting color on hose.

clocking. A traffic count made inside or outside a store on selected days or hours. Usually done to check the desirability or viability of a store location based on average daily traffic.

clodhopper. A coarse, heavy shoe or boot; a plowman's boot.

clog. A thick-sole wooden shoe, sometimes with leather upper. Clogs have periodic cycles in fashion popularity. See also *klompen.*

Clog.

Clubfoot shoe.

close grain. A tight formation of the surface grain on leather.

closed back. Any shoe with a closed rear section, as with most footwear.

close-edged sole. A sole whose edge is trimmed closely to the upper, with little or no extension. Seen in many men's and women's fashion shoes.

closed mall. A large shopping center where all the stores are enclosed under one roof and air-conditioned, with rents paid to the mall owners.

closed pump. Any pump with closed toe and heel.

closed seam. See *seam*.

closet shoe rack. A rack with shoe-holding brackets on which to place multiple pairs of shoes. The rack is usually on the closet floor. The rack may also be a cloth or plastic sheet with a series of pockets for the shoes, hung on the closet door.

closing. The stitching together of two or more parts of the upper; more generally refers to the stitching operation of the shoe's backpart with a closed seam. The shoe factory has a closing department for this operation.

closeout. A discontinued stock number, model, or line from the vendor's inventory, offered to retailers at reduced prices.

closing the sale. The important final steps in making a sale to a customer.

closure. See *fastener*.

cloth-top boot. See *boot*.

clown shoes. Shoes made exclusively for wear with clown costumes. Made by only a few specialists, usually with specifications from professional clowns. The styles and color combinations are usually grotesque for humor.

clubfoot. A congenital foot deformity in which the foot is severely turned inward so that the arch faces upward and the outer-upper border of the foot be-

comes the walking surface. Appearing at birth, clubfoot is correctible by surgical and other means. Medical name: *talipes equinovarus*.

clubfoot shoe. A shoe designed specially for club-footed infants, used as an adjunct to medical or surgical treatment.

clutch handbag. See *handbag*.

cnemis. A combination sandal and legging worn by soldiers of ancient Rome.

coarse grained. A leather surface showing large, widely separated wrinkles and uneven grain pattern. It reflects inferior quality.

coated fabric. A fabric coated or impregnated with a polymeric substance to give it firmer texture, durability and some water resistance. Some imitation leathers, used for shoe linings and uppers, are coated fabrics.

cobbler. A repairer or mender of shoes; also an apprentice shoemaker not yet a craftsman.

cobbler's seam. See *seam*.

cobcab. A sandal-like shoe with a thick platform sole, worn by women of some Asian countries, especially at public baths.

cocker. An obsolete term for a high shoe or half boot; also a high laced boot worn by hunters and fishermen in the 16th century.

code markings. See *shoe size codes*.

collagen. White protein fibers of the derma layer of hide and skin; a vital component of leather.

collar. 1) a narrow strip of material around the top-line of the shoe for ornamental effect. 2) a padded collar as used on many sports shoes around the rear-part topline for protection against friction or rubbing.

collection. A vendor's or designer's line exhibited to retailers, or at a clientele fashion showing.

colonial buckle. A large, square metal buckle worn over the instep of a shoe of colonial times in both America and Europe. Wealthy persons wore buckles of genuine silver.

colonial shoe. A black, low-cut shoe with square toe

and a large, square, ornamental buckle, sometimes with a high, broad tongue extending over the instep. Worn in colonial America.

colonial tie. A bow or ribbon worn over the high tongue of a colonial shoe to hold the shoe onto the foot.

colonial tongue. See *tongue*.

color. A fundamental element of footwear and fashion. Color dictionaries list over 17,000 different color variations, all stemming from just three primary colors: red, yellow, and blue. Color is associated with many subtle variations or terms important in the expression of footwear fashion and the presentation and selling of fashion. Among them are:

  cast. One color imbued with a hint of another; e.g., gray with a blue cast.

  chromatic. Color having hue as opposed to achromatic colors—white, black, gray—which are neutral and without hue.

  complementary. One of two colors which appear opposite each other, one highlighting the other, as red with blue-green.

  cool. Hues associated with a feeling of coolness, such as tones of blue, violet, blue-green, but not red or yellow.

  coordinated. Colors brought together in harmonious relationship.

  hue. The particular shade or tint of a given color.

  neutral. A color that has none of the primary colors; color without hue. Pongee is a neutral color.

  ombre. Shaded or graduated color, usually going from light to dark tones in one color range, as from light to dark blue.

  palefoot. A fashion term for grays, beiges, off-whites, and pastels; popular for wintertime wear.

  pastel. A soft, delicate tint or pale tone of a color.

  rich. A color with luxuriant expression, such as deep scarlet or purple.

  shade. A gradation or varying degree of a color; the darker tones of any color.

  tint. The lighter tone of a color—the opposite of shade.

  tone. A color's tonal depth or modification of a particular color.

  warm. Hues associated with heat, such as yellow, orange, and red.

color card. A card or chart issued seasonally or periodically by manufacturers of textiles, apparel, leather and footwear to acquaint their respective industries or retailers with the season's new colors and color names. Official color cards are issued by the Textile Color Card Association in the United States and the British Colour Council. The official color cards are issued to prevent chaos of color introductions in the apparel and allied industries and to provide a reasonable color unity and direction each season.

color fastness. The ability of a material to retain its dyes and color without changing or fading with wear or storage.

calfskin leather. See *leather*.

coltskin leather. See *leather*.

combat boot. See *boot*.

combination last. A last departing from standard measurements in the forefoot/rearfoot ratios. E.g., a B width at the ball and AA at the heel. Used to accommodate feet with narrow heels.

combination lasting. The use of more than one lasting method of the same shoe. E.g., moccasin construction shoes are often slip-lasted in the forepart and cement-lasted at the heel.

combination tannage. See *tannage*.

comfort shoe. A loose designation for a conservatively styled shoe with a fuller last, a low to medium heel, a broad toe, soft upper leather, and often a cushioned bottom. Designed for those whose chief priority is foot and shoe comfort.

comma bar. See *bar*.

comma heel. See *heel*.

commisary. A general store, usually on the grounds of a military base or a large factory, whose merchandise is sold to affiliated personnel. E.g., safety shoes sold to factory employees at little or no profit.

commission. Payment of a percentage of the money taken in on sales to a salesperson or sales agent, in addition to wages or salary. A form of sales incentive.

community relations. A stores involvement or participation in community improvements or affairs as a form of local public relations.

common sense heel. See *heel*.

common sense shoe. A loose designation for a shoe of moderate fashion design or in heel height; a basic comfort shoe.

competitive pricing. Setting prices to match or beat those of competitive stores for the same or similar merchandise.

component. Any part involved in the shoe's construction. E.g., heel, outsole, insole, counter, box toe.

Compo process. See *shoe construction*.

composition. Scraps of leather or other materials pulverized, compressed, and held together with a binder to form a sheet material for insoles, midsoles, heel bases, etc.

Computer-aided design (CAD).

compression mold. Shaping materials by heat and pressure.

compression set. The amount of permanent deformity resulting from weight load, pressure, or abrasion, such as an outsole or cushioned insole or midsole.

computer-aided design (CAD). The use of computer graphics to assist the creation or modification of a shoe or last design. A modern technology to greatly increase speed and versatility in the design of lasts, shoes and other products. CAD programs rotate two-dimensional drawings through three dimensions, allowing a "drawing" to be seen from all perspectives.

computer-aided manufacturing (CAM). The use of computerized machinery or equipment for the manufacture of products such as footwear. A modern computer/electronics technology used in factory operations.

computer-integrated manufacturing (CIM). The coordination and integration of a group of computerized machines in a factory for a sequence of related functions in production.

computerized shoe. A shoe containing a small electronic device with computerized elements that record certain performance factors of a runner or walker, such as distances traversed, weight impact on the foot and shoe, stride length, etc.

concealed heel. See *heel*.

concentration. The degree of market share or penetration owned by one or several companies.

concept store. A store specializing in one product category, such as sports footwear; also applies to a store focused on just one brand.

conductive shoe. A shoe without any metal parts (tacks, nails, shank) that can cause a spark. Used by doctors and nurses in operating rooms where a spark could cause ether vapors to explode; or in a chemical or industrial plant where a spark could ignite or explode dangerous chemicals. Also known as an *anti-static shoe*.

condyle. A rounded prominence of a bone at a joint, especially when occurring in pairs, as with the condyles of the tibia in forming the knee joint.

cone. The part of the last corresponding to the foot's instep; important in shaping the shoe for proper fit.

congenital. Genetic, existing at birth, as in some foot disorders or deformities.

conformability. The ability of a material to conform to the shape and movements of the foot with shoe wear.

congress boot. See *boot*.

conservative styling. Restrained, basic, mid-road in design and color; leaning toward classic looks.

construction. See *shoe construction*.

consumerism. A consumer movement, organized or otherwise, demanding some change or improvement in a product category, services, or prices.

consumer spending. A statistical record of consumer spending on footwear annually or for a lesser period. Calculated for a total of all footwear combined or by any given category (men's, women's, juvenile, etc.), or on a per capita basis. See also *per capita*.

consumer price index (CPI). A government issued measurement of inflation or deflation based on the average retail prices of a selected array of goods and services (including footwear). Based on the theory that market-wide trends are accurately reflected by the price of individual goods. The CPI uses an index based on 100 for a given two-year period.

consumption. 1) Total footwear pairage consumed by the public or a nation, state or other demographic area on an annual basis. 2) Total consumption of any particular category of footwear, such as men's, women's, children's, athletic. 3) Consumption on a per capita basis. See also *per capita*.

contact dermatitis. See *shoe dermatitis*.

contemporary fashion. A fashion existing and popular during the current time period.

contests. 1) A competition conducted by store management as an incentive for the salespeople to increase sales, with some tangible reward for the winners. 2) A competition or drawing for the store's customers to spur sales or introduce a new product or line, with a tangible reward for the winners.

continental heel. See *heel*.

continental shoe sizes. See *Paris point*.

contoured insole. Innersole contoured to conform to the sole of the foot. Usually cupped at ball and heel, with contoured cushioning under the arch.

contract shoe manufacturing. 1) A contract or agreement by a large volume retailer or chain with a footwear manufacturer to produce a specified amount, type and price of private label footwear for the retailer. 2) An agreement in which one manufacturer pays another to produce footwear to be sold under the first manufacturer's brand name. Also known as *subcontracting*.

contract system. An 18th- and 19th-century system of American shoemaking in which a small shoe manufacturer cut the uppers, then contracted with another shop to sew the uppers, and contracted with still another shop to apply the soles and heels. The finished "contracted" shoes were returned to the original source, ready for packing and selling. This enabled a low-financed and minimally equipped business to operate profitably and to eventually grow into a full-fledged, self-contained enterprise.

contract tanning. Tanning leather from hides and skins furnished by the customer, usually a large shoe manufacturer. The tanner himself may subcontract a particular operation, such as finishing, to an outside leather finisher.

convalescent shoe. See *surgical boot*.

conveyor. A long belt attached to mechanized rollers to provide a moving platform and continuous transport of materials or components to a sequence of work stations, thus eliminating the need of manual movement of these items on wheeled racks. Also known as a *transport system*.

cookie. A small pad, usually foam rubber or felt covered with leather or other material, used as an arch cushion inside the shoe. It can be built into the shoe or used as a separate insert. Sometimes called a *scaphoid pad*.

cooperative advertising. An arrangement in which a vendor usually provides finished advertising with blank space left to include the retailer's name and logo. The retailer may prepare his own advertising featuring the vendor's brand. The vendor shares in the cost of the advertising.

cooperative money. Money contributed to the retailer by the vendor to help promote the vendor's merchandise or brand, not necessarily only through advertising.

cooperative retailing. In a store with a number of branded departments, each brand vendor is responsible for setting up, maintaining and paying for the displays in his area. He becomes a partner in the inventory, with the store providing the space and salespeople.

coordinated. The assembly or arrangement of all parts of the costume, including footwear, into a harmonious unit of design, color, materials, etc.

copper toe. A copper toe cap used in the 19th and early 20th centuries on children's, police, and firefighters' shoes to protect the toe against abrasion. See also *Appendix I*.

copy. 1) The words or text part of an advertisement. 2) The duplication or simulation of an existing shoe or design. See also *piracy*.

cordoban. A soft, brilliantly dyed leather made by the Spanish Moors of Cordova. In old England it was called "cordowan," and eventually it evolved into the American "cordovan."

cordonnier. French word for a skilled shoe craftsman or cordwainer. The term is derived from Cordova, Spain, which in the 11th and 12th centuries was a famous center for fine shoemaking.

cordovan leather. See *leather*.

cordovanner. Original name for cordwainer. See also *cordwainer*.

cordowan. In the 11th and 12th centuries, the English name for the soft and beautiful leathers imported from Cordova, Spain.

corduroy. See *fabrics*.

cordwain. Tanned and dressed goatskin or split horsehide from Cordova, Spain. Used during the Middle Ages in Europe for boots for the wealthy. An old name for cordovan leather, but not related to today's cordovan leather.

cordwainer. British name for an artisan shoe craftsman or leathermaker.

Corfam. The proprietary name for the first poromeric, man-made shoe upper material. Similar in appearance and texture to leather, it was introduced by DuPont in the early 1960s after 25 years and $125 million in R&D investment. Despite early commercial success, its later dwindling sales forced abandonment.

cork. The outer bark of certain evergreen trees in Mediterranean countries, chiefly Spain and Portugal. A semi-spongy material, it is used in footwear for soles, wedge heels, platforms and bottom filler.

cork boot. See *boot*.

corn. See *heloma*.

coriaceous. Resembling leather in appearance, texture, and performance; a leather-like, man-made, poromeric material. The term was introduced by DuPont for its Corfam material.

Cork sole shoe.

Shoe with cork heel and platform sole.

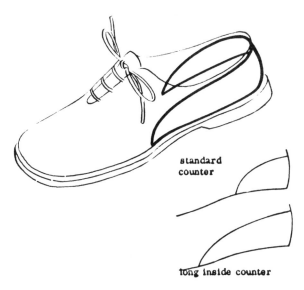

Shoe counter or backpart stiffener.

corrected grain. Leather which has had the outer surface of the grain removed by an emery wheel to delete or "correct" blemishes. Also known as "snuffed finish." (See also *snuffed leather*).

corrected leather. See *corrected grain*.

corrective shoe. An orthopedic-type shoe with orthotic features designed to prevent or correct foot disorders. Sold in some specialty shoe stores. The term is now outmoded and is seldom used. (See also *prescription shoe*).

corset. See *ankle corset* and *arch corset*.

cost price. The wholesale price paid by the retailer.

costing. A factory procedure used to calculate the cost of producing a product. The factory or wholesale price is determined by adding all production costs—materials, labor, overhead, plus sales costs, and profit.

cothornos (also kothornos). The first shoe to use a heel and also the first platform shoe. Said to have been introduced by Aeschylus, the Greek dramatist, in about 450 B.C.E. to distinguish actors and roles by body height—the higher the platform the more important the actor and the role. The platforms ranged up to six inches in height. The cothornos started as a sandal with thongs and straps, then later evolved into a buskin or half boot.

cottage industry. A system of farming out certain factory operations, such as sewing of shoe uppers, to women who did the work in their homes or "cottages." A common practice among shoe factories or shops in the 18th and 19th centuries. It continues today in minor use in some segments of the shoe and apparel industries.

cotton. See *fabrics*.

counseling. A procedure of professional shoe salespeople in counseling customers about fashion, shoe care, foot care, product information, etc., as part of the selling service.

counter. The stiffener or reinforcement in the backpart of the shoe to retain shoe shape and offer stability and support to the heel of the foot. The counter may range from soft to rigid. It can be premolded or flat and then molded to the last by pressure.

counter lining. British for counter pocket.

counter pocket. A piece of lining material attached to the inside face of the counter to conceal the counter which is in the "pocket" between the upper and lining.

counter splint. A strip of flexible material attached to the counter to limit pronation or rotation of the heel of the foot inside the shoe.

court pump. A plain, seamless pump.

court shoe. 1) British term for a plain pump style. 2) A shoe used for court sports such as tennis or basketball.

court tie. A men's oxford, usually in patent leather with black silk bow or tie, used for ceremonial dress in England and other countries. Also applies to a women's two- or three-eyelet tie shoe, usually on a blucher pattern.

couture. Sewing or needle work; the work of a seamstress; dressmaking. Also a collective term for French designer and dressmaking houses.

couturier. French for a male costume designer, usually high fashion.

couturiere. A female costume designer, usually high fashion.

cover cloth. Fabric used to cover shoes during manufacture to prevent soiling.

covered heel. A heel with the same material and color

covering as the upper, or in contrasting material and color.

cowboy boot. See *boot, western.*

cowboy heel. See *heel.*

cowhide leather. See *leather* and *side.*

cow's mouth shoe. See *duckbill.*

crack. The break so that fissures appear on the surface. Usually refers to leather under the strain of lasting, or on the surface of rubber resulting from weathering or deformation.

cracking (or crabkin). A term of the early 18th century, meaning to break into or burglarizing a shoemaker's shop—a common crime of the time.

crackowe. Originally an elegant soft shoe of fine leather and thin sole, sometimes protected with a removable wood slab under it, worn by the upper classes. Introduced in Crackow, Poland, in 1360, it gradually acquired a toe of exaggerated length to become a grostesque style. See also *poulaine.*

crafted. Made or constructed by hand, or as if by hand.

crazing. A surface effect, such as on leather or rubber, characterized by many minute cracks.

creasing. Deliberately impressing creases across the vamp of the shoe, either as a decorative feature or to make shoe flexing easier. Often done with western boots.

credit. 1) The acknowledgment of a debt paid, or a sum deducted from an amount owed, or added favorably to one's account as with a bank or vendor. 2) An allowance given to a customer for a previous purchase. 3) A loan given to a person on the basis of trust.

credit department. The department in a business charged with the billings and keeping records of accounts and payments due. The department which establishes the customer's credit line.

credit line. A customer's credit status with a vendor or bank.

credit manager. The person in charge of the credit department.

credit rating. The level of credit reliability of an individual or business.

creedmore. A cheap, heavy, blucher-cut shoe with gussets, laces and bellows tongue, worn by workmen.

creep. An action of the shoe's bottom filler which, under the combination of the foot's heat, pressure and moisture, softens and "creeps" to the sides to form bumps conforming to the foot's sole tread pattern.

creole. See *boot.*

Crepe sole.

crepe rubber. Latex rubber specially compounded for use as soles or heels. There are various types: natural, blown, plantation, and neoprene.

crepida. A half boot and half sandal which leaves the toes uncovered. It has a thick leather sole like a low platform. A shoe of ancient Greece and Rome.

crest. A ridge or prominence on the insole, filling the groove between the foot's ball and toes and serving as a cushion-like grip surface.

cretati. Referring to the slaves of ancient Greece and literally meaning "chalked people." The soles of the slaves' feet were chalked white when they were sold in the slave markets. The ancient Greeks also slashed the Achilles tendon of slaves who attempted to escape, resulting in permanent crippling.

crib shoe. A soft-sole shoe or knitted bootee worn for warmth by a baby in the crib.

crinkle leather. Usually patent leather with a unique wrinkled or crushed look, achieved with a special tanning method.

Crispianus. See *Saint Crispin.*

Crispin. See *Saint Crispin.*

crocking. The rubbing off or staining from leather, such as suede, or a fabric whose dyes "run."

crocodile leather. See *leather.*

crooked shoes. Derogatory name give to left-and-right shoes when first introduced in America in the early 19th century. All conventional shoes were made on "straight" lasts, meaning shoes that could be worn on either foot. By contrast, shoes made for left and right appeared "funny" or crooked.

crop. A side of hide or leather after the belly and shank portions have been removed or cropped.

cropping. The mechanical process of producing a crop, done before the finishing operations.

croquet shoe. The original name for the first rubber-sole canvas-upper sneakers when introduced in 1868. They were expensive and affordable only by the rich, who used them for playing croquet on their expansive lawns. Also known as a croquet sandal.

cross-over straps. See *strap shoe.*

cross training shoe. A sports shoe of versatile design that can be used for training purposes in two or more sports.

cross travelers shoe. An all-purpose shoe, though the term is now outmoded.

cross wedging. Combination shoe wedging; e.g., a medial heel wedge with a lateral sole wedge.

croupon. An untanned, whole cattlehide with belly and shoulder portions removed.

crown. The lateral contour or convexity across the ball of the last on the bottom surface, creating a mild cavity bed for the ball of the foot.

crumbing. The deterioration of a cushion insole with wear, with sections breaking up into small crumbs.

crushed leather. A leather boarded in several directions to create a unique bumpy grain surface similar to a blistered fabric; a wrinkled, crushed effect. Usually refers to kidskin.

cruiser. See *boot*.

crust. A vegetable-tanned but not finished leather. In this state it is called "in the crust."

caravan. A primitive, thong-laced brogue with untanned upped leather, unlined, and heelless.

Cuban heel. See *heel*.

cuboid. 1) A squat, chunky bone of the tarsus section of the foot. 2) in the shoe trade, the curve or roll of the outside border of the last or shoe at midfoot, corresponding to the shape of the foot in that area.

cuff. A band of leather stitched to the top of the shoe's quarter to increase its height or bulk; a collar. Also used in some boots as a decorative feature in contrasting material or color.

cuir bonilli leather. Hard leather molded to shape while soft from soaking or boiling. Used during the Middle Ages for parts of armor, now used for some decorative leather articles. In French, literally meaning "boiled leather."

cunieform bones. Any of the three small, chunky bones (inner, middle, and outer) in the front section of the tarsus. These bones are jointed with the back ends of the metatarsal bones.

cupped heel. A saucer-shaped heel seat that forms a comfortable and secure bed for the foot's heel.

cupped sole. A saucer-shaped area on the forepart of the insole to provide a contoured bed for the ball of the foot. See also *shell sole* and *contoured insole*.

curing. The treatment of raw hides and skins to prevent putrefaction and bacterial decomposition. It includes the tanning operations of brining, green salting, and pickling.

curling. Curling of the edges of the insole, midsole or outsole with wear, due to heat, perspiration, chemicals, and pressure. It causes the shoe bottom to warp, curl, and crack around the edges.

currying. A tanning operation to soften, strengthen, or waterproof a lightly tanned leather. Performed by manipulating the material and adding fatty substances.

curule. A black and white leather shoe, usually kidskin, with turned-up toe and a side fastening. Worn by the magistrates of ancient Rome as an insignia of their profession.

curved last. A shoe made on a last with a curved or flared design.

cushioning. The use of a resilient material, particularly as an insole or midsole, to absorb step shock and provide a comfort zone between the sole of the foot and the ground. The cushioning may be built into the shoe or may be used as a separate insert.

custom-molded shoe. A shoe made over a last based on a plaster mold of the foot.

custom shoe. Usually made at least partly by hand, either to the customer's design specifications or selected from styles in stock. Meticulous measurements are taken of the foot, which are translated into the customer's last and shoes.

customer benefits. The particular benefits of a shoe accruing to the customer, such as comfort, wear satisfaction, style or design, fit, value, or price, as cited by the salesperson.

customer communications. Any form of communication between the customer and the store or salesperson intended to cement customer service and loyalty.

customer relations. A part of the store's public relations program to create good will and allegiance to the store.

customer record. A record maintained by the store of each customer's name, address, shoe size, dates, types and prices of purchases, etc.

customer research. Demographic study of customers and prospects within the local trading area. The data is used for various purposes: marketing, advertising, type of inventory, etc.

customer service. Any form of service helpful to the customer, such as fitting, counseling, free parking, honoring credit cards, free holiday wrapping, etc.

customer turnover. 1) For a store, the rate of change in the demographic makeup of the store's clientele, such as from younger to more mature customers, over a period of time. 2) A salesperson who is having difficulty satisfying or selling a customer, "turns over" the customer to another salesperson or to the manager in an effort to save the sale.

customs. Duties or tariffs imposed by a government on imported merchandise, usually as a measure of

Cutouts used as design treatment.

Cutouts on shoe upper.

protection for domestic producers of similar merchandise, or as a means of government revenue.

cutoff vamp. See *vamp*.

cutout. One or more small pieces of various shapes cut from the upper pattern, leaving empty spaces as a decorative feature. Cutouts may go through both upper and lining, or through the upper only.

cut price. A selling price below regular or standard price, or below competing prices.

cut soles. Soles cut from a large piece of firm leather or other material. Soles are cut to prespecified sizes in accord with sizes and types of footwear.

cut stock. Particular components of the shoe furnished by suppliers to footwear manufacturers; e.g., insoles, counters, heels, box toes.

cutter. One who operates a clicking or cutting machine in the shoe factory; or one who hand-cuts upper materials.

cutting. In the shoe factory, the process of cutting a material into prespecified sizes and shape in accord with the shoe's pattern. This is done with dies attached to a cutting or clicking machine which can cut either single or multiple layers of material.

cutting dies. The metal blades designed to a prespecified shape, used to cut upper and lining materials.

cutting room. The department in the shoe factory where the cutting operations are done.

D

D. The letter symbol for a D-width shoe size, which is medium for men, medium-wide for women.

damask. See *fabrics*.

dance shoe. A shoe or slipper-shoe. The design and construction varies for different types of dancing—tap, ballroom, ballet, etc.

Men's formal dancing pump with grosgrain bow.

dancing clog. A low-cut shoe with leather upper and a light wood sole, used for some ethnic, such as Irish, dancing.

dash leather. A patent leather finish on a cowhide split.

dash system. See *shoe size*.

database. A large collection of records stored in a computer system from which selected data may be extracted, organized and manipulated; any organized and structured collection of data.

dating. The date on a vendor's invoice; also, a change of the actual purchase date usually to an advanced one, to be used on the vendor's invoice.

daub coat. The first coat or varnish or lacquer applied in finishing patent leather.

Daughters of St. Crispin. A labor union of women shoe workers founded in Lynn, Massachusetts, in 1869. The nation's first women's labor union.

David. Trade term for a D-width shoe.

daytime shoe. A loose designation for shoes worn for daytime occasions in contrast to an evening or more formal shoe.

dealer. A merchant who sells merchandise at the retail level.

dealer aids. Any form of aid provided to the retailer by the vendor, such as point-of-sale displays, counter or window cards or signs, special promotion materials, training programs, fixtures, etc. Provided free or for a nominal sum.

dealer service. The type or quality of services provided to the retailer by the vendor.

deck shoe. See *boat shoe*.

deer foot. A delicate fashion demi-boot with a high wedge heel. Popular with Chinese women of the early 20th century because it made the foot look small, it was worn by women with unbound feet who wished to appear to have the still-admired bound or "lily" foot. Very difficult to walk in, the boot/shoe required the precarious, fragile steps of the sensuous "willow walk" used by boundfoot women. Also known as a *theatre boot*.

deerskin leather. See *leather*.

degrained leather. 1) Leather in which the grain surface has been removed by buffing. 2) Suedes finished on the flesh side from which the grain has been removed by splitting.

delineator. A fashion forecaster. Now a largely outmoded term.

Del-Mac Process. See *shoe construction, skeleton insole shoe*.

demi-boot. See *boot*.

demi-sock. A half or short sock, not showing above the top rim of the shoe.

demographics. A statistical representation of the geographic and socioeconomic makeup of a given population, widely used in marketing.

denier. The designation of yarn sizes in silk and manmade fibers. The finer yarns have lower denier numbers.

denim. See *fabrics*.

Dennis Browne splint. A mechanical orthopedic device attached to the soles of infants' shoes and worn to bed at night. The splint is used in conjunction with medical treatment to correct a deformity or abnormality of the feet, legs or hips.

density. In a midsole or outsole material, a measure of firmness.

Denver bar. See *bar*.

Denver heel. See *bar, heel*.

department. 1) In a shoe factory, a section focused on a particular segment or sequence of the shoe-making process, or a group of related operations. Also known as a "room"; e.g., stitching room. 2) in a large, multi-merchandise store, such as a department store, a section given over to one particular category of merchandise; e.g., men's or women's shoes.

department store. A large retail store containing a variety of separate departments or smaller "stores" under one roof and one management. Sometimes a department, such as a shoe department, may be leased to an outsider.

derby pattern. A shoe pattern with its facings and quarters overlaid and stitched onto the vamp; the reverse of an oxford. The shoe may or may not have a tongue. Introduced in the 18th century for men and women by England's Earl of Derby.

derma. The second and deeper underlayer of skin or hide.

dermatitis. An inflammation of the skin, sometimes caused by shoe chemicals.

dermatology. The branch of medicine specializing in the diagnosis and treatment of skin diseases.

dermis. Skin.

designer. A stylist who creates the design of the shoe.

designer label. Apparel, footwear or other merchandise identified with the designer's name. The label or name is usually associated with a prestigious designer.

detailing. 1) Planning or programming the details of a shoe—pattern, last, colors, materials, heel, silhouette, ornamentation. 2) Creating a special customer order for a shoe, with variations in color or material, in accord with the customer's specifications. E.g., an original black and white model detailed in two shades of brown or a different upper material.

diagonal fitting. A method of fitting shoes that takes into account that in a group of different sizes and widths the inside-shoe volume or space is about the same. For example, a 7 1/2AAA, 7AA, 6 1/2A and 6B would provide about the same inside-shoe space for the foot. But they would not fit equally well because there would be differences in size/width proportions, and also a difference in the distribution of the same volume. Diagonal fitting is often used

in shoe stores, though usually the salesperson or fitter does not recognize it by its name.

diamond tip. See *tip*.

die. A metal cutting piece shaped to cut pieces of material to a pattern.

dieing out. Cutting shoe parts or cutouts with a die by hand or machine. Also called die cutting. See also *clicking*.

digit. A toe or finger.

digitigrade. Walking on the toes with the heel off the ground. The gait manner of horse, deer and other hooved animals.

dinking. The machine-cutting of heavy leathers or other materials. The dies used for dinking are heavier and thicker than dies used on clicking machines.

dink toe. A colloquial term for toeing in.

direct mail. Any advertising material such as letters, postcards, brochures, leaflets, calendars, catalogs, etc. sent through the mail by a vendor or retailer or mail order house to customers and prospects.

direct selling. Door-to-door selling of a product or service by a salesperson.

discalced. Unshod, barefoot, as traditionally with some monks and friars; also some who wear simple sandals but never shoes or boots.

discontinued merchandise. Merchandise in stock that will not be reordered by the retailer. Also, vendors' merchandise no longer available to retailers.

discount. A reduction from the list or regular price. Various forms include quantity discount, trade discount, cash discount, and credit discount.

discount store. A store selling merchandise at below standard mark-on or regular price.

discretionary spending. Purchases made by consumers with the money left over after all essential bills or expenses are paid.

dish sole. See *shell sole*.

display. Any exhibit of merchandise or promotional effects related to merchandise inside the store or in the store windows. The act or process of exhibiting merchandise or promotional effects.

display case. Usually a glassed-in unit displaying merchandise inside the store.

display form. A light, plastic, foot-shaped form inserted in the shoe to hold the shoe's shape for window or other display.

distal. The part farthest from the center, such as the toe tips from the center of the foot.

distress merchandise. Merchandise still in stock after undergoing several markdowns or clearances. Hard-to-dispose merchandise, sometimes sold to jobbers or given to charity organizations.

distribution. The process of moving merchandise from the vendor's or supplier's shipping point to the retailer; the network system for the movement of goods.

distributor. The vendor or supplier who distributes the merchandise or who uses the distribution system.

divide system. See *shoe sizes*.

diversification. The spread or assortment of merchandise categories made available to customers to serve a broader range of customers or customer needs.

Doctor of Podiatric Medicine (D.P.M.). The title and degree of a medical practitioner specializing in the diagnosis and treatment of foot disorders. A podiatrist.

doctor shoe. A shoe designed by or conforming to the specifications of a medical practitioner, usually in the orthopedic category, for the prevention or alleviation of foot problems. It may be sold under the doctor's name.

doeskin. See *leather*.

dog. A hard-to-sell shoe.

dogs. Slang for feet.

dogskin. See *leather*.

dogtail quarter. An extension of the top of the back of the outside quarter, overlaid and stitched to the inside quarter to reinforce the backseam. Also known as a *half hurley*.

dog walloper. A young boy hired to keep stray dogs away from the merchandise on open displays outside the store or in outside stalls. The boy brandishes a stick with which he "wallops" the offending dog before damage is done. The term is Australian in origin. This "system" is used by some shoe stores and other merchants in open bazaars in different parts of the world.

dollar round. An out-of-date term for a round-toe shoe with the toe shape resembling half of a silver dollar.

doll's shoe. A miniature shoe of very thin leather or other material designed for a doll's foot.

Dom Pedro. A heavy, cheap, single-buckle men's work shoe with bellows tongue. Named for Brazilian Emperor Dom Pedro.

dongola kid. See *leather*.

door-to-door selling. See *house-to-house selling*.

d'Orsay pump. A shoe with a circular vamp and quarers that curve downward into deep V-cuts at the sides for foot exposure. Introduced by Count D'Orsay, a French dandy, about 1840.

dorsiflexion. An upward-rearward motion of the forefoot with the toes pointed toward the leg.

dorsum. The top surface of the foot.

double-header. A sale of two pairs of shoes to one customer in the store.

doubler. An interliner between the toe lining and vamp of the shoe. Commonly made of flannel and cotton nap fabrics in twill, drill or sheeting weaves.

double sole. Two layers of soling on the shoe for extra heft or durability.

dowel. A thin shaft of metal or plastic which runs through the core or shaft of a higher heel to reinforce against heel breakage.

dowie slipper. See *slipper*.

downtime. The time in which a machine or piece of equipment is idle because of temporary failure.

down to the stick. On the last, the length measurement heel to toe tip. Some shoe fitters allow extra length beyond the actual foot size, especially in fitting shoes for children. Many lasts have no extra shoe length allowance. In the lastmaker's language such lasts are "down to the stick," meaning the actual stick size measurement.

D.P.M. See *Doctor of Podiatric Medicine*.

drape. To cover with a fabric or other material, gathered in folds, as on a shoe's vamp.

draped heel. See *heel*.

draping. The draped arrangement of fabric, leather or other upper material as on a shoe's vamp.

drawn grain. See *grain, shrunken*.

dress shoe. A general designation for any shoe worn for business or dress-up occasions, daytime or evening, but not formal wear. Opposite of a casual shoe.

dressed kid. Kidskin leather with a smooth or glacé finish, generally on the grain side.

dressing. 1) The application of special finishes to leather chiefly to render the leather more flexible and waterproof. 2) The application of special finishes to a shoe to enhance color and shading, and also for cleaning and polishing.

drill. See *fabrics*.

D-ring lacing. A D-shaped metal or plastic ring serving as an eyelet to provide more flexibility and a more comfortable adjustment of the lacing.

dropoff. The front vertical edge of a rocker bar. See also *bar, rocker*.

drum. In tanning, a revolving cylindrical container for hides and skins, usually equipped with pegs for lifting the stock. Used for such operations as washing and dyeing.

dry loft. Storage space for dried leather awaiting selection for further processing.

drying. Applied to hides, skins, leather and shoes to

remove moisture by use of dry hot air, or direct heat from special equipment in the shoe factory or tannery.

dual density. A shoe component with two different sections having different degrees of resilience or flexibility, such as sole and heel on a unit sole, to meet the functional requirements of the different parts of the foot.

dual tone. A shoe made of material in two shades of the same color.

duck. See *fabrics*.

duckbill shoe. A shoe with an extremely broad toe up to 12 inches wide. The top of the toe and vamp is liberally decorated with slashes or cutouts. A popular upper-class fashion of the 16th century, especially in England. The style is also known as a *bear's paw* and *cow's mouth*.

dumb shoe. Trade term for a plain, conservatively styled shoe without any particular design or fashion character. Usually applied to women's shoes.

Duo process. See *shoe construction*.

duplication of lines. At retail, carrying of brands or lines that overlap or are similar in style, quality, and price.

durability. The ability of a material, component, or shoe to resist wear or abrasion.

durometer. A pointed instrument for measuring the resistance of a material to penetration or puncture.

durometer scale. A system for determining the degree of resistance to penetration or puncture of a material and its density on a scale of 0 to 100, with the lower readings indicating lesser resistance or softness. Used to test and rate shoe materials such as outsoles.

dusting powder. An ordinary talcum powder used to prevent adhesion. Often sprinkled inside the shoe to enable the foot to slip in easily when the foot or hose is damp. Commonly used in shoe stores.

dutchboy heel. See *heel*.

Dutch foot. Trade term for a short, extra-wide foot.

dutchman. A thin wedge of leather or fiberboard inserted between the insole and outsole, or between the lifts of a heel, to tilt the foot to correct a faulty balance or tread.

duty. A government tax or tariff imposed on imports, exports or manufactured goods.

duty shoe. A uniform-type shoe usually worn by nurses and others in medical occupations, and also by waitresses, hairdressers, laundresses, etc. Usually a white oxford with low heel and broad toe.

dwell time. The amount of pressure time applied by machine to bond parts of the shoe, such as sole to upper.

dyeable shoe. A shoe made of a material that readily accepts dye. Often used by bridesmaids so that all the shoes are in a matching color.

dynamic fitting concept (DFC). A system of geometric last grading to improve shoe fit with fewer sizes and widths. Developed in the early 1960s by Genesco, a Nashville, Tennessee shoe manufacturer. The last widths are graded about 1.5 times the usual geometric width increment, and also different from the 1/4-inch increments used in arithmetic width sizing. See also *geometric last system*.

Dynametric systems. A last-grading system (Dynametric I and II) designed by Battelle Memorial Institute in the early 1960s to combine the best features of the dynamic fitting concept and a geometric system for improved fit with fewer sizes and widths.

dysfunction. The incomplete or faulty function of a body or product part.

E

E. Letter symbol for an E-width shoe.

early bird discount. A discount from the regular price given by a store on purchases made during designated early morning hours. A promotional tactic to attract customers during slower business hours.

early buy. Purchases made from a vendor or supplier to assure early delivery.

earned discount. See *purchase discount*.

earnings. 1) Net profit for a business. 2) Combined wages or salaries plus commissions, bonuses, and fringe benefits for salespeople.

Earth Shoe. Proprietary name for a shoe with an oblique toe and a negative heel. A comfort and cult shoe popular in the early 1970s. The shoe design was copied or pirated by an estimated fifty manufacturers.

Earth Shoe.

eclipse tie. A one-eyelet tie shoe for women, with closed stitching at the throat and with a small, pointed tongue.

écrasé. Crushed, as in crushed leather.

ecru. See *color*.

ectrodactyl. The fusing of the bones of the toes and/or fingers with accompanying webbing of the toes and/or fingers.

Eddie. Trade term for an E-width shoe.

edema (or oedema). A swelling of a body part such as a foot or ankle.

edge. The full edge of a shoe's sole.

edge finishing. The trimming, staining, dressing, or burnishing the sole edge. The finished sole edge can have any of several shapes such as beveled, round, square, extension, fudged, feather.

edge setting. See *edge finishing*.

edging. Beveling a very narrow scarf from leather or fabric, particularly where upper parts are joined by seams, or where upper edges are finished by burnishing. The work is done on a skiving machine.

educational selling. During the selling process in the store, "educating" the customer about the shoe—its construction, materials, fashion features, the fit, last, etc. Also called *informational selling*.

EE to EEEEEE. Size designations for progressively wider shoe widths beyond an E width.

egg heel. See *heel*.

Egyptian sandal. A simple soled sandal held onto the foot with a thong between the big and second toe, attached to an ankle strap. One of the earliest sandals dating back at least 5,000 years. Lefts and rights were first introduced in such sandals, though only for wealthier or upper-class individuals.

elastic threads. Threads made from stretchable materials. Used in weaving shoe goring and backing cloth for elasticized shoe materials.

elasticized leather. Shoe upper leather backed with flexible, yarn-woven fabric whose threads contain rubber to give stretch and contraction.

elasticized materials. 1) Elastic goring used as shoe panels or inserts. 2) Upper leathers or fabrics backed with elastic-thread materials.

elastomers. 1) Any substance or mixture containing natural rubber and having rubber-like qualities; 2) Synthetic rubber.

electric foot massager. A small mechanical device

Examples of simple, ancient Egyptian sandals.

on which the feet rest while being massaged with vibrators.

electric shoe shiner. A mechanical device with black and brown brushes which revolve and polish shoes held against them.

electrodynogram. An electronic apparatus using sensors for testing stance and gait pressure points on the foot. Used by gait laboratories, podiatrists, and other medical practitioners for testing and diagnosis

Vibrating electric foot massager.

of foot and gait problems related to foot balance, tread, faulty pressures, etc.

electronic data interchange. (EDI). An electronic communications system between manufacturer/vendors and volume shoe retailers. It allows vendors and retailers to quickly transmit important information such as invoices, purchase orders, shipment notices, inventory status, etc.

elevation. 1) The material or height added onto the sole or heel for extra height, or to elevate one foot when the leg is shorter; used in shoe therapy. 2) The heel measured from floor to heel seat at the back of the heel.

elevator shoe. A proprietary name for a men's shoe with raised features concealed inside the heel seat of the shoe, plus a moderately higher heel, to increase the wearer's height.

elkskin leather. See *leather*.

elongation. A lengthening or extension, such as with a muscle or tendon.

embossed leather. Any smooth leather on which any kind of grain or design is imprinted by an embossing machine under heavy pressure. Also known as *printed leather*.

embossing. The process of imprinting designs or grain patterns on the surface of smooth leather or man-made shoe upper materials by embossing machines with design plates that imprint the design onto the materials under heat and pressure.

embroidery canvas. See *art canvas*.

embroidered fabric. See *fabrics*.

emu leather. See *leather*.

enameled leather. See *patent leather*.

end of month (EOM). An inventory accounting system referring to inventory status at the end of the month versus beginning of month (BOM). The difference in overall inventory, or any selected portion of it, between the beginning and end of the month represents the number of units sold and also the numerical state of the inventory.

endromis. See *boot*.

energy return. The rebound effect when weight is removed from the foot's spring apparatus (arches, muscles and tendons, ligaments) or the shoe's cushioning materials. The stored energy is released to create the elastic spring effect. Usually associated with sports footwear or athletic activities.

engineered last. A last incorporating certain functional features designed to facilitate shoemaking operations such as standard heel seat shape, back cone height, plane relations.

engineer's boot. See *boot*.

40

engineer's boot. See *boot*.

English foot. Hose with a side seam in the foot portion.

English jockey boot. See *boot*.

English last. A last with a low heel and a long recede toe.

English shoe sizes. Similar to the American system with one-third inch (8.466 mm.) between each full size. However, English infants' size 0 begins at exactly four inches while the American size 0 begins at 3 and 11/12th inches.

ensemble. A coordinated costume—dress, coat, hat, handbag, shoes, gloves, etc., creating a harmonious effect of color and line. The word is from the French, meaning "together."

envelope handbag. See handbag.

epicondyles. The bony prominence above the condyles where the ligaments attach. (See also *condyle*).

epidermis. The top or outermost layer of the skin.

equinovarus. A clubfoot deformity in which the foot is turned inward and the toes are on a lower plane than the heel. See also *clubfoot*.

equinus. A deformity in which the foot is pointed downward and the walking is done on the toes, as with a horse's hoof. See also *toe walking*.

equine leather. See *leather*.

ergonomics. The study of the relationship between humans and machines or working environment from physical and psychological aspects. Workplace engineering.

escarpine. A simple, low-heel pump with a very long pointed or square toe.

Eskimo boot. See *boot*.

espadrille. A rope-sole shoe with canvas or strap upper for casual wear. (See also *alpargata*).

Espadrille.

estivan. See *boot*.

estivaux. See *boot*.

ethyl vinyl acetate (EVA). A foam material commonly used as midsole cushioning, usually in sports shoes.

etiology. The cause of an injury or disease.

eupodology. The art or practice of foot esthetics or beautification.

Europoint. A metric system of measurements and sizing of lasts and shoes, developed by the British Shoe and Allied Trades Association (SATRA), and designed as a universal shoe sizing system. Now superceded by the Mondopoint system. (See also *Mondopoint*).

EVA. See *ethyl vinyl acetate*.

even pricing. Setting even dollar prices; e.g., $5.00, $10.00), in contrast to odd or off-cents pricing.

Everett slipper. See *slipper*.

eversion. An outward motion or movement of the forefoot.

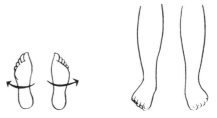

Eversion of foot.

exclusivity. A retailer's agreement with a vendor for exclusive territorial rights to the selling of a particular brand or product.

exercises. See *foot exercises*.

exhibit. A vendor's display of merchandise or services at a trade show.

exostosis. A bony outgrowth from the surface of a bone; a bone spur.

exotic leathers. Unusual leathers made from the hides or skins of such creatures as reptiles, sea turtle, iguana, llama, yak, ostrich, walrus, penguin.

expanded rubber. Rubber infused with air, hence lighter, softer, more resilient and less durable than hard or natural rubber. See also *blown rubber*.

expanded vinyl. Soft, nonbreathable, stretchy base polyvinylchloride material. Softer and more flexible than nonexpanded vinyl.

expenses. The costs involved in the operation of a business.

export. The sale and shipment of goods to foreign customers or markets.

extended counter. See *long counter*.

extended eye stay. A shoe with an eye stay that extends downward or forward to form the toe cap.

extension. A forward stretching of the foot or any of its parts such as the toes or foot, or a muscle or tendon, on weight bearing.

extension edge. A sole edge that projects outward more than average. Also known as an extended sole.

Extra-depth shoe to accommodate orthotic insert.

extracts. Vegetable materials (wood, bark, leaves, nuts, etc.) from which tannin is extracted and used in vegetable tanning.

extra-depth shoe. A shoe made on a special last that allows for more inside-shoe volume or space to accomodate a thick/fat foot or an orthotic insert.

extra pairage. Purchases or sales of two or more pairs of shoes by the consumer customer.

extremes. 1) Categories of hides classified by weights outside the standard ranges. E.g., country hides 23 to 45 pounds, or extreme light Texas steers 23 to 48 pounds. 2) Shoe sizes extending beyond the regular size range in a given footwear category. E.g., youths' regular sizes 1 to 3; extremes 11 to 3.

eyelet. A small, flat ring of metal or plastic attached to the upper along the eye stay to provide holes for the laces to pass through.

eyelet facing. See *eye stay*.

eye stay. A facing or strip of leather, fabric or other material attached to the rim of the shoe upper along the front or eyelet edge. Also known as an *eyelet tab*.

eyelet tab. See *eye stay*.

eyeletting. The factory operation of inserting eyelets in a shoe upper, or of embroidering eyelets.

F

fabricate. To make, manufacture or assemble a product.

fabrics. Cloths that are knitted, woven or felted from a natural or man-made fiber. The most common types of fabrics used for footwear are:

brocade. A rich, decorative fabric with dimensional design, often woven from metallic threads to give the effect of embroidery or raised stitching.

canvas. A strong, coarse cloth of cotton, flax, or other fibers closely woven in a basket weave.

corduroy. A pile fabric with cords of cotton, or wool ribs, of either plain or twill weave.

cotton. The most common of shoe fabric fibers, used alone or mixed with other fibers for shoe uppers and linings.

denim. A strong, coarse, washable cotton fabric in a twill weave.

drill. A heavy cotton fabric with a diagonal weave.

duck. A tight-weave cotton or linen fabric with a flat or ribbed weave.

embroidery. An ornamental design in silk, cotton or metallic threads.

faille. A silk with a carded effect.

flannel. A lightweight, loose-woven wool, or cotton fabric in plain or twill weaves, usually lightly napped.

flax. A soft, silky fiber of the flax plant, woven into linen. (See *linen*).

foulard. A soft, serviceable, washable, satiny silk with fine twill; plain or printed, but usually has figures on a contrasting background.

gabardine. Tightly woven, deep-twilled fabric in wool, cotton or rayon, or a mixture of these.

glitter. A fabric with glistening flakes adhered to the surface to give it a sparkling appearance.

grosgrain. A tightly woven fabric with heavy corded finish, with the cords rounder than those of faille.

jacquard. A figured fabric woven on a special loom, giving the same effect as brocade.

khaki. A stout cotton cloth of dull, brownish color.

linen. A plain or damask woven fabric made from flax, easily dyed.

madras. A firm cotton fabric, usually striped, woven with basket or figured weaves.

mesh. Lattice-like design woven with either natural or synthetic fibers.

metallic. A fabric in which metal-covered threads have been woven to given a unique look of interwoven metal and fabric.

moiré. Silk, cotton or rayon with a "watered" look obtained in the finishing process. The material is usually ribbed.

novelty. A broad range of fabrics which are printed, embroidered, embossed, or otherwise ornamented.

nylon. A generic term for a synthetic fiber filament, used in full or mesh weaves.

peau de soir. A firm, soft, durable silk in twill weave with a dull, satin-like finish.

poplin. A firm, durable, medium-weight fabric in plain weave, with fine cross ribs. Made of cotton, silk or wool, or combinations.

pongee. A thin, soft, undyed fabric in plain weave, made of irregular yarns of silk, cotton, rayon, etc., smooth or slightly rough in touch.

orlon. A proprietary name for a synthetic fiber filament.

rayon. From cellulose, it embraces many types of man-made fibers.

sateen. A satin-imitation cotton fabric.

satin. Silk or rayon fabric made by the satin-weave process.

serge. A wool fabric with a pronounced twill weave on both sides; cotton or rayon may also be used.

shantung. A fabric made of silk, rayon, or cotton and having a rough, nubby surface.

43

silk. A natural fiber from the cocoon of the silk worm and producing a smooth, soft luxury fabric with a sheen finish.

tapestry. A fabric where a design is woven in colors into the weave.

terry cloth. A cotton fabric with uncut loops formed by the addition of an extra warp thread.

velvet. A fabric with a fine, short pile, made from silk, nylon, cotton or rayon.

whipcord. A fabric with a type of twill weave and with a heavier ribbing than gabardine.

fabric shoes. Any footwear having uppers entirely or mostly of fabric.

facing leathers. Lightweight leathers used for facing seams or for binding the edges of shoe uppers.

facing rows. Ornamental stitching on the eyelet tabs of the quarters.

facing stay. A reinforcing material placed under the tabs of the quarter and pierced by the eyelets to strengthen the shoe at the place where the fastening occurs.

factor. One who renders a factoring service for a business.

factoring. Selling of accounts receivable outright to a factoring or brokerage house, thereby providing the manufacturer or other business with working cash. The factor investigates credit risk and assumes all responsibilities for the accounts receivable. The amount of the factor's "loan" to the manufacturer or business is based on the value of the accounts receivable.

factory damaged. (FD). Shoes received by the retailer from the factory with some kind of defect. Also, footwear sold by the store or factory and marked as FDs, then sold at a discount price.

factory defect. See *factory damaged*.

factory department. See *department, factory*.

factory-owned store. A retail outlet owned and operated by a manufacturer which sells only merchandise produced by the manufacturer.

factory outlet. 1) A store, usually situated near or on the property of a factory, that sells a manufacturer's discontinued or factory-damaged merchandise to the public at discounted prices. 2) An independent operation not associated with a manufacturer but buying closeouts and discontinued merchandise from a variety of manufacturers and selling at discount prices to the public. Usually a large volume retailer with a large-space rack store.

factory run. See *table run*.

factory sole leather. One of the two main types of sole leather. Tanned and finished to have more flex-

ibility and compressibility for use with shoemaking machinery in making new shoes. See also *finders sole leather*.

factory system. Assembly line shoe production using a corps of workers, each employed at a specialized task for the sequence of the assembly process, in contrast to one workman making the shoe from start to finish. The system was introduced in 1750 by John Adams Dagyr, a Welshman, in Lynn, Massachusetts. With the advent of shoe machinery in the latter half of the 19th century, the factory system dominated in the production of low-cost, mass-produced footwear, and became the model for mass production systems for virtually all products thereafter.

factory value. The wholesale price of a shoe based on costs for materials, labor, equipment, overhead, and the manufacturer's profit.

fad. A popular, cult-type fashion or idea that appears abruptly, then quickly fades. A passing fancy usually associated with the young.

faille. See *fabrics*.

fair stitch. Stitching that runs around the top edge of the sole of a McKay construction shoe to give the appearance of a Goodyear welt. See also *stitched aloft*.

fake. A manufactured imitation or substitute of a natural material. E.g., fake fur or fake leather.

fallen arch. A depressed or flattened long arch of the foot. Not to be confused with a normal low arch or flat foot.

family shoe store. A store selling men's, women's, and children's shoes. Also known as a "gender store."

fancy leathers. Leathers with an unusual grain or finish or other special character, whether natural or the result of embossing or processing.

fancy stitching. Stitching that is primarily ornamental, as distinguished from functional stitching.

fascia. A sheet or band of tough fibrous membrane connecting bones or joints or serving as a protective layer. See also *plantar fascia*.

fashion. A temporary, prevailing or accepted style or group of styles in current vogue. Fashion is ephemeral and cyclical.

fashion coordinator. One who coordinates or harmonizes current fashions, colors or materials. Sometimes employed by shoe manufacturers, tanners, materials producers, or large stores to help guide store buyers in regard to fashion trends.

fashion cycle. The periodic turn and return of any fashion, such as certain toe shapes, heel shapes or heights, materials, designs, etc. Cycles usually swing gradually from one extreme to another over a period of time.

fashion delineator. A fashion forecaster or writer.

fashion flat. Flat-heel shoes currently in vogue.

fashion forecast. A prediction as to which fashion or trends will be popular during the coming season or year.

fashion piracy. See *piracy*.

fashion show. A presentation of new apparel or accessories lines by designers and manufacturers for retail buyers and members of the press.

fastener. Any device that holds together or fastens separate parts, such as a button, buckle, zipper, strap, lacing, velcro.

fat ankle shoe. A trade term referring to a comfort or orthopedic shoe made with uppers fitted especially for fleshy or fat ankles.

fatigue. Deterioration of a material caused by repeated stress or deformation.

fat pad. 1) A large fatty pad covering the long inner arch of an infant's foot during the first few months after birth. 2) A marble-size mass under the talonavicular joint. 3) A fleshy pad on top of an infant's foot behind the toes.

fat wrinkle. Tiny folds or markings on leather caused by fat accumulation under the original hide or skin. When the skin is tanned the tiny fat wrinkles remain as a natural part of the leather's character.

faust slipper. See *slipper*.

feather. The line around the shoe in the crevice where the upper abuts with the outsole or midsole or welt.

feather edge. A very thin sole edge used mostly on women's fashion shoes. The term also applies to some shoe components such as counters. See also *skived edge*.

feature shoe. A shoe with one or more orthopedic or orthotic features such as a metatarsal pad, cookie, contoured insole, special last, etc.

FD. See *factory damaged*.

fell. A hide, skin or pelt.

fellow. One of a pair of shoes or lasts.

felt. Matted fibers of wool, cotton, or hair, compacted by pressure into a sheet. Used for uppers on some slippers and also as insoles or cushioning for heel pads, cookies, tongue linings, and bottom fillers.

fenestration. See *cutouts*.

fetish. 1) An intense sexual fixation on some particular part of the body or on a particular article of clothing or material. 2) Foot fetishism is a strong sexual affinity for the foot of a person of the opposite sex. 3) Shoe fetishism is the powerful sexual attraction of the fetishist to the shoes of a person of the opposite sex. 3) Leather fetishism is a sexual arousal by the touch or smell of leather or leather apparel such as clothing or shoes. Of the fifty known sexual fetishisms, foot and shoe fetishisms are the most common. Almost all sexual fetishists are male and heterosexual.

fiber. A slender, thread-like structure associated with leather or plants (cotton, flax) or animals (wool, hair). Or the fiber made be synthetically produced (nylon, dacron, orlon). Leather fibers are formed into interwoven bundles for great tensile strength.

fiberboard. Loosely applied to cover a wide range of composition materials used in footwear. It usually consists of fibers from such materials as hemp, leather, flax, etc., combined with paper and binder, compacted under pressure to form a firm sheet or board. Used for counters, insoles, heel bases, and built-up heels. Also known as *leatherboard*.

fiber optics. A communications technique where information is transmitted in the form of light over a transparent fiber such as a strand of glass. The communication is noise free and not susceptible to electrmagnetic interference. The technique has application to industrial production, including footwear.

fibula. The outer of the two leg bones and the smaller of the two. It is not a weight-bearing bone.

FIFO. See *first in, first out*.

filigree. Delicate, ornamental open design such as lace-like jewelry. Sometimes used on shoe ornaments, or on fabrics or leather.

filler. 1) Any material used to fill cavities in a shoe, such as a bottom filler to fill the cavity between insole and outsole. 2) A substance used to add weight and body to leather.

fill-in sizes. Missings sizes reordered by the retailer to fill in stock absent from the size range.

findings. Small parts used in making shoes, such as nails, eyelets, lacings, buckles, heel pads. Also, incidental items like polishes, arch cushions, laces, etc. in a shoe store.

finders sole leather. One of the two main types of sole leather. Less flexible and compressible and more suitable for shoe repairing. See also *factory sole leather*.

finger-foxed. Having a pierced quarter cut so that the heel foxing extends forward to the throat in a narrow strip below the upper part of the quarter. The lower piece looks like a hand with the forefinger extended.

finger gore. See *goring*.

finger stitching. A short double row of stitching which reinforces a blucher pattern at the corner where the quarter overlaps the seam.

finish. A top coating applied to the upper to give the surface a particular visual effect. A finish can also be applied to the outsole. The common upper leather (or man-mades) finishes are:

    aniline. A transparent, mirrored look, usually applied to full-grained leathers. Perhaps the most common of shoe finishes.

    antique. A subtle, two-toned effect usually associated with fine woods or old leather bookbindings.

    burnished. Similar to antique finish but with less shadowing. Produces an effect like hand-rubbed wood grain to give a rich, polished depth to the leather.

    glazed. A high lustre accomplished by passing a glass cylinder at high speed over the leather. Applies chiefly to kidskin or calfskin.

    gun metal. A semi-bright, blue-black finish similar to the color of new gun barrels. Used on some better grade shoes.

    lustre. A transluscent glow with a subtle inner reflection much like the soft glow of a pearl. Also known as *pearl finish*.

    matte (or mat). A flat, dull, eggshell look for a subdued tone.

    metallic. Similar to the natural surface look of any of various metals—gold, silver, bronze, copper. Commonly used on evening shoes, and also on some flamboyant boots.

    napped. A buffed surface in any of different degrees of nap, from fine suede to coarse brushed.

    patent. A shiny, sparkling, high-gloss finish with dimensional depth. Also known as a *gloss finish*.

    pearl. See *lustre* finish.

    pigment. An opaque surface for color fullness.

    satin. A dull finish, (See *matte* finish).

    suede. See *napped* finish.

    waxy. A dull, rustic look with a subtle waxiness to the touch. Used on heavier glove-type leathers for casual shoes and work/outdoor boots.

finishing room. One of the major departments in the shoe factory, where the bottom of the outsole is finished, lasts removed from the shoes, sock linings and heel pads inserted, inspections and other finishing operations performed, Also known as *packing room*, *treeing room* and *shoe room*.

finnesko boot. See *boot*.

firm grain. A leather or other material with a tight fiber and grain structure.

first in, first out (FIFO). A system used in accounting which assumes that the first merchandise put into the warehouse or inventory is the first to be sold.

first steppers. Shoes worn by infants for the initial stages of walking.

firsty. Trade term for an infant's first walking shoe.

fishing boot. See *boot*.

fishskin leather. Leathers made from the skin of smaller fish such as eel, salmon, stingray, sea bass, or carp, but does not include shark or porpoise.

fishtail toe. An extremely long, turned-up-toe shoe design like a fish tail. Popular in 11th- and 12th-century Europe.

fit. The ability of the shoe to conform to the size, width, shape and proportions of the foot. Sizing that allows for proper fit and foot function inside the shoe.

fitness walking. Walking for exercise and health benefits.

fitter. A person skilled in the proper fitting of shoes; one whether skilled or not, who fits shoes to customers in a store.

fitting. The procedures of ensuring proper shoe fit for the foot.

fitting allowance. Extra space allowed in a shoe, especially for length, for foot-stretch or expansion. Especially important in children's shoes to accommodate foot growth.

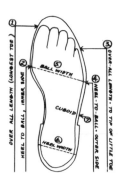

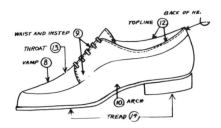

Test points in professional fitting of shoe.

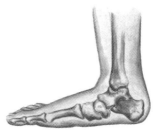

fitting mirror. A floor or wall mirror in the store to allow the customer to view the shoe on the foot.

fitting platform. A long, raised platform on which the customer can stand and take a few steps, enabling the fitter to judge the fit of the shoe in profile. Most often used in stores specializing in juvenile or orthopedic footwear.

fitting room. The factory department where various parts of the shoe upper are prepared for fastening together by skiving, folding, marking, and sewing. Also called the *stitching room*.

fittings. The buckles, studs, ornaments, or other functional or decorative attachments to a shoe.

fitting scale. The progressive increments of length and width sizes in a fitting plan or system.

fixed assets. Any asset of a business with collateral value, usually of continuing or permanent worth, such as property or cash.

fixed costs. The basic costs or expenses of a business that do not fluctuate with revenues, such as rent, utilities, insurance, and depreciation.

fixture. Any stand, bracket, support, shelving or other device or equipment for storage or displaying samples of the store's stock.

flaccid foot. A flabby, slack, loose-jointed foot lacking firmness.

flagship store. The main or central headquarters store, as in a department store chain.

flange heel. See *heel*.

flanged lasting. See *flanging*.

flanging. The edge where the rim of the upper is turned or flared outside for attachment to the outsole or midsole rim, as in a stitchdown construction.

flanky. See *pipey*.

flannel. See *fabrics*.

flapper. See *Appendix II*.

flared heel. See *heel*.

flared outsole. An outsole with a rim or edge that flares or extends outward for increased stability. Most common in some sports shoes.

flash. The extra plastic material appearing on the edge of a molded edge, as on a vulcanized or injection-molded sole when removed from the mold. It must be removed to give the shoe a finished look.

flat foot. A foot with no visible long inner arch. Flat feet can be congenital, in which case the condition may be normal, not affecting foot function. Flat feet as a result of a gradual breakdown of the arch structure is generally accompanied by foot distress and faulty function resulting in a labored, shuffling gait. The medical term for this is *pes planus*.

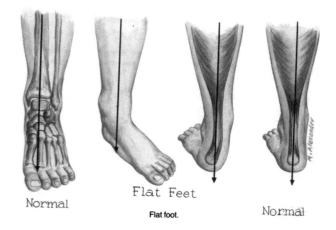

Normal

Flat Feet

Flat foot.

Normal

flat heel. See *heel*.

flat lasting. A shoe lasting method in which the upper is pulled over the last and fastened to the insole with quick-drying cement, tacks, or staples, first at the toe, then at the heel, then along both sides under the last. Flat-lasted shoes are form-fitting and provide a flat base and stable tread with good torsional rigidity.

flattie. Women's or girls' shoes with a low, broad or pancake-like heel.

flax. See *fabrics*.

fleece. The coat of wool or hair covering sheep, llama, alpaca, camel, vicuña or cashmere goat. Also, a textile fabric with a soft, fleecy pile. Fleece refers only to fabrics containing fibers classified as wool. Fleece is used as linings for some slippers and some weather or outdoor boots.

flesher. The underlayer of a split sheepskin.

fleshing. A tannery operation in which the fat and other fleshy parts are removed from raw hides and skins.

fleshy foot. A foot with a thick covering of tissue, including fat, especially on the top surface.

flex angle. The angle across the ball of the foot, or across the ball of the shoe corresponding to the foot's flex angle.

flex grooves. Strategically placed grooves in the midsole or outsole under the ball area to increase shoe flexibility.

flexible flat foot. A foot that is mildly arched with the foot at rest, but whose arch flattens on weight bearing without foot distortion. Usually it is a normal foot anatomically and functionally.

flexible shank. A shoe shank that yields or flexes under pressure; a shoe without a rigid shankpiece.

flexible sole. A shoe sole that flexes easily with the flex action of the foot. The foot's flex angle at step takeoff is about 55 degrees. For a shoe to be fully flexible it would have to flex to about the same 55-degree angle with the same natural ease as the foot.

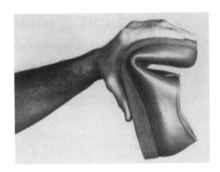

Flexible sole.

flexion. The bend action of the foot across the ball, or of a shoe or outsole across the ball and vamp. The degree of the flex action is an indication of the functional normalcy of the foot or the walking ease of the shoe.

flexion energy. The propulsive energy released when the foot takes a forward step from a fixed point.

flex life. The relative ability of a material or shoe to withstand repeated bending stresses.

flight boot. See *boot*.

floater. A customer in a store who leaves while the salesperson is in the stockroom getting shoes. Also, a customer who habitually shops from store to store seeking the merchandise he or she wants.

flock. A short fiber of cotton or wool used as filler for molding materials.

floor manager. The person in charge of the selling floor or a department, and responsible for personnel, department procedures, and stock.

floor space. Total square footage of a store or other business. It may be divided into selling space and storage or stockroom space.

Florentine leather. Fine-tooled leather often worked with gold and another color. Used for belts, handbags, book bindings, and decorative accessories. Originally made in Florence, Italy.

flow embossing. See *flow molding*.

flow molding. 1) Shaping heated, viscous plastic with a mold. 2) The process of molding a design into the surface of a plastic or vinyl shoe upper, using a silicone mold under pressure to emboss a leather grain design on a man-made material. Also known as *flow embossing*.

fluffing. Producing a soft texture on either the grain or flesh side of leather.

fluting. A narrow pleating applied to the flat surface on the upper; a series of parallel channels cut into the upper.

flying buttress. See *heel, flying wedge*.

flying wedge. See *heel*.

foam. Any of various resins in sponge or cellular form with an open or closed cellular pattern. Softer foams such as polyurethanes are used for shoe cushioning, while denser foams are used for midsoles and outsoles to provide resilience and shock absorption.

foam rubber. Spongy rubber made from latex by whipping or foaming the rubber before the vulcanization process. Usually used for shoe cushioning in insoles.

focused retailing. See *niche retailing*.

folding. Turning over the edge of a shoe upper to form a finished edge. Also called *pressing*.

followup sale. Any additional sale following the initial purchase by a customer.

foot anatomy. The structure or morphology of the bones and other tissues of the foot and their design as a unit. The human foot consists of 26 bones, plus two pea-sized sesamoid bones, 19 muscles and tendons in addition to 13 more coming down from the

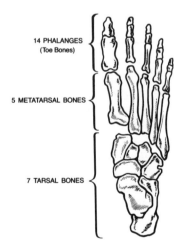

14 PHALANGES
(Toe Bones)

5 METATARSAL BONES

7 TARSAL BONES

Bones of foot (not including two pea-sized sesamoid bones under great toe joint).

leg and attached to the foot. It also has 38 joints and 107 ligaments, in addition to several bursae, a plantar fascia, arches, nerves, blood vessels and sweat ducts. The foot is divided into three sections: the rearfoot with seven tarsal bones, midfoot with five metatarsal bones, and the toes with 14 phalangeal bones. The foot also has four arches, two of which are "true" arches.

foot aids. Commercial products sold for relief or prevention of various foot problems such as corns, ingrown nails, arch ills, etc., and consisting of balms, lotions, powders, pads and, arch supports.

foot angle. The angle formed by the space between the two feet in standing or walking, determined by the direction of the toes, such as angled outwardly or inwardly or with the feet in parallel positions.

foot appliance. See *appliance*.

football shoe. See *sports shoe*.

footbed. The area and shape of the shoe on which the foot directly rests; the insole and midsole.

foot binding. See *bound foot*.

foot coolant. Any substance that gives the skin of the foot a cool, refreshed feeling.

foot frame. An extension on the surface of the midsole, or an additional piece that cradles the foot, for extra support and to prevent the foot from running over.

foot exercises. Any of a variety of motion patterns of the foot to strengthen muscles and tendons and improve the condition of other tissues or functions, such as blood circulation. Sometimes prescribed by medical therapists to increase functional efficiency of the foot and as an adjunct to medical treatment.

foot exerciser. Any device designed to exercise the foot or any of its parts to develop strength and functional capacity.

footgear. Any form of footwear. Usually applies to coverings for protection and utility rather than for dress or fashion wear.

foot growth. The pace or amount of foot growth in juveniles from infancy to maturity.

foot health. The general health status of the foot.

footie (or footy). See *footsie*.

foot measurements. The measurement of the foot as a whole or any of its parts or sections. In the shoe store, usually only two or three measurements are taken (overall length, ball width, sometimes heel-to-ball). For custom-made shoes a dozen or more measurements may be used. In scientific (anthropometric) work, 20 or 30 measurements may be taken. See also *podometrics*.

foot measuring device. Any device used to measure the foot or any of its parts.

foot mold. 1) A plaster or plastic cast from which a duplicate mold of the foot is obtained. 2) An appliance orthotically shaped to the sole of the foot.

foot orthopedics. The science or study of foot biomechanics; the diagnosis and treatment of mechanical foot disorders.

foot shield. See *instep guard*.

footsie. An old and universal gesture between male and female of rubbing their feet and/or legs together for sexual signaling and mutual exchange of sensual contact. Usually the foot action is concealed, such as under a table.

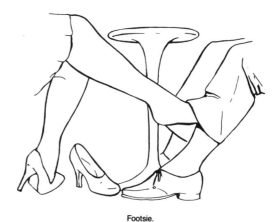

Footsie.

foot strike. The action or impact of the foot or any of its parts striking the ground in walking or running.

foot structure. The anatomical structure of the human foot.

foot talc. See *dusting powder*.

foot type. The design or shape traits of the individual foot classified by a particular anatomical type. Among shoe people and medical practitioners feet are classified by such loose labels as short-wide, long-narrow, bony, fat-fleshy, inflare, outflare, etc. In anthropometry, however, the types are more precisely designated based on measurements or geometric shapes. Foot type may be classified anatomically or functionally or both. Anatomical foot type is believed to be related to foot function and a predisposition or resistance to various foot disorders.

foot warmer. Any article or device designed to keep the feet warm in cold temperatures. Often used by persons with poor foot circulation.

footwear. Any foot covering in the form of shoes, boots, slippers, or hose used for utility and/or dress wear. Not necessarily synonymous with shoes, which are simply one category of footwear.

force lasting. See *shoe construction: slip-lasted, California process*.

force platform. Testing equipment used to measure the impact forces on the foot in standing, walking, or running.

forecast. A projection of anticipated sales or fashion developments.

forefoot. The part of the foot from the ball or metatarsal heads forward.

forefoot control. A shoe or orthotic designed to control the direction of movement of the forefoot in walking or running.

foreman. The head or manager of a manufacturing department in the factory.

formal shoe. A shoe for wear with formal attire.

forty-four boy. A junior helper to the salespeople in the store, such as returning shoes to the shelves. Origin unknown.

foulard. See *fabrics*.

foxing. A reinforcement or covering at a point of particular stress or wear. Usually a piece of material forming or covering the lower part of the quarter or attached to the top of the back seam.

franchise. The right to market a manufacturer's product or service, usually exclusively for a specified area or territory.

Franco-Cuban heel. See *heel*.

freak last. A last of unusual or grotesque shape, sometimes used for theatrical or circus footwear.

freestanding store. An unattached building occupied by a single retail outlet; a store not in a mall or shopping center or in company of other stores.

freight cost. A vendor's shipping charge to the retailer, or from a supplier to a manufacturer.

French-American sizes. See *shoe sizes*.

French binding. See *French cording*.

French calfskin. See *waxed calfskin*.

French cording. A narrow fabric binding, usually in contrasting material, applied to the top edge of the shoe upper.

French falls. See *boot, cavalier*.

French foot. Hosiery with a center sole seam.

French heel. See *heel*.

French kid. Originally fine quality kidskin imported from France. Currently applied to any alum- or vegetable-tanned kidskin with a finish resembling French kid. The term is little used today.

French seam. See *seam*.

French sizes. See *shoes sizes*.

French toe. A narrow-square recede toe, usually on men's dress shoes.

fringe benefit. Any earnings of an employee other than salary, wage, commission, or bonus. It can include employer-paid medical or life insurance, paid vacation and sick leave.

fringe tongue. See *tongue*.

frized leather. See *leather, mocha*.

frogskin leather. See *leather*.

front. The forepart of a hide or skin, particularly horsehides.

front strap. See *strap*.

front gore. See *goring*.

frostbite. A condition caused by prolonged exposure to extreme cold and affecting the toes, foot, finger, ears, nose. Accompanied by swelling and consequent damage to tissues.

fudge edge. A sole edge that does not protrude beyond the lasted upper but closely hugs the shape of the last.

fudging. Wheeling the protruding edge of the shoe's sole in imitation of Goodyear welt stitching. See also *wheeling*.

full brogue. A bal or blucher pattern featuring a long wing tip extending back to the throat of the shoe, trimmed with bold pinking, perforations and stitching, usually on men's shoes. See also *brogue* and *half brogue*.

full-fashioned. Hose knitted to shape on a flat machine and later seamed up the back.

full grain. The outer or grain surface of leather from an unblemished hide or skin. Top quality "uncorrected" leather with a natural flawless surface. Also known as *top grain*.

full regent pump. A pump with a circular vamp and a full quarter. A narrow collar extends from the forepart of the quarter around the throat of the vamp. The collar, which is part of the quarter, may extend without a seam to the remaining quarter, in which case the two quarters and collars are cut from a single piece and the shoe is a "full" regent pump. See also *three-quarter regent pump* and *split regent pump*.

full vamp. See *vamp*.

functional shoe. 1) A shoe designed for a particular use or purpose, such as an athletic shoe. 2) A shoe designed to conform to the functional requirements of the foot. 3) A shoe for active wear in contrast to a strictly dress or fashion shoe.

fungus. A parasitic growth on organic matter, which causes mold or mildew to form on leather. Also, a skin infection such as athlete's foot.

furniture heel. See *heel*.

fur-trimmed shoe. The top edge or collar of a shoe, boot, or slipper trimmed with fur for warmth or ornamentation.

futures. Purchases made or contracted for on the commodities markets in advance of availability or production of the product based on anticipated price on a given forward date. Hides and skins are commonly purchased in this manner.

fuzzie-wuzzie (or fuzzies). A category of slippers using a mass of fleece or shearling inside or outside.

G

gabardine. See *fabrics*.

gain. The difference when the materials actually used are less than the materials cut, as in leather or cloth.

gait. The manner of moving on foot, as in walking or running.

gait cycle. The sequence of a single step or stride, start to finish, seen as separate segments of the sequence.

gaiter. A cloth or leather covering for the leg, buttoned or buckled or laced on the side and usually secured by a strap under the foot. Sometimes also an ankle-high leather boot with elastic goring at the side and a cloth top.

gait laboratory. A place for scientific testing with special equipment to record and analyze gait.

gait mechanics. The structure and "engineering" of the gait.

gallacia. A wooden sabot worn in the country or wet weather in ancient Rome.

galosh (or galoshes). 1) In the Middle Ages, a wooden clog held onto the foot with a strap or thong over the instep. 2) In more recent times, a protective rubber overshoe fastened with buckles or a zipper.

galuchat leather. See *leather*.

gamashes (or gamoshes). Gaiters. Also, a high boot worn in the late 17th century.

gams. Colloquial term for women's legs. Derived from the French *gambe* for animal leg.

gang. A group of shoe workers who went from factory to factory to perform needed work. Often consisted of specialists in one or more operations, such as lasting or heeling. This kind of employment used in America until the mid-19th century was known as the "gang system."

gang room. The bottoming department of a shoe factory. Archaic.

Ganges leather. Printed leather simulating small-grained snakeskin.

gape. Said of a shoe when the toplines do not cling closely to the foot when in motion.

garment leather. Leather used to make apparel such as coats, jackets, skirts, pants, etc. Usually such leathers as sheepskin, pigskin, cabretta, kidskin, or horsehide.

gastrocnemius. The largest of the calf muscles.

Gaulish shoe. A wooden sabot of ancient Gaul. The term evolved into "galosh."

gem duck. A heavy fabric cemented to leather insoles to support the lip for stitching and attaching to the welting and upper. Used in Goodyear welt shoes. See also *fabrics*.

gem insole. A leather insole reinforced with gem duck for making Goodyear welt shoes.

gender store. See *family shoe store*.

gentle craft. In centuries past, a name given to shoemaking when it was a hand craft, and when shoemakers sat quietly doing their work.

gentlemen's shoe. Dress shoes for business executives, professional and white-collar employees as distinguished from footwear worn by blue-collar workers. A common designation of the 19th and early 20th centuries, though occasionally used today.

genu. Referring to the knee.

genu valgus. Medical term for knock knees.

genu varus. Medical term for bow legs.

geometric grading. A last-grading system in which the increments per size and width are specified as a constant percentage of the dimension. The increments are in geometric points. One geometric point is 0.003 times the original dimension, which increases for each point. The increment between full sizes in all dimensions is 10 geometric points. Girth dimensions grade 8 points between widths, or approximately 0.24 times the original dimensions.

geometric last system. An engineered last using a geometric proportional system of grading between sizes in a size run—designed to match the traditional arithmetic system as closely as possible. The main difference between the geometric and arithmetic systems is that with the geometric the size-to-size changes conform closer to the proportional changes in the foot with size progressions.

gēta. Native clog of the Japanese. A platform-like shoe raised 2 to 12 inches above ground and held onto the foot with leather or cloth thongs. There are no lefts and rights and no front and back.

ghillie (or gillie). A low-cut, laced sport shoe without a tongue, often with corded lacing which passes through loops crossed over the instep and frequently around the ankle. The name is for the Scottish hunt attendants or "gillies" who wore a cruder form of the modern ghillie shoe.

Gibson. See *blucher*.

Girl Scout Shoe. A brown laced oxford with broad toe. The "official" shoe of the Girl Scout uniform.

girth. Any of several circumference measurements taken on the last, such as around the ball, waist and instep; or similar measurements on the foot used for custom-made shoes.

give-away. See *premium*.

glacé. French for frozen or iced. For leather, it refers to a smooth finish on a glossy, polished surface, as in glazed kid or patent leather. (See also *glazed kid*.)

glazed kid. Chrome-tanned kidskin, usually in black, given a glazed or glacé finish.

glazed leather. Leather finished with a high polish by means of friction under pressure, a process known as glazing. Usually applied to kid and calf leathers to distinguish brightly finished leather from duller finishes.

glitter fabric. See also *fabrics*.

gloss finish. See *finish, patent*.

glove leather. Leathers such as cow or steer hide, kid, sheep, deer, pig, and horse treated with a special oil tannage to give the leather a soft, plumpish feel with a waxy finish. Used for some casual footwear, deck shoes, work and outdoor boots.

golf shoe. See *sports shoe*.

golfer's foot. Discomfort under the outer border of the foot, or under the ball, experienced by some golfers.

golf spike. Special studs or spikes applied to the sole of the golf shoe for traction.

gondola last. A low-wedge, platform-type shoe with turned-up Turkish toe that gives the shoe a gondola-like appearance.

Goodyear welt. See *shoe construction*.

goosestep. The stiff movement of the lower limbs marching in cadence, the foot slapping the ground and leg swinging like a pendulum. Used by 18th-century Prussian troops as a military parade exercise, and later adopted by the troops of Nazi Germany in the 1930s and 1940s.

gore panel. See *goring*.

gore pump. A pump with an elastic goring, concealed or visible, at the throat or sides.

goring. A fabric woven with rubber threads to form an elastic material. Used in footwear in various applications. The main ones are:

finger. Used mainly in high-front shoe styles. The goring is used between the lining and upper leather.

front. Concealed, with a top opening of not less than three-fourths inches, applied at the shoe's throat or instep for snug, clinging fit.

side. Applied in V-shape or U-shape at the sides of the shoe.

sleeve. A single piece of concealed goring extended from one side strap around the back of the shoe to the end of the other side strap, for snug fit.

gore panels. Double rows of stitching sometimes used where added support or strength is needed.

grab. See *knock-down*.

grade. 1) The change between sizes and/or widths of any portion of the last. 2) To increase or decrease the length of shoe patterns to form a set.

grading. 1) Appraising hides, skins, and leather by quality and size, which determine their value or price. 2) The process of grading the last proportionately by size, width, and other measurements. 3) The measuring method used by designers or pattern makers to size the original or model patterns of a shoe.

grain. 1) The outer surface pattern of a hide or skin which includes the hair follicles and pores just beneath the thin layer of epidermis. During the tanning process of unhairing the epidermis is removed and the underlayer becomes the grain surface. 2) On finished leather, the nature and design of the surface. 3) The grain character produced by special tanning operations on leather, such as boarded or crushed, or the embossed or printed patterns on man-made materials. The more common types of grains are:

boarded. A mechanically produced grain that accentuates the grain surface and also softens the leather. The grain is fine-lined and remains intact throughout the wear life of the shoe.

drawn. See *shrunken grain*.

marbled. A natural mosaic pattern of indentations

visible on the surface, corresponding to the network of tiny blood vessels beneath the surface, leaving a marble-like pattern.

open. A coarser or more open grain, in contrast to a small, tight grain. Open-grain leathers are usually stretchier and of lesser quality.

pebbled. A grain design with multiple raised dots created by embossing.

pin seal. A natural fine grain on highgrade sealskin, often imitated by embossing, and called "pin grain leather" to distinguish it from the genuine.

scotch. A coarse pebbled grain embossed on heavy leather; originally from Scotland.

shrunken. A special chrome-tanned treatment that shrinks the leather to give the surface a unique fine-wrinkled effect. Used chiefly on kid, calf, or other light leathers. Also known as "drawn grain".

grained leather. Leather finished by a chemical or mechanical method (boarding, embossing) to create a particular surface grain pattern.

granny boot. See *boot*.

grass shoe. A homemade shoe of plaited straw with a rope sole. Worn by peasants in Asian countries.

gray goods. Fabric prior to bleaching, dyeing or finishing.

greaves. A legging made from leather or knitted cloth (or sometimes light metal plates), worn by soldiers for leg protection in battle during the 12th to the 17th centuries. See also *Appendix II*.

Grecian heel. See *heel*.

Grecian sandal. A leather sole cut to the foot's sole shape, the upper consisting of any of a variety of styles or patterns of straps attached to the foot, ankle, or leg. Worn by the ancient Greeks and related civilizations.

green salted hides. Raw, wet hides weighing 40 to 70 pounds, ready for salting (called green salting) and curing prior to tanning.

grid layout. A layout arrangement to direct store traffic along a pre-determined path or course. A supermarket layout is an example. "Grid" is for gridiron, a football field design.

grid sole. A rubber, plastic or composition sole with a grid-like pattern on the surface for traction.

grinning seam. A shoe seam that opens because the thread breaks, or a seam not tightly closed.

grommet. A metal or plastic eyelet used on leather or cloth. See also *aglet*.

grosgrain. See *fabrics*.

gross margin. See *margin*.

gross margin return on inventory (GMROI). A measure of retail inventory productivity. Obtained by dividing the gross margin dollars by the average inventory at cost. It reflects the number of margin dollars earned for each dollar invested in inventory.

group buying. An arrangement in which a group of independent retailers buy merchandise as an organized group to obtain lower prices because of bulk orders.

growing girls' shoe. A juvenile footwear category for girls' shoes in sizes 21/2 to 9 (extremes 2 to 10).

growth. Refers to the rate of foot growth from infancy to about age 16. While there are "average" foot growth rates, growth tends to occur in spurts, thus digressing from the averages. Foot growth is an important consideration in fitting children's shoes.

guild. An organization of persons of the same craft or skills to uphold craft standards and protect the mutual interests of the members. Usually more selective than a labor union. Guilds date back to ancient times.

gum boot. See *boot*.

gum rubber. Raw rubber made from a gummy sap drawn from the rubber tree during the sapping season. Formerly used for some rubber footwear. Today, most footwear rubber is synthetic and vulcanized.

gumshoe. A police officer or detective. Derived from the gum rubber shoe soles they wore around the early 20th century. Now outdated.

gun metal. See *finish*.

gusset. An insert of leather or rubber webbing at the upper sides or back, or concealed at the throat, of some shoes and boots, such as a congress boot, to provide fitting adjustment.

gusset leather. Pickled sheepskins.

gym shoe. Sneaker-type footwear used for gymnasium activities or sports.

gypsy seam. See *seam*.

gypsy vamp. See *vamp*.

H

hair-on leather. Leather tanned without the removal of the hair from the hide or skin.

half boot. See *boot*.

half brogue. A bal or blucher pattern featuring a wing tip extending halfway between the normal tip line and the throat of the shoe, trimmed with pinking, perforations, and stitching.

half hurley. See *dogtail quarter*.

half-length sock. A sock not covering the toes or ball, extending only to the waist or instep of the foot.

half pair. 1) A single shoe in any stage of manufacturing. 2) A single shoe of a pair.

half size. The increment between a full shoe size. In American or arithmetical sizes, a half size amounts to one-sixth of an inch.

half sole. A sole extending from the toe to the front of the shank, but not covering the shank. Applied in shoe repairing.

half Wellington. See *boot*.

hallux. Medical term for the great toe.

hallux rigidus. A stiff, inflexible great toe, caused sometimes by such conditions as arthritis.

hallux valgus. A great toe abnormally bent toward the other toes, often accompanied by a bunion over the joint.

halter. See *jimmy*.

halter strap (or halter back). See *strap shoe*, *slingback* and *open back*.

hammer toe. A toe deformity in which the toe is

Hallux valgus of big toe joint.

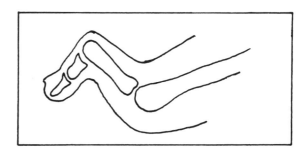

Hammer toe.

drawn back in claw-like position. The cause may be congenital, or due to habitual wearing of short or pointed-toe shoes.

hand. The texture or feel of leather or fabrics by which the character or quality is appraised.

handbag. A pouch or bag carried in the hand or on the arm of women. Size and shape vary with contemporary fashion. First popularized in about 1910. The more common or basic types are:

attache. Flat with a hard frame; a smaller version of an attache case.

backstrap. With a strap at one end of the bag.

barrel. A cylindrical, barrel-like shape with a stiff frame. It may have either a handle or an over-the-shoulder strap.

box. Rigid and opening like a box. In round, square or oval shape with single or twin strap handles.

clutch. Soft, medium size, shaped like an envelope and carried in the hand.

envelope. With a flap closing like an envelope and snap-fastened. It may or may not have a handle.

melon. Round, with fullness allowance via goring, shaped like a melon.

mesh. Small and made of flexible or metallic fabric of linked wire mesh, often gold or silver. Sometimes known as a "whiting bag."

muff. A combination of handbag and muff, usually of fur or fur-like fabric with a lined opening for

57

attache   box

clutch

inserting the hands between the bag section and the outer surface.

pancake. Made of two flat circles of leather or fabric, joined halfway up, with double handle.

parachute. A pouch type shaped as if made from a flat piece of material plaited into a closing. Resembles an open, upside-down parachute.

pillow. Semi-soft, partially pleated, shaped like a small, rectangular pillow.

pouch. Small or medium-size bag with a pouch-like shape, with zipper or cord or snap closure.

reticule. A small to medium-size drawstring handbag popular in mid-19th century America. The term is outmoded. Similar styles in larger sizes and called drawstring bags are used today.

round robin. Semi-circular with a top handle and an envelope flap.

satchel. Shaped like a small valise.

shoulder strap. With a long strap, worn hanging from the shoulder; sometimes adjusted for under-the-arm use.

tamburine. Round and flat with a strap handle, similar to a pancake bag.

top handle. With one or more handles at the top.

umbrella. With a pocket at the bottom of the pouch for a stubby umbrella, which is usually sold with the bag.

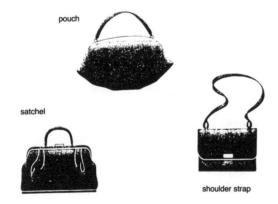

pouch

satchel

shoulder strap

underarm. Flat, handleless, and carried under the arm, sometimes with a flat back strap.

vanity. Rigid, box-like bag with built-in sections for lipstick, compact, comb, coin purse, etc. Usually with a mirror inside the cover.

whiting. See *mesh*.

handcrafted shoe. A shoe made entirely or mostly by hand.

handout. Shoe patterns or soles cut by hand instead of by machine.

Handcrafted shoemaking in 19th century.

hand cutting. A skilled, slow, and costly method of cutting shoe upper patterns, used before the advent of faster, more efficient and economical machine cutting.

hand lasting. Lasting the upper by hand instead of by machine. The upper is attached by hand to the insole by tacks, nails, cement or stitching.

handsewn. A method of construction in which the sole is attached to the upper by hand. Also, a construction of a moccasin plug at the vamp to give a unique raised seam or puckered look. Machines can simulate a handsewn look to some degree.

hand stitched. See *handsewn*.

hand-turned shoe. See *shoe construction*.

hand welted. The welt and upper sewn to the insole rib by hand.

hang tag. A label or tag attached by string to a shoe to describe the special features of the related product.

hard sell. Aggressive, pushy selling by either the store

Hand sewing of moccasin.

Heart shoe.

or the salesperson, with the customer pressured to make the purchase.

hard-toe shoe. A shoe with a hard, usually raised, box toe. See also *safety toe*.

hard goods. Usually larger, bigger ticket items made of wood, metals, or plastic (home appliances, furniture, etc.), in contrast to soft goods (shoes, clothing, etc.). The term is used for economic classification.

hard-to-fit foot. A foot of unusual size or shape, or with some serious anatomical defect, that is difficult to fit with conventional shoes.

hardware. Decorative or functional metal or plastic trims on footwear, such as buckles, zippers, horsebits, large eyelets, or hooks.

harness. See *saddle*.

harness boot. See *boot, motorcycle*.

hashing. In the store, broken lots of shoes combined as clearance merchandise into categories of colors, sizes, materials, heel heights. Usually arranged in bins or on racks for self-service or self-selection.

haute couture. Fashionable, expensive clothing of top-name designer houses of Paris or other fashion centers. Sometimes applied to shops or commercial houses of internationally known footwear designers.

haute monde. High, elitist or fashion society; the world of that society.

haute ton. French for high fashion.

Hauser bar. See *bar*.

hayfoot. See *strawfoot*.

health shoe. An orthopedic or prescription shoe, or a conventional shoe with special orthotic or comfort features. A now outmoded term.

heart sizes. The best-selling sizes or size/width combinations in the center of the size run.

heart shoe. A shoe with a heart carved or imprinted on the sole to leave an imprint on the ground. A popular European women's or girl's style of the 17th and 18th centuries. Sometimes hearts were embroidered on the shoe's vamp or tongue.

heat sealing. Applying viscid, warm, flowing plastic under pressure to seal sole and upper, as in the injection molding process.

heat setting. The application of heat to lasted shoes to allow the upper material to stretch for better shape adaptation and retention.

heavy duty footwear. Boot or shoes designed and constructed for heavy-duty wear; usually water-resistant and with rugged leathers and soles.

heavy leather. A somewhat general term that includes sole leather and heavy-duty upper leathers.

heavy stitching. Stitching done by machine with heavy thread and large stitches in imitation of hand seams used in saddlery.

heel. The raised component under the rear of the shoe, consisting of any of a wide variety of shapes, heights, styles and materials. The raised heel has origins dating back at least 3,000 years and was used in a utility manner to prevent the feet of horsemen from slipping out of the stirrup, and also to increase the wearer's stature and status. The modern high heel (two or more inches in height) dates back to the 16th century and has evolved into a primary fashion feature in a shoe, but also has retained its original purpose of increasing stature and status. Among the common heel types or styles are:

ashley. With flared sides and the breast set forward. The heel is pitched forward for arch support. Usually for orthopedic use.

baby Louis. A lower Louis heel. See also *Louis heel*.

barrel. Of nearly cylindrical shape, resembling a barrel in profile.

block. Long, set-forward heel about 10/8 in height. Used mostly on western boots.

boulevard. A higher, slimmer, and lighter Cuban heel; usually covered with a material matching or contrasting with the shoe's upper.

built-up. High and slender with stacked layers of leather to give a layered look. Usually used with spectator-type pumps. Also known as a "stacked" or "spectator" heel.

comma. Instead of falling in a straight line, the center of the heel's shaft is deeply curved inward toward the arch, then sharply curved rearward at the bottom, becoming crescent-shaped like an inverted comma.

common sense. Any low, broad heel, especially on women's shoes.

concealed. See *inside heel*.

continental. High (16/8 to 19/8) slender heel with straight/flat breast and less back curve than a Louis heel, with a lip extended part way under the shank.

cowboy. Any of various styles worn on western boots, usually 10/8 or higher.

Cuban. Medium height (14/8 to 16/8), with a rectangular shape from any perspective, and usually covered.

draped. Bound in back to the foot with a kerchief-like draping.

dutchboy. Low, rounded heel with a long seat and broad toplift. The breast is angled low and covered with a thin portion of the sole.

egg. Flat and oval shaped.

flange. Medium height, flaring out at the bottom for a wider base.

flat. Very low (4/8 to 6/8), broad, worn with flattie shoes.

flared. See *flange heel*.

flying buttress. See *flying wedge heel*.

flying wedge. A wedge heel with an oval opening or space under the shank area. Also known as "flying buttress," "loop," and "tunnel."

Franco-Cuban. A narrower, mare slender Cuban heel.

French. Covered and high, very curved at the breast; similar to a Louis heel but higher.

furniture. Originally made of natural furniture woods and clear wood grains, shaped to conform to contemporary designs in furniture legs. Now made of plastics. First introduced in the 1930s.

Grecian. High with a wide heel cup and small toplift, with the breast and back lines flaring out from toplift to cup.

half wedge. Essentially a wedge heel but with a small "air space" under the shank, instead of the whole sole and heel resting flat on the ground.

high. Any heel above 16/8 (two inches) in height.

hourglass. With a narrow neck and flaring out at the top and bottom, shaped like an hourglass.

inside. The raised section concealed inside the shoe so that the shoe appears heelless, and a sole flat from toe to back.

lavoratory bottom. British term for a curvy, squattish heel of medium height, shaped like the outside bottom portion of a toilet bowl.

little. Mid-height, with a curvy, slender shaft, flaring wide up to the heel cup.

loop. See *flying wedge heel*.

Louis. High, with a graceful curved back and sides; the lip extends part way under the shank, creating a curved breast, and the heel pitched forward toward the shank. Sometimes called a French heel. Named for King Louis XIV for whom it was designed.

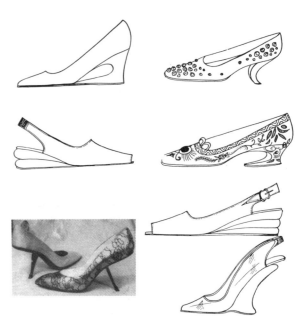

Examples of novelty heels.

mid. Slender and flared, of medium height. See also *little heel*.

military. A low heel stacked with built-up layers of leather; a heavy, squat look.

museum. Low, thick and curvy, of various shapes.

negative. Lower in back than in front to create a back-slant plane. An orthopedic feature originally designed to help straighten body posture. A standard feature of the Earth Shoe.

outside. Any heel visible on the outside of the shoe, as opposed to an inside or concealed heel.

oval. See *egg heel*.

pancake. Flat and rounded, shaped like a pancake or silver dollar.

pinafore. Very low, curving and blending into a low shank or arch; used on some girls' shoes.

pompadour. A very high, curvy heel designed es-

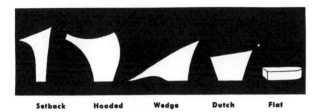

Various types of heel styles

Thomas heel.

pecially for the tiny foot of Madame de Pompadour of France, who introduced it.

riding. A leather heel 12/8 to 14/8 in height with a forward pitch. Often used on western and riding boots.

rocket. A high, straight, setback heel of the 1950s and 1960s.

Sach. Cushioned with sponge or soft crepe rubber. An orthopedic heel used with a rocker bar to facilitate a more natural gait from heel strike to step pushoff.

sensible. A general term for a low, broad heel on women's shoes.

setback. Medium height and pitched toward the rear of the shoe, with a straight back shape.

shock. Another name for a stiletto heel. The name was first used by designer Roger Vivier in 1955.

Spanish. A high, curvy and covered heel similar to a French heel but with a straighter breast, broader base and toplift area.

spectator. See *built-up heel*.

spike. Very high (20/8 and up), with a long, slender shaft.

spool. Shaped like a thread spool with a series of wide, horizontal grooves; medium to high in height.

square. Squared off at the back and front so that the heel has four corners. Sometimes matched with a square-toe shoe.

spring. Very low (2/8 to 3/8) with the lip extending into the shank. Used on infants' shoes to provide forward "spring" to the step.

stacked. See *built-up heel*.

stiletto. See *spike heel*.

Thomas. A low rubber heel or toplift with a small,

tongue-like extension on the inner front to offer support under the arch. Used on some prescription-type shoes.

tunnel wedge. See *flying wedge heel*.

ultra. Extremely high, ranging from 5 to 8 inches, usually on specially made shoes.

Ultra 6-inch heel.

walking. Broad, built-up leather heel, 10/8 to 12/8, worn with some western boots.

wedge. Extending forward and curving down to fill the entire shank area of the shoe so that the sole is a continuous flat tread surface toe to heel, with no space under the shank. It can range from low to high, with any of various style treatments.

wrestler. Low and roundish, worn with western boots. See also *block heel*.

heel angle. The down slant or angle of the heel seat upon which the foot's heel rests.

heel base. That part of the heel next to the sole, usually shaped to fit the heel seat; the body of the heel.

heelboard. Leather or compressed scrap leather formed into sheets from which pieces are cut out

61

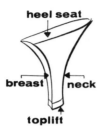

Basic anatomy of a heel.

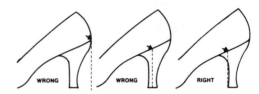

for the layers forming leather heel bases; also used for some counters and insoles.

heel brace. A right-angled metal brace attached to the heel breast and sole shank to keep the heel straight or to strengthen a weak heel.

heel breast. The front face of the heel.

heel breastline. The edge on either side of the heel breast.

heel burnishing. Polishing the inked, stained, or waxed heel to a hard finish.

heel cover. Leather, fabric or man-made material, matching or contrasting with the shoe upper, used to cover the raw surface of the heel.

heel cup. A cupped-shape insert to cradle the foot's heel for motion control or cushioning.

heel curve. The back curve of a shoe from heel seat to the top rim to conform to the back curve of the foot. The curve shape varies in accord with heel height, style, or construction of the shoe or boot. The heel curve must be precise to avoid shoe slippage or biting at the heel. Also known as *back curve*.

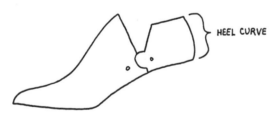

HEEL CURVE

Heel curve.

heel elevation. The height of the heel measured from the extreme rear. Not to be confused with heel height.

heel girth. The distance around the foot from the rear base of the heel to the top of the instep. A measurement taken on the last.

heel guard. A protective device to cover the back of

the shoe heel and counter, especially on women's shoes, from abrasion while driving a car.

heel height. The height, floor to shank, measured at the heel breast. Heel height is measured in increments of 1/8th inches. Hence an 8/8 heel is one inch, a 20/8 is 2 1/2 inches, etc.

heel lift. A single layer of leather or other material forming part of a built-up heel. Not to be confused with top lift.

heel lip. The thin flap of heel cover material extending from the heel breast and attached to the shank of the shoe.

heel liner. A special lining around the inside back of the heel's counter, usually to prevent heel slippage.

Heel liner inside shoe to prevent slippage.

heel neck. The shaft or middle section of a high heel.

heel pad. A thin layer of leather or other material covering the heel seat to protect the foot's heel from chafing against the rough surface beneath. Also, a thicker cushioned pad for shock absorption on heel strike.

heel pitch. The vertical slant or angle of the heel at the rear from heel seat to floor. Not to be confused with the heel angle.

heel plate. The metal plate covering the heel seat on the last during shoemaking as protection against machine pounding.

heel plug. A section or spot of hard rubber or plastic on the heel surface (usually the outer rear rim) for extra wear or durability.

heel point. The rearmost and center point of the heel on the last; a reference site in measurements.

heel position. The position of the heel under the shoe; of considerable importance for properly engineered

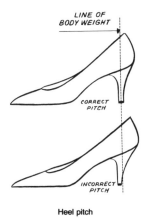

Heel pitch

heel support and balance, especially with higher heels. It is dictated to some degree by the type or style of heel.

heel rand. A narrow strip of leather or other material around the top edge of the heel; used to fill the crevice between the heel and sole. It resembles a very thin strip of welting.

heel seat. The slightly cupped section of the shoe on which the foot's heel rests; also the section of the shoe to which the heel is attached.

heel seat lasting. One of the various shoe lasting operations in which a machine fastens upper, counter and lining to the heel seat of the insole.

heel seat width. The greatest width across the heel seat on a line perpendicular to the center line from the heel point.

heel shaft. See *heel neck*.

heel spring. The small space between the rear-bottom surface of the shoe heel and the floor. This is incorporated into the last, especially with lower heel shoes, to lessen heel strike impact and to allow better leverage for the step.

heel spur. An abnormal, knob-like growth of bone on the bottom or lower front area of the heel bone. A painful condition often requiring surgery for removal.

heel stay. An insert of suede or reversed leather placed inside at the back of the shoe against the quarter lining to prevent slippage of the foot's heel. Also known as a "non-slip."

heel stabilizer. An orthotic heel inlay which helps to correct an imbalance of the foot's heel.

heel strike. The manner and impact force with which the heel of the foot and shoe strike the ground with each step or stride.

heel style. The shape, design and height character of a heel.

heel tip. A metal or plastic reinforcement attached to the outer-rear edge of the heel's top piece to resist heel wear or abrasion.

heel-to-ball. A measurement taken on the last, and sometimes in the shoe store, from the back of the heel to the inner ball joint. Ideally, in this measurement the foot and shoe should correspond.

Heel-to-ball fitting is important to the correct length fitting of any shoe.

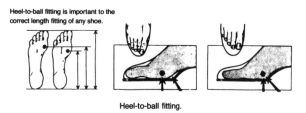

Heel-to-ball fitting.

heel-to-toe. The measurement taken on the foot to ascertain shoe length size; from the back of the heel to the tip of the longest toe.

heel-to-toe bar. See *bar, rocker*.

heel width. The width of the heel of the foot across its two widest points on weight bearing.

heloma. Medical term for a corn; also known as *clavis*. The four main types are:

heloma durum. A hard corn, usually on the surface of a toe.

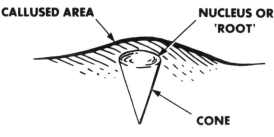

CALLUSED AREA — NUCLEUS OR 'ROOT' — CONE

Anatomy of a hard corn.

heloma molle. A soft corn in the web between two toes.

heloma miliare. A small excrescence, usually found in clusters on the sole of the foot, or around the great toe joint.

heloma vascular. A reddish, painful growth usually on the sole or on the tip of a toe. Sometimes called a *blood corn*.

hemline. The height of a skirt or dress hem from the floor. Hemlines shift with fashion trends and influence shoe fashions and heel heights.

Hessian boot. See *boot*.

hidden gore. See *goring*.

hide. The thick skin taken from a large animal (cow, steer, ox, etc.). It is classified as a hide only if it weighs 25 or more pounds.

hide pack. A pile of salted hides stacked to allow for an efficient curing process. The buildup of heat mixed with the salt between the hide layers generates the curing process.

high end. Merchandise in the upper price ranges of a line.

high fashion. Refers to more expensive or elitist fashion merchandise, including footwear, that usually innovates fashion trends that eventually seep down to popular or mass level at lower prices. Ironically, while we speak of "high fashion" we never refer to "low fashion."

high front. A shoe with a high vamp or tongue extending over the instep.

high heel. See *heel*.

highgrade. Any product or service of above-average quality and price.

high-low boot. See *boot*.

high-riding front. See *high front*.

high-riding tongue. A high flared tongue over and beyond the instep, usually on a slip-on shoe.

high shoe. Any over-the-ankle shoe; a boot.

high tech. Any product employing state-of-the-art technology, such as the application of biomechanical principles in the design of athletic shoes.

hightop. See *high shoe*.

highway store. See *freestanding store*.

hiking boot. See *boot*.

hinge. A movable metal piece connecting the front and rear sections of the last, allowing the last to be easily inserted into or removed from the shoe.

Hittite shoe. An ancient clog-type shoe worn by the Mongols prior to 500 B.C.E., later adopted by the Greeks. Made with a wooden or thick leather sole with wood or leather upper, attached with a thong or strap. Still worn in some parts of the world today by peasants and highland soldiers.

hobnail. A heavy nail with a large head which is driven into the soles of some work or military boots. Originally used by Roman legions on their long marches. The nailheads resist abrasion and make an intimidating sound.

hobnail boot. See *boot*.

hollow foot. See *pes cavus*.

hoofer. A theatrical or show business term for a tap dancer. The term dates back to 17th-century England when young dandies wore metal taps on heels and toe tips, making a sound like a horse's hooves on the cobblestone streets.

hook eyelet. A hook-shaped eyelet to catch and hold the lacing. Used mostly on work and outdoor boots.

horizontal retailing. Employment of stock spread over a variety of footwear categories and/or lines. The opposite of more specialized focus of inventory known as "vertical retailing."

horsehide leather. See *leather*.

hose. A fabric (sometimes leather) foot and leg covering, usually knit or woven.

hosiery. More sheer types of hose, chiefly women's, such as nylon or silk, worn thigh-high or as pantyhose.

hot melts. Heated blends of petroleum and wax that form an adhesive used to bond the upper lasting margin to the insole.

houseaux. A leather gaiter of 17th-century France. Covering the shoe and lower leg, it was laced in front or at the side and held in place by a leather strap passing under the shoe shank.

house shoe. A lightweight, thin-soled, low-heel, comfortable shoe worn around the house, a bit dressier than a house slipper. Now obsolete.

house slipper. See *slipper*.

house-to-house selling. A method of selling shoes to consumers by going house-to-house with samples or a catalog. Once the customer has made a selection, the foot is measured for size and the shoes are later delivered by mail. A few companies specialize in this business.

huarache. A woven leather shoe or sandal native to Mexico.

hue. See *color*.

hump foot. A foot with a prominent hump or bump at the peak of the instep at the metatarso-cunieform joint. A hump foot is functionally normal but can experience discomfort when fitted in a high-front slip-on shoe with front goring, or from lacings tied tightly.

hunting boot. See *boot*.

hussar boot. See *boot*.

hyperidrosis. Medical term for excessive sweating of the feet.

hypermarket. A supermall; a huge mall containing many more stores than an ordinary large mall, plus restaurants, theatres and other entertainment features to attract mass numbers of shoppers.

hypermobile foot. A foot with excessive mobility or movement of the joints; loose-jointed; a foot that does not act as the usual firm lever at step pushoff.

hyperpronation. Excessive pronation of the foot. See also *pronation*.

hypertrophy. Excessive enlargement or swelling.

hypoallergenic. Allergy-causing. Shoe dermatitis is a common skin ailment that afflicts the foot. Some people are allergic to rubber cements and rubber-related chemicals, plus chromate salts, all of which are involved in footwear and are a source of shoe dermatitis. For such persons, the shoe should have vegetable-tanned upper leather, a box toe of pyroxylin material, and contain no rubber cement in the construction. A hypoallergenic shoe is constructed with such features.

I

ice creeper. A metal, sole-shaped device attached to a shoe for traction on an icy surface.

illusion heel. See *heel*.

image. The character, personality or reputation of a store, product, company, brand or person as seen by others.

imbalance. A faulty or abnormal balance or tread manner of a foot or shoe.

imitation leather. Any nonleather material treated chemically and/or mechanically to simulate leather in appearance and texture.

imitation moccasin. See *shoe construction*.

imitation tip. See *tip*.

imitation welt. See *shoe construction*.

impact strength. The ability of a material to withstand shock loading, as with a cushion insole or midsole.

importer. One who buys goods, such as footwear or leather, from a foreign country for resale.

impulse buying. An unplanned purchase; a purchase made spontaneously on sight.

in the blue. See *in the crust*.

indenture. A legal agreement between the parents of a boy and a skilled craftsman or artisan. The craftsman provides instruction in his craft, plus board, room, and clothing (but no wages) in return for the boy's services and assistance. Indenture contracts usually lasted six or seven years. It was a common method of entering and learning shoemaking and other skilled crafts in 17th- to 19th-century America. This apprentice system was brought over from Europe by the early American settlers.

independent retailer. One who owns and operates one or several stores as an unaffiliated enterprise.

Indian moccasin. A genuine moccasin construction with a vamp plug and puckered plug stitching, with or without fringed collar or decorative beading. A design associated with the American Indian. See also *shoe construction*.

infants' shoe. A soft- or firm-sole shoe or boot in sizes 5 1/2 to 8 (extremes 4 to 9).

inflammation. The reaction of living tissue to irritation or infection, accompanied by pain, redness, heat and swelling.

inflare. An inward curve or angle, such as the inward swing of the forepart of the foot, last or shoe.

Child's corrective inflare shoe.

infooted. A toeing-in gait.

informational selling. See *educational selling*.

ingrown nail. A toenail (usually of the big toe) whose edge has grown down into the flesh at the side of the toe, causing infection and pain. The medical term is *onychocryptosis*.

initial buy. The first buy or order by the retailer for the approaching season. Usually consists of basic inventory which can be purchased earlier with less risk. It also may include purchases on new fashions as a preliminary or test order.

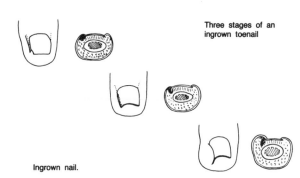

Three stages of an ingrown toenail

Ingrown nail.

initial mark-on. The first mark-on imposed on new merchandise.

injection molding. See *shoe construction*.

inking. See *staining*.

inlay. 1) A contrasting piece of leather or other material inserted under cutouts, punchings or perforations of a shoe upper for decorative purposes. 2) In prescription footwear, an arch support or orthotic inserted in the shoe.

inner long arch. The foot's main arch on the inner border.

innersole. See *insole*.

in-process time. The time required for a particular shoe factory operation, or the full sequence of operations, to be completed.

inseam. See *seam*.

insensitive foot. A foot afflicted with certain disorders, such as diabetes, in which all or most of the sensation or feeling is absent, leaving it subject to injury or infection.

insert. Any extra component or piece of material inserted in the shoe for functional or ornamental purposes. E.g., a cookie, arch or heel cushion, orthotic, decorative inlay.

inside heel. See *heel*.

insole (or innersole). A layer of material shaped to the bottom of the last and sandwiched between the outsole (or midsole) and the sole of the foot inside the shoe. It is the shoe's structural anchor to which is attached the upper, box toe, linings, and welting.

insole rib. On a Goodyear welt shoe, a strip of canvas attached to the underside of the insole to form a ridge to which the welt and upper are attached.

inspection. 1) In the shoe factory, the process of examining the shoes in process to detect defects. 2) In the shoe store, examination of incoming shipments for defects, or for fulfillment of the original order.

instep. The top inner portion of the foot at its crest, formed by the articulations of the bases of the first three metatarsal bones with the navicular and the first two cunieform bones.

instep guard. In safety shoes or boots, the metal or plastic guard plate or shield over the top of the foot for protection against injury from falling objects.

instep girth. The circumference around the foot at the instep, an important last measurement.

in-stock. The on-call merchandise of the shoe manufacturer or distributor available at once on order from the retailer, and including specified stock

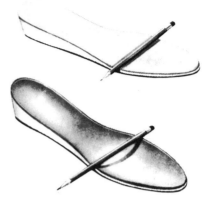

Contour insole (bottom) in contrast to flat insole (top).

CUSHION INSOLE

numbers, colors, sizes. Such vendors are known as in-stock houses.

insulated shoe. A shoe using a construction, design or components to insulate the foot and shoe against excessive heat or cold.

interlaced. A sheet made from weaving strips of leather or other material and used for making the whole or part of the upper, simulating but not duplicating a woven shoe upper.

interlining. See *doubler*.

interest. Fashion detail in shoe design focusing on a particular section or feature, such as toe interest, heel interest, etc.

interior display. Any organized display or display unit used inside the store to attract customer interest and stimulate sales; or simply as an in-store decorative feature.

in-toeing. See *toeing in*.

inventory. The merchandise in stock and available for sale in the store or factory. In a broader sense, all tangible or physical assets within the store or factory, exclusive of operating equipment.

inventory breadth. The spread or assortment of an inventory in styles, sizes or brands. In some stores, inventory breadth is achieved at the sacrifice of inventory depth.

inventory control. The systematized management and maintenance of stock in as salable and updated condition as possible, without overload or underload. A vital and continuing process in the shoe store or department to keep markdowns and losses at a minimum.

inventory depth. The stock more intensively focused on more selection of sizes and widths; or size depth on selected styles.

inventory management. See *inventory control*.

inventory-to-turnover ratio. The ratio between inventory and stock turnover rate. The lowest amount of stock required to meet customer demand without loss of sales is the ideal inventory-to-turnover ratio.

inversion. Elevation of the inner border of the foot, or turning the sole of the foot toward the other foot.

INVERSION

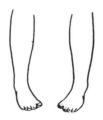
INVERSION

invoice. A billing, or an itemized listing of merchandise shipped to a buyer, with cost, fees or other charges, and request for payment.

iron. A measurement used in reference to the thickness of an outsole, or of sole leather. One iron equals 1/48 inch. Hence a 12-iron sole is 1/4 inch in thickness.

ironing. In the shoe factory, an operation to remove wrinkles from the upper leather by use of a hot iron.

iron tonnage. See *tannage*.

irridescent. Providing changing rainbow colors as in mother-of-pearl.

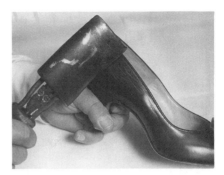
Hand ironing to remove wrinkles from shoe upper.

island. See *modular system*.

isoporo. Body balance or equilibrium; sometimes applied to the foot.

Italian sizes. See *shoe sizes*.

item. A particular footwear style or stock number selected and purchased by a retailer out of a vendor's line because of its appeal or for a special promotion.

itinerant shoemaker. In the early days of America (1690–1830), a shoemaker who traveled with his tools and leather by horse or wagon, stopping at farms or villages to make or repair shoes and boots of families. He was paid for his work and given meals and lodging.

J

jack boot. See *boot*.

jacked leather. Usually horsehide, waxed and coated with tar or pitch to give it a black, waterproof surface. Formerly used to make jack boots.

jacquard. See *fabrics*.

japanned leather. Leather finished with successive coats of varnish to produce a high gloss surface known as japan. See also *finish, patent*.

Japanese sandal. A sandal of plaited straw raised on a small pedastal.

Japanese shoe sizes. See *shoe sizes*.

jellies. Cheap, all-plastic or rubber shoes and sandals for beach, poolside or shower wear.

jerkin leather. Clothing leathers, usually in the British trade.

jewelling. Ornamenting of footwear with jewels, real or fake.

jimmy. A piece of material shaped like the forepart of an insole, inserted in the shoe for a snugger fit.

jobber. A middleman or wholesale merchant who buys merchandise in quantity from manufacturers or importers and sells them to retailers. He may also buy out the stock of a liquidating retailer for resale.

job lot. A bulk of merchandise bought or sold by the jobber, or bought from the jobber by the retailer.

jockey boot. See *boot*.

jodhpur. See *boot*.

jogging. A slow, rhythmic running pace, usually with different foot strike patterns from walking or running.

jogger's ankle. A strain or mild sprain of the ankle from jogging.

jogger's foot. A loose term for any of a variety of foot injuries or disorders resulting from jogging.

jogging shoe. See *sports shoe*.

jockey seam. See *seam*.

joint. The abutment of two or more bones hinged by one or more ligaments to provide a hinge-like movement.

Jones bar. See *bar*.

Juliet slipper. See *slipper*.

jumps. Outmoded term for leather heels in which layers of leather were pasted together to form a heel.

jungle boot. See *boot*.

junior misses' shoes. Low-heel shoes for girls in sizes 12 1/2 to 3. Usually the first grouping in which there is a separation of styles between shoes for little boys and girls.

just in time. 1) Supplies or materials delivered to the manufacturer to arrive on a precise date at the factory. This eliminates accumulation, storage and cost of not-in-use supplies inventories while allowing for a time-efficient, uninterrupted flow of production. 2) At the retail level, the delivery of finished merchandise to the store precisely on a pre-arranged date, again to prevent accumulation and storage of merchandise not yet ready for sale. Also known as *quick response*.

jute. A glossy fiber of either of two East Indian jute plants. Used for some rope-type shoe soles.

K

kabuli. An Afghanistan sandal made with two wide strips of leather crossing over the vamp, attached with narrow strips to form a slingback.

kamik boot. See *boot*.

kangaroo leather. See *leather*.

Keds. A trademarked, proprietary name for sneaker-type footwear, especially for children.

keystone. The retail price with a full, normal mark-on.

keystone bone. See *navicular*.

khaki. See *fabrics*.

kickoff. Leather drawn and stitched at the back of the shoe's quarter and extended downward. Used mostly on unlined, unstructured, loafer-type footwear with no counter as protection for the place where the shoe is pushed or "kicked" off with the toe of the other shoe.

kidskin leather. See *leather*.

kiltie. A casual or sport shoe with a slashed tongue overlapping the lace rows at the instep. Originated in Britain in 1640 but introduced as a modern fashion in 1925 by the Prince of Wales. See also *shawl tongue*.

kipskin. See *leather*.

kissing cousins. Jocular term for fake or imitation reptile leather shoes.

kiss spot. A light spot or blemish left on vegetable-tanned leather after two hides have rubbed together during the tanning stage, preventing full access of tanning liquor to those spots.

kitchen shoemaking. In early American colonial days the shoemaker handmade shoes in the kitchen of his own home, sometimes aided by family members.

klomp. See *klompen*.

klompen. A dutch wooden shoe or clog.

knee-highs. Hose reaching just below the knee. Sometimes also refers to knee-high boots.

knight's slipper. See *slipper*.

Knights of St. Crispin. The first labor union in the footwear industry, formed in Lynn, Massachusetts, in 1865. See also *Crispin* and *Crispianus*.

knob sandal. Of ancient Indian or Persian origin, a large knob with a flat head extending up from the sole, the knob fitting between the big and second toes. The sole was either of wood or leather and often platform height, worn by both men and women. It became the custom for the knobs on the women's sandals to be connected with a small chain to require small, mincing steps, signifying the bride's subservience to her husband.

knock-down. A salesperson in the store who waits on a customer out of turn. Also known as a *grab*.

knockoff. See *copy* and *piracy*.

knock-knees. See *genu valgus*.

knuckle walking. Walking on the knuckles of the forelimbs, as with the gorilla and some other apes.

knurl. To imprint a serrated design on the surface edge of the shoe's sole by use of a wheeled tool. See *wheeling*.

knurled bottom. The shoe bottom or sole finished with ornamental tooling.

kothornus. See *cothornus*.

krepida. See *crepida*.

krepis. A toeless, sandal-like shoe with straps, worn in ancient Greece. The straps passed around the ankle and leg to above the calf. See also *soccus*.

kroupeza. A musical shoe invented by the ancient Greeks. It made musical sounds when stepped on. The sole was split with a narrow metal wind pipe inserted in the middle. Depending upon the manner and pressure of the step, the sole emitted different sounds, and with a little practice a simple tune could be played.

kubab. A knobbed wooden platform shoe, or sometimes a leather-sole sandal, worn by brides in wedding ceremonies in the Middle East. The knob passed between the first and second toes and served as a phallic symbol, and the web between the toes as a vaginal symbol.

kuhmaul. An extremely broad-toe shoe that origina-ted in 16th-century Germany. The vamp had several slashes to expose the foot with each flexing step, or sometimes the vamp having an underlay of material of different color. The name in Old German means "cow's mouth." See also *cow's mouth*.

L

label. 1) The paper label attached to the front of the shoe box to identify stock number, brand, size, style, color. 2) The brand name printed inside the shoe on the quarter or sock lining. 3) a prestigious brand name referred to as a "label."

laced boot. Any boot fastened by lacings.

lace hole. The hole through which the shoe's lacing passes. It may be with or without an eyelet.

laced shoe. Any low-cut shoe fastened by lacings, such as an oxford or tie.

lace keeper. See *tongue guide*.

lacings. Flat or rounded cords with which the shoe is laced or fastened. The lacing material may be fabric, leather, plastic, braided, etc.

lace locks. Plastic devices on the upper that maintain tension on the lacings.

lace-to-toe. A low shoe or boot with eyelets and lacings to the toe. Usually found in sports footwear.

lacquer. A leather varnish or coating made from various substances such as resin, cellulose or shellac, combined with a plasticizer.

ladies' shoes. A term for women's shoes, but in declining use. Formerly referred to quality dress shoes for upper-class women.

lambskin. The skin of a lamb, or leather made from lambskin or sheepskin. Fine-grained, soft and supple, not durable enough for shoe uppers, but used for slippers or linings, and also for garment leather.

lamelift. A sheet of material such as cork, used to add a layer inside the shoe for persons with one limb shorter than the other.

laminated. Composed of two or more layers joined together, as with two fabrics, or leather with fabric.

Lancaster clog. A clog with wood sole and heavy, coarsely tanned leather upper, worn by English farmers during past centuries but rarely today.

landed cost. The amount that an imported pair of shoes or other product costs the buyer or importer after all duties, tariffs, and other charges are paid.

language of fashion. The fashion terms, phrases and expressions used by designers, buyers, retailers, or salespeople, and understood within the trade or by the consumer. A mode of communicating the concepts of fashion.

lap seam. See *seam*.

lap stone. A slab or stone, slate or iron resting on the lap, upon which the old shoemaker craftsmen beat sole leather or seams or folded edges with a flat-faced hammer.

larrigan leather. See *leather*.

laser cutting. A method of cutting out shoe patterns or components with a laser beam.

last. Used as a noun, the plastic, wood or metal foot-shaped form over which the shoe to conform to the prescribed shape and size of the shoe. The term is from the Old English "laest," meaning a footprint. Used as a verb, it refers to the process of shaping

Last in "raw" form on way to finishing.

75

A. Cross Section of Last with Wide Tread Area

B. Last of same Size and Width with High Waist and Narrow Tread Area

the shoe to the last. The last is the single most important element in the shoemaking process.

lasting. The operations in the factory involved in forming all the parts of the shoe to the last, including such special operations as toe lasting, side lasting, heel seat lasting.

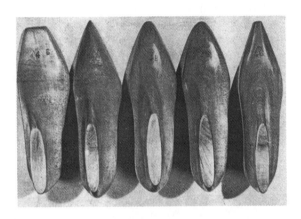

Last styling focuses on toe shapes. The toe may be square-snipped, round-flat, oval or crescent, pointed or blunt-squared, depending upon current mood or mode. And each single type of toe may have many subtle variations, such as narrow-snip or wider-snip, single needle or triple needle. The main styling character of the last and shoe is usually in toe shape, and its character may wear many faces.

lasting allowance. The amount of upper material extending around and under the edge of the last so that it may be anchored to the insole for a firm bonding.

last lathe. The special machine used to turn the last as it is shaved and trimmed to conform to the master model whose dimensions are pre-coded into the lathe to produce duplicates on a production-run basis.

last measurements. 1) The numerous measurements taken on all parts of the last to determine proper size and fit of the shoe, and also proper tread and shoe performance. 2) The standard measurements for sizes and widths for each footwear category such as infants, children's, misses', boys', men's, and women's shoes. 3) The standard measurements designated for the girth of ball, waist, and instep for given shoe sizes relative to the type of footwear.

last pulling. The operation of firmly pulling the upper material over the last to conform precisely to every

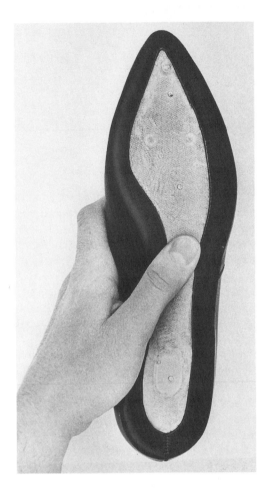

Upper tucks under bottom edge for extra margin or lasting allowance.

part of the last. Formerly a skilled operation done by hand, now done by lasting machines.

last remodeling. The repair of worn or damaged lasts, or the remodeling of the shape of used lasts.

last systems. Different methods of grading and sizing lasts, such as arithmetic, geometric, dynametric, Mondopoint, etc.

latchet. Any strap fastening on a shoe.

lateral. 1) Anything situated or done to the side. 2) The outer side. See also *medial*.

latex. The milky, sap-like fluid exuded from the rubber tree; a main ingredient of natural rubber.

laundry leather. A proprietary name for washable leather. See also *washable leather*.

lavoratory bottom heel. See *heel*.

lawyer. A shoe trade term for a friend accompanying

76

Last turning lathe shaving coarse last to pre-calculated shape and size.

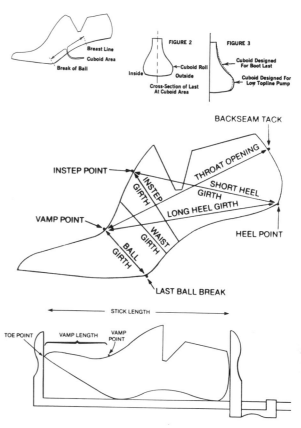

Examples of last measurements.

a customer to advise on the purchase when buying shoes in a store.

lease. 1) The contract between landlord and tenant for use of property for a specified time for a specified rent. 2) The process of drawing up such a contract.

leased department. A section of a large store leased by a tenant from the store owner to operate a specialized department, such as footwear, within the store. The arrangement can vary, but usually includes rent, a share of the sales income or profits, plus abidance to store policies or rules.

leasing. A system once unique in the footwear industry whereby the shoe manufacturer leased machinery on a per-pair-produced royalty basis rather that directly purchasing it from the machinery manufacturer. The system was started by Gordon McKay and the McKay Sewing Machine in 1861, and later became standard practice throughout the footwear industry. It is known today as the "unit system."

leather. The end product of a hide or skin after conversion by a combined chemical and mechanical process known as tanning. Leather itself comes in numerous varieties and forms, depending upon the original hide or skin, plus the method of tanning and finishing. Next to toolmaking, leathermaking is the oldest craft known to man and dates back several hundred thousand years. Leather can be made from the hide or skin of any living creature—bird, beast,

or fish—from about the size of a frog to anything larger. The important leathers are as follows:

alligator. The tanned hide of an alligator or crocodile. The leather has a box-like grain pattern with indented outlines separating the sections of the grain. For shoes, skins of smaller alligators are used because of the smaller grain. Skins of larger alligators are used for luggage. The leather is extremely durable and takes a high polish.

antelope. Fine, soft and velvety in texture, with a mild sheen, usually suede-finished on the flesh side. Very little antelope leather is available or used in footwear.

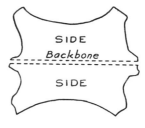

Side upper leather.

77

Alligator leather shoe.

bucko. See *reverse leather*.

buck sides. Cowhide side leather tanned to simulate genuine buckskin.

buckskin. Tanned deerskin, mostly oil-tanned to produce a soft, pliable leather with a buff color. The leather commonly used for clothing and footwear by the American Indians, plus hunters and trappers. Because of the very limited supply of deerskins, most "buckskin" leather today is suede-finished cowhide tanned to simulate buckskin.

buffalo. Tanned mostly from domestic buffalo hides such as found in India. A tough, heavy leather with a rough grain, used chiefly for soles or rugged upper leathers.

buffalo calf. Tanned skins from the calves of water buffalo.

cabretta. Made from the skins of Brazilian hair sheep. The leather is smooth and tight-grained, with a firm fiber structure similar to kidskin. Used for shoe uppers, gloves, and garments.

calfskin. Made from the skins of calves, it is one of the finest quality of all leathers. Calfskin is soft, light, pliable, durable, with firm texture and fine grain.

capeskin. Made from South African hair sheep, the leather superior to ordinary sheepskin. The leather is light, soft, fine-grained, durable, and used mostly for garments and gloves.

carpincho. Made from the skins of carpinchos, large water rats found chiefly in South America. It is usually chrome-tanned and is classed commercially as pigskin because of the similarity in texture and grain surface. Used mostly for men's fine gloves.

cattlehide. See *side leather*.

chamois. A sheepskin leather made from the flesher or inner layer of sheepskin, oil-dressed and suede-finished. The leather is soft, pliable and fabric-like.

coltskin. Leather made from the skin of colts. A softer, finer grain than horsehide.

cordovan. The only leather not made from a hide or skin. It is produced from an oval, ligament-like tissue under the butt hide of the horse (also mule and zebra). A very durable leather with low porosity, used mostly for men's expensive shoes. "Cordovan" is also used in a generic sense—the burgundy-like color and smooth, glossy finish of genuine cordovan. Today, most cordovan leather is actually cattlehide tanned to simulate cordovan. See also *shell cordovan*.

cowhide. Leather from the hides of mature cows, with the hide weighing over 25 pounds. See also *side leather*.

crocodile. See *alligator leather*.

doeskin. Leather made from the skin of the female deer. It is soft, supple, light and has a fuzz-like nap. The term, however, more usually refers to white lambskin or sheepskin leather tanned with alum or formaldehyde.

dogskin. The skins of various wild dogs used to make leather. The leather is similar to capeskin, but tougher.

deerskin. Leather made from deerskin and almost identical to buckskin.

dongola kid. The skin of sheep, goat, or kangaroo tanned a finished to resemble French kid.

elephant. Only the large ear is suitable for making leather. The elephant hide itself is four to five inches thick.

elk. A trade name which does not mean leather tanned from real elkskin (which is buckskin). The leather known as elk is actually cattlehide leather with a special tannage and finish. The leather is sometimes known as "elk sides" or "smoked elk" (originally known as "Los hide"). Used chiefly for work and sport shoes, it is very similar to side leather. See also *side leather*.

emu. A smaller species of the South African ostrich family. The leather is commercially classified as ostrich. See also *leather, ostrich*.

equine. Leather made from the hide of a horse, mule, colt, zebra, and other equine animals. See also *horsehide*.

frogskin. Leather from the skin of a giant frog found in Brazil. It has a distinctive grain pattern. Used as uppers and trims for some expensive women's shoes. Imitations are classified as "frog-grain leather."

galuchet. A kind of sharkskin tanned without removal of the hard, pebbly surface. Similar to boroso leather but with a coarser grain. See also *shagreen leather*.

horsehide. A tough, durable leather from the hide

78

of a horse or colt, generally used for work boots or work gloves. Very limited amounts are available.

kangaroo. Leather made from any of the 100 species of Australian kangaroos. It is soft, lightweight, supple, very durable, scuff-resistant, with a firm, close-fibered grain. Used in some better grade sports and comfort shoes. In limited supply and relatively expensive.

kidskin. Leather produced from the skins of young, immature goats. Very lightweight, soft, porous, and durable. Commercially, the term applies to all goatskin leathers.

kipskin. The skin from a young bovine animal. The skin weighs between 15 and 35 pounds. The animal's maturity is between a calf and a cow, and the quality of the leather between calfskin and side leather.

lambskin. Leather made from the skin of a lamb, though some sheepskins pass commercially as lambskins. The leather is soft and fine-grained, used for some infants' shoes and booties, uppers for slippers, and some linings.

larrigan. Light, oil-tanned cattlehides, used chiefly for moccasins.

lizard. Leather from the skin of any of the many species of lizard found in tropical countries. The leather is very durable and has a unique speckled grain. Embossed imitation lizard is commonly made from cowhide. Genuine lizard is used for expensive shoe uppers and trims, also handbags.

mocha. Leather produced from the skins of hair sheep from Saudi Arabia, Iran, and Africa. It has a heavy, suede-like finish on the grain side, with a fine nap. It is also sometimes made from goatskins.

morocco. Tanned goatskin, or its imitation in sheepskins, with a special tannage. Originally made in Morocco and stained red.

napa. Chrome, alum or combination tanned sheepskin glove leather with a waxy finish, drum-colored.

ostrich. Leather made from the skin of the South African ostrich. The surface has a unique quill-hole grain pattern. The leather, always in limited supply, is light but strong and is used mainly for women's shoe uppers and handbags. Imitations or prints are made from cattlehide leathers.

patent. Commonly referred to as a kind of leather, which it is not. It is a kind of finish. See also *finish, patent*.

peccary. The tanned skin of wild boar found in Central and South America, similar in texture and grain pattern to pigskin.

pigskin. A tough, durable and versatile leather with a distinctive grain of three-hole clusters formed by the skin's follicle pattern. The leather can be natural grain or buffed with a sueded nap. Used for shoe uppers, insoles and linings.

pin seal. Boarded leather made from the skins of baby seals.

porpoise. Genuine porpoise leather is similar in

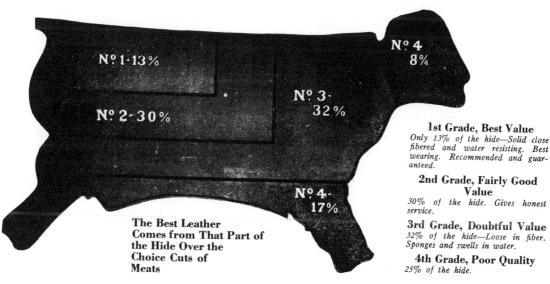

No 1·13%
No 2·30%
No 4 8%
No 3· 32%
No 4· 17%

The Best Leather Comes from That Part of the Hide Over the Choice Cuts of Meats

1st Grade, Best Value
Only 13% of the hide—Solid close fibered and water resisting. Best wearing. Recommended and guaranteed.

2nd Grade, Fairly Good Value
30% of the hide. Gives honest service.

3rd Grade, Doubtful Value
32% of the hide—Loose in fiber. Sponges and swells in water.

4th Grade, Poor Quality
25% of the hide.

Source of leather quality derived from hide.

character to sharkskin. Most of what is called porpoise leather is actually made from the hide of white whale and is used mostly for outdoor boots.

reptile. Includes leathers made from the skins of alligator, lizard, snake, and other reptiles. Usually very durable and with distinctive grain patterns of the particular species.

reversed calf. Heavier weight calfskin, suede finished on the flesh side and containing oils to increase water resistance. In England it is called "French calf" or "hunting calf."

reversed side leather. Cattlehide side leather finished like reversed calf but with a coarser texture and nap.

reversed split. Split leather finished like reversed calf or side leather but with a much coarser texture and nap.

roan. A low-grade, unsplit sheepskin leather dressed to imitate ungrained morocco leather. Used for uppers on some slippers.

russet. 1) An unfinished calfskin leather, vegetable-tanned with natural russet color. 2) Russet sheepskin leather originally tanned with hemlock bark, resulting in a russet color and used for shoe linings; now is sheepskin given a russet color as though tanned from vegetable extracts.

Russia calf. A full-grain calfskin leather usually made in brown and tan shades and always smooth. It originally meant a vegetable-tanned leather made in Russia, but now applies to a smooth, chrome-tanned calfskin resembling the texture of the original Russia calf.

sealskin. A strong, soft leather from the skins of adult hair seals, though sometimes also from the skins of young seals or "harps."

shagreen. 1) Formerly untanned leather prepared in 18th- and 19th-century Russia and Eastern Europe from the skins of various animals, given a granulated, pebbly finish and dyed in bright colors. 2) Tanned sharkskin when covered with the hard armor of small, close-set tubercles to give the appearance of shagreen leather. This surface is usually removed in tanning but is left intact in smaller species such as galuchet and boroso leathers.

sharkskin. A very durable leather from the skin of any of several species of shark. Used for the toe caps of some children's and boys' shoes because of its scuff resistance.

shearling. Leather made from sheepskin or lambskin with the wool left on. A soft leather with fur-like surface; the hairs can be short or long. Artificial or man-made shearling simulates the look of natural shearling but not the texture and warmth. Used for slipper uppers or linings, or for fleece linings on weather boots.

sheepskin. A soft, stretchy leather from sheepskin after the wool is removed. Used for shoe linings and slippers, and some garments.

shell cordovan. The full and correct name for genuine cordovan leather, distinguishing it from imitation cordovan leathers not made from the unique oval-shaped tissue under the butt hide of the horse (also mule, zebra). Shell cordovan is glossy-smooth, extremely durable, usually finished in a burgundy color, but low in porosity.

side. Usually refers to cattlehide leathers. The large hide is cut down the spine into two halves or "sides," and hence the name "side leather." In Western countries it is the most used of all shoe leathers.

side upper. This usually refers to the lighter weight side leathers, or the lighter portions of side leather.

snakeskin. Made from the skins of some of the 2,000 species of snake, usually the larger ones. Snakeskin has a very distinctive surface pattern, varying with the species. The leather is used for shoe uppers, trims and handbags. Snakeskin grains are frequently simulated by embossing on smooth leathers such as side leathers.

snuffed leather. See *corrected grain*.

split. Any leather made from the underlayer of a thick hide or skin that has been split into two or more layers. The split refers to leather made from a layer other than the grain or surface layer. Split leather, though serviceable, is of lower quality.

steerhide. A member of the cattlehide family whose hides are converted into side leather. See also *side leather*.

suede. Not a kind of leather but a kind of leather finish. See also *finish*.

veal. Leather made from large calfskins, similar in quality, texture and grain to kipskins.

veau velours. Soft-finished calfskin, the surface of which has been brushed and worked until it resembles the texture of velvet. Used for some women's fine shoes and gloves.

vici kid. A proprietary name which later became generic for a brand of chrome-tanned, glazed kidskin. The name was later applied to all types of chrome-tanned kidskin.

wallaby. Leather from the skin of the Australian

wallaby, a small to medium-sized kangaroo. The leather is strong, soft, supple and scuff-resistant.

walrus. A thick, tough hide which is split to make leather for bags and luggage. The grain is sometimes simulated by embossing cowhide.

waxed calf. Calfskin leather with a waxed finish on the grain side, one of the earlier methods of finishing calfskin. Also known as "French calf."

willow calf. Calfskin leather with a boarded grain.

leatherboard. Leather sheets made from pulverized leather scrap held together with a binder and compressed into sheet form; used for heel bases and midsoles.

leather chemist. One specializing in leather chemistry.

leather chemistry. A specialized branch of chemistry dealing with the nature and composition of hides and skins and the chemical aspects of the tanning processes and materials involved in the conversion of hides and skins into leather.

leatherette. A trade name for imitation leather composed of paper, fabric, or other materials.

leather gauge. An instrument for measuring the thickness of leather in ounces, millimeters, or irons.

leatherine. Imitation leather made from calico with a rubber or plastic coating.

leathering out. Attaching pieces of leather over certain parts of the last to alter the shape or dimensions of that part to accommodate a needed adjustment in the shoe, such as a longer or wider fit or some foot lesion.

leather lined. A shoe that is wholly or partly lined with leather.

leather novelties. A broad term applied to small leather goods or items not classifiable within the major groups of leather products. E.g., desk articles, lapel ornaments, souvenirs, etc.

leather scrap. The scraps of leather left over after cutting out shoe upper patterns, soles, etc., from larger pieces of leather. The scrap is either recycled for other uses such as making leatherboard, or discarded as waste.

leather sorting. In the shoe factory, the sorting of the amount and quality of leathers required to cut for each order. After sorting, the leather is sent to the cutter.

leather substitute. Imitation leather.

leg boot. See *boot*.

legging. A leather or cloth leg covering extending from ankle to knee, strapped or laced at the side, secured with a strap under the shoe's shank. See also *puttees*.

leg warmer. Any leg covering of any material to keep the legs warm.

leisure footwear. A loose term for casual footwear used indoors or outdoors.

leisure slipper. See *slipper*.

length. The length measurement of the foot from the back of the heel to the tip of the longest toe. Also the length of the shoe from heel to toe tip but not including the shoe's sole.

leotard. A complete body-covering garment foot to neck, snug fitting, with or without sleeves. Worn by acrobats, trapeze performers, and dancers.

lesion. An injury or ailment of a part of the body, usually impairing function of the part or the body.

leveling. Shaping the sole to the bottom of the last by using heavy rollers or molds.

leverage. The force or thrust of the foot against a firm object such as the ground to achieve locomotive power for forward or other motion.

Levy mold. A full-length insole inlay conforming to the foot's sole surface or contour; an orthotic.

licensing. A contract between the owner of a property, business or service and another individual, allowing the latter to use it under specified terms.

LIFO. Last in, last out (LIFO). An accounting method used to evaluate inventories. Based on the premise that the last merchandise put into the inventory is the last to be sold. See also FIFO.

liftoff. The moment or action of step pushoff.

ligament. A tough, fibrous, semi-elastic tissue connecting two bones across a joint.

light leather. Leather made from skins rather than hides, or split leather from hides, both of which are lighter weight than hide leather. Light leathers are used for women's shoes or men's lightweight shoes.

light native cows. Cowhides free of brand marks, sold in weights under 54 pounds, used for making shoe upper leather. A standard designation for trading in hide futures on the commodity exchanges.

light native steers. The same as for light native cows except that steerhides are used as the standard.

lightweight trainer. An athletic training shoe weighing less than 10 ounces. Used for racing or special training, but not as durable or supportive as a regular training shoe.

ligula. A light sandal worn by athletes in ancient Greece. See also *krepis*.

liming. The use of lime as the principal agent for removing hair from the raw hide or skin in preparation for tanning.

lingula. A sandal/shoe of ancient Greece, having a wide slitted tongue lapped over the instep, with straps through the slits. The more ornate versions had the tongue plated with gold, silver, or ivory. Slaves were prohibited from wearing them.

line. The manufacturer's or distributor's branded or unbranded merchandise in a given category. In footwear, the line usually changes seasonally.

line builder. A stylist. The person responsible for developing the company's new seasonal lines.

linen. See *fabrics*.

lining. The inside covering of the shoe or boot or any of its interior sections. It may consist of any of various materials: leathers, fabrics, man-mades. The main shoe linings are:

    quarter. Covering the inside backpart of the shoe from the midfoot rearward.

    skeleton. A strip of leather around the edge of a fabric quarter lining on a men's shoe.

    sock. Covering the insole as a buffer between foot and insole. This may be full (heel to toe) or a half lining (heel to front of shank).

    strap. The inside or back covering of a strap.

    toe. See *vamp lining*.

    tongue. The underlayer of the shoe's tongue.

    vamp. The inside covering of the shoe's forepart.

lining leather. Any leather used for shoe linings. E.g., kid, sheep, split cowhide.

liquidation. Conversion of the assets of a business into cash or collateral. To sell or dispose of merchandise or property as in the closing of a business.

lirippe. An exaggerated long toe on the grotesque poulaine or cracowe shoe styles of the 11th and 12th centuries. From the Flemish "leer-pyp," meaning a point of leather. See also *poulaine*.

little gents. A standard footwear category for little boys' shoes in sizes 8 1/2 to 13 (extremes 8 to 13 1/2).

little heel. See *heel*.

Littleway process. See *shoe construction*.

Littleway lockstitch. See *shoe construction*.

livestock. Herds of domesticated animals maintained for eventual slaughter for their meat, hides and skins.

loafer. A laceless slip-on shoe with moccasin style forepart and a saddle over the instep. Once a proprietary name, the term has become generic.

lockstitch. A double thread stitch that locks the threads together so that damage to one thread does not damage or split the seam.

lockstitch process. See *shoe construction*.

logo. The distinctive signature, symbol or insignia of a business as a kind of trademark.

long counter. The forward portion of the counter, either on the inner or outer side, extending beyond the usual or standard length. Used in some orthopedic or prescription shoes for added support to the arch or foot.

long heel girth. The tape measurement on the last from the rear base of the heel to the throatline of the vamp.

longitudinal arch. See *arch, long inner* and *outer*.

look. Refers to a particular style or fashion character reflected by the shoe or the apparel as a whole.

loop heel. See *heel*.

looker. Retail trade term for a browsing, "just looking" customer.

Los hide. See *leather, elk*.

lotus foot. One of the numerous flattering terms used by the Chinese for the bound foot. See also *bound foot*.

Louis heel. See *heel*.

lounge slipper. See *slipper*.

low-cut. Any below-the-ankle shoe.

low end. The cheaper or bottom range of prices in a line or store. Merchandise low in quality and price.

lug sole. A pattern of cleating covering the entire bottom of the sole, usually rubber or man-made material, similar to the tread pattern on an auto tire. Used for traction and durability on work and outdoor boots.

lumberman's boot. See *boot*.

lunula. A long, decorative tongue used especially on military footwear in ancient Greece and Rome.

lustre finish. See *finish*.

M

M. A loose designation or symbol for a medium-width shoe, ranging from C to D in men's and boys' shoes, and B to C in women's and girls' shoes.

macaroni. A showy, over-dressed London fop of the 17th and 18th centuries. During the American Revolution, gaudily dressed British troops in Maryland.

madras. See *fabrics*.

machine-sewn shoe. A shoe in which the sole is attached to the upper and insole by a seam stitched through the insole by machine.

mail order. Merchandise advertised via catalogs or in small advertisements in newspapers and magazines, and sold through the mails.

make-good. A manufacturer to a retailer, or a retailer to a consumer—giving a refund, a new pair of shoes, or a credit for shoes returned because of some defect or other dissatisfaction.

makeup. Shoes not in the manufacturer's stock but produced on order for specific customers in accord with the customer's specifications and terms. The opposite of in-stock.

making room. The department in the shoe factory where the heels are attached, the sole edges finished, and other finishing operations completed.

malleolus. The knob-like tip of the ankle on either side, formed by the lower end of the two leg bones (tibia and fibula). The plural is malleoli.

man-made materials. Materials made of properties other than natural fibers, usually to simulate natural-fiber materials such as leather or silk. They are usually lower priced than the natural and are commonly used for shoe uppers, linings, insoles, outsoles, and other components. They are generally lower in breathability and esthetics but have greater durability. The three most common families of man-made shoe materials are polyvinyls, polyurethanes and poromerics.

manipulation. A pressure action or massage technique used by medical practitioners and physical therapists on the foot to relieve or correct lesions or loosen adhesions. See also *acupressure*.

manufacture. Literally meaning to make by hand (from the Latin "manu" for hand and "facture" for make). Today it refers to producing by machines, a process which began in the shoe industry in the middle of the 19th century.

manufacturer's representative. A road salesperson who represents and sells the lines of one or more manufacturers whose merchandise is not competitive with each other. The representative functions as an independent entrepreneur rather than as an employee of any one company exclusively. See also *shoe traveler*.

marbled grain. See *grain*.

march foot. A term common during World War I that referred to general foot soreness, aching, or other symptoms during long marches by soldiers.

margin. The difference between the cost of the merchandise and the selling price. That from which operating expenses are paid and profit derived. Gross margin is the spread between cost of merchandise and selling price. Net margin is the remaining margin after markdowns or other depreciation.

markdown. A marking of merchandise for sale at a reduced price or below original or normal mark-on level; the amount of the price reduction.

market. 1) A gathering place for display of merchandise and the exchange of buying and selling. 2) A demographic segment of a mass market. 3) A selected trading area.

marketing. All activities or operations involved in movement of merchandise by the seller to the prospective buyers, including advertising, displays, promotions, services, and direct selling.

market position. The competitive standing of a business among competitors of similar merchandise in the same marketplace.

market price. The price the market or consumer is willing to pay for the merchandise offered.

market research. The study of the demands or needs of consumers in relation to particular merchandise or services.

market share. The share of a given market earned or owned by an individual business in a competitive situation.

market value. The best price that a product or service can be expected to bring, regardless of cost to produce, relative to supply and demand.

marking. The stamping or printing of the size, stock number, etc. on the shoe lining for identification; or the stamping of brand names or logos on sock linings, heel pads, or elsewhere; sometimes called "branding."

markon. The difference between the cost of the merchandise at wholesale and the selling price at retail. The difference provides for all the operating expenses plus profit.

markup. See *markon*.

Mary Jane. A classic style for little girls, consisting of a low heel patent leather shoe with an instep strap.

mass market. The all-inclusive market that embraces the full demographic range of persons of all ages, incomes, lifestyles, occupations, etc. More symbolic than real.

master model. The pilot or original model of the last which serves as the dimension guide from which a production run of lasts is produced.

mat (or matte) finish. See *finish*.

mat. An indented paperboard sheet, usually provided by a branded vendor or an advertising agency, imprinted with picture and copy for reproduction in a newspaper, for the retailer to use in local advertising.

mat kid. Kidskin leather with a mat (or matte) finish.

match marking. A consecutive numbering of colored shoe upper parts by the cutter to allow proper matching of the parts when they are stitched together in the factory. Matched marks are usually stamped on the inner surface to ensure proper mating of shoes in the packing room.

mates. The left and right of a pair of shoes of identical size, color, material, style, brand.

matrix. A mold built on the bed of an embossing press to enhance the design of the pattern to be reproduced on the material by the embossing plate.

matte finish. See *finish, mat*.

mature-age market. A flexible demographic term referring to 50-and-over age groups.

Mayo bar. See *bar*.

McKay construction. See *shoe construction*.

measurement. The dimensions of a foot or last applied to the size, shape, and fit of the shoe.

measuring leather. Ascertaining the dimensions of a hide or skin or finished leather for square footage or area, or by weight or thickness, done by a measuring machine or device.

medallion. See *tip*.

medial. The inner side of an object, such as the inner or medial side of the foot.

medical referral. A patient referred by a doctor, hospital, or clinic to a shoe store to be fitted in accord with prescription instructions.

medical shoe. See *prescription shoe, orthopedic shoe*.

mellow. A subjective response or evaluation to the touch and feel of leather—a soft, buttery feel. A common trade or fashion term.

memory. The ability of a material, such as leather, to stretch or expand under pressure, then return to its original dimensions when pressure is removed. An important quality for conformability in shoe fit. Some materials, such as some man-mades, lack this capacity.

men's shoes. A trade category of adult men's shoes sizes 6 to 12 (extremes 4 to 16).

merchandise. Goods, products, or wares, usually bought to be resold to consumers.

merchandise manager. In the department store, the individual in charge of one or more lines of merchandise and who is responsible for the profitable movement of those lines.

merchandise mix. The styles, brands, and prices content or mix of a store's inventory.

merchandising. The broad scope of buying and selling merchandise by utilizing all the necessary techniques of moving and disposing of it most effectively and profitably.

mesh. See *fabrics*.

metal last. Used for making vulcanized or injection molded shoes where high heat and pressure are involved. Also known as a *mold*.

metatarsal. 1) One of five long, slender bones in the midfoot between the tarsal and toe bones. 2) The midfoot section of the foot forming the area between the ball and instep. From the Greek "meta," meaning between or in front of.

metatarsal arch. See arch.

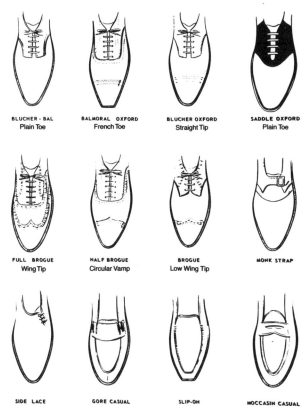

| BLUCHER - BAL | BALMORAL OXFORD | BLUCHER OXFORD | SADDLE OXFORD |
| Plain Toe | French Toe | Straight Tip | Plain Toe |

| FULL BROGUE | HALF BROGUE | BROGUE | MONK STRAP |
| Wing Tip | Circular Vamp | Low Wing Tip | |

| SIDE LACE | GORE CASUAL | SLIP-ON | MOCCASIN CASUAL |

Selected classic styles of men's shoes.

metatarsal bar. See *bar*.

metatarsalgia. Any pain, soreness, or aching in the front metatarsal area of the foot, or under the ball. "Algia" is Greek for pain.

metatarsal pad. A small, heart-shaped pad inserted under the foot just behind the heads of the metatarsal bones to lift the metatarsal "arch" and provide relief for soreness there. The pad may be attached there by strapping, or may be inserted in the shoe. Some prescription shoes are made with a pre-inserted metatarsal pad.

metatarso-phalangeal joint. The joint formed by any one of the heads of the metatarsal bones abuting the

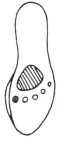

Metatarsal pad just behind bone heads.

rear surface of a toe or phalangeal bone in front of it. The abutment of all the metatarsal bones with the phalanges form the ball of the foot.

metatarsus. The five metatarsal bones together as a unit. The term is from the Greek, meaning "in front of the tarsus."

metric shoe sizing. Any system using a metric rather than an arithmetric method of measuring the last, foot or shoe sizes. Metric shoe sizing is used in most nations of the world, with the U.S. one of the few remaining countries using the arithmetic system. See also *shoe sizes*.

microcellular sole. A rubber or plastic sole with tint cells or "bubbles" dispersed throughout the material to give a cushioned effect. Depending upon the density of the cellular structure, the cushioning can be firm to spongy.

midfoot harness. See *saddle*.

midheel. See *heel*.

mid-road fashion. Conservative or classic fashion that is neither conspicuous nor dowdy.

midsole. The layer of soling between outsole and insole. Used on some rugged work or outdoor boots to add heft and durability, or on some running or athletic shoes to provide a layer of cushioning. Midsole materials can be leather, rubber, plastic, or foam.

mildew. Any fungus that attacks or appears on organic material such as leather, resulting in a thin, fuzzy, whitish coating, especially when it is exposed to prolonged dampness indoors.

millinery shoe. A fashion term to describe a women's shoe with numerous styling details or trims, or intricate pattern designs. It applies especially to more ornate fabric footwear.

military footwear. Embraces all categories of footwear used by the armed forces.

military heel. See *heel*.

mineral tannage. See *tannage*.

miner's boot. See *boot*.

miniature shoe. Any tiny replica of a regular shoe or boot, reproduced in leather, ceramics, metal, fabric, wood, or plastic. Used for ornamental purposes. Accumulated by some collectors.

misses' shoes. A juvenile footwear category in 11 1/2 to 2 size range (extremes 11 to 3).

misfit. A shoe that does not fit the foot properly.

mismates. 1) Applied to the foot, it refers to the two feet of a pair that are seriously mismated in size, width, proportion, or shape. 2) Applied to footwear,

85

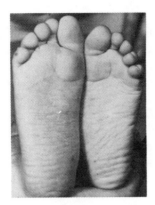

Mismated feet.

any two shoes of a pair that are mismatched in size, width, style, or other manner.

missy. Trade term for a misses' shoe.

mitten. See *shoe mitten*.

mobile display. 1) Any interior store display that can be easily moved on wheels or other means to a different location. 2) An animated display. See also *animated display*.

mobile shoe store. A van containing a stock of footwear, usually with one or two seats inside for fitting customers. Used mostly for a particular footwear category such as children's or work shoes, with the van moving within a metropolitan area to serve a particular clientele such as shut-ins, or families with limited time or access to regular stores.

moccasin. A shoe of unique design originally made of a one-piece construction. Perhaps the oldest form of footwear, dating back at least 12,000 years. Adopted by the American Indians who introduced the moccasin plug, plus decorative colored beads and other ornamentation that signified rank or status. The word "moccasin" is American Indian in origin. The moccasin is one of the seven basic styles from which all footwear fashions emerge. (See also *basic shoe styles*).

moccasin construction. See *shoe construction*.

moccasin front. See *tip*.

moccasin plug. See *plug*.

moccasin seam. See *seam*.

moccasin toe. See *tip*.

mocha leather. See *leather*.

mock moccasin. See *imitation moccasin*.

mock welt. See *shoe construction*, *imitation welt* and *pre-welt*.

mode. A formal term for fashion.

model. 1) A sample shoe, usually of a new fashion or a new entry into a line. 2) A live individual who models shoes in a model size for a fashion show or in a showroom.

modelist. See *stylist*.

model last. See *master model*.

modellista. French term for a designer of apparel, footwear, or accessories.

modelmaker. The highly skilled technician responsible for making the original model of the last upon which the production runs are based. He is a combination of engineer, architect, sculptor, and artist.

modification. An alteration or change made in a shoe to accommodate or correct some foot problem. Usually associated with prescription footwear, or with the modification prescribed by a doctor.

modular system. In the shoe factory, a team of self-supervised workers responsible for a number of operations. Each member of the team is capable of two or more operations in case one worker is absent. Also known as "quality circles" or "islands."

module. 1) Machines and a team group working within the modular system. 2) In a store, specially designed shelving units that can be moved around

Examples of Indian moccasins.

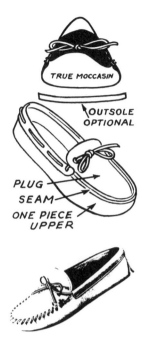

Basics of moccasin construction.

easily on wheels or rails to rearrange the layout or look of the store. It may also include display or other units.

moiré. See *fabrics*.

moisture absorption. The capacity of a material, such as leather, to wick up, absorb, and pass off foot moisture, though not necessarily through the pores. Known loosely as "breathability."

moisture transmission. See *moisture absorption*, also *breathability*.

mold. 1) A bacterial or fungal growth on organic material such as leather, causing a whitish, fuzzy stain. 2) A matrix or negative mold for a shoe sole design, into which is poured soft plastic or rubber which, when cooled and hardened, duplicates the matrix design. 3) A cast of plaster or other material covering the foot, which when hardened is removed, producing a replica of the foot and serving as an exact model for which an orthotic or custom shoe can be made.

molded insole. A pre-molded insole designed to conform to the foot sole. Also, a custom-molded insole used as an orthotic.

molded shoe. A shoe sized and shaped to a plaster or other mold of the foot, usually for problem feet.

mom-and-pop store. A small retail store or shop owned and operated by proprietor and his wife and family.

Mondopoint. A system to designate the size of the

last and/or shoe, which includes a girth measurement and uses the metric system. Designed by Britain's Shoe and Allied Trades Research Association (SATRA), its objective is to be universally adopted as an international shoe sizing system. It is now used in various countries, but not yet in the U.S.

Mongolian boot. See *boot*.

monk. A closed shoe, usually men's, with plain toe and held onto the foot with a wide, buckled instep strap. Also known as a "monk strap."

Monk strap.

monk strap. See *monk*.

morocco leather. See *leather*.

Morton's foot. A foot with a shortened first metatarsal bone, whereby undue weight and pressure are borne on the head of the second metatarsal bone with consequent pain there.

Morton's neuralgia. See *Morton's toe*.

Morton's toe. A painful condition of the fourth metatarso-phalangeal joint at the ball, with excessive pressure on the nerves there. Also known as Morton's neuralgia.

mother-of-pearl. A hard, irridescent layer on the inside of a mollusk shell, used for buttons, buckles, and ornaments on shoes and apparel.

motif. A unit of design which, when repeated, forms a pattern on apparel or footwear.

motion control. Control of excessive motion in the foot, such as pronation, supination, eversion, inversion, etc., by use of orthotic inserts in the shoe or special shoe design.

motorcycle boot. See *boot*.

mountain boot. See *boot*.

mouton. Pressed lambskin or sheepskin used in making certain fur types of apparel, usually with the wool straightened.

Mrs. McKensie. A retail shoe trade term for a customer who consumes the salesperson's time but does not buy. Seldom used today.

mudguard. A separate piece of leather wrapped around the sole edge (usually a low, platform sole), matching or contrasting with the shoe's upper material. Originally designed to protect the upper from soil and dampness, but is now used as a trim or style feature.

mudguard tip. See *tip*.

mukluk. See *boot*.

mule. A backless shoe or slipper with or without a heel. One of the oldest known types of footwear.

muleback. See *mule*.

muleskin. A split of leather from the flesh side of the hide. A misnomer and now seldom used.

mulleus. In Latin, meaning a red shoe. An elegant shoe in bright red, purple, or violet worn by the patricians of ancient Rome on ceremonial occasions. Later adopted by the public in general as a dress shoe.

mulling. The process of dampening the leather while the shoe is on the last, to get a more precise form fit of the leather to the last.

multicolored. A shoe pattern or design utilizing two or more colors.

multiple cutting. Layers of the same material superimposed for cutting at the same time with one machine stroke.

multiple-line store. A store carrying a variety of lines or brands.

multiple-pair selling. A sale of two or more pairs of footwear to a single customer during one transaction. Also, the sales technique of accomplishing this feat repeatedly. Also known as "extra-pair selling."

multiple pricing. A store offering or advertising a lower price for purchases of two or more pairs. E.g.; one pair $40, two pairs $70.

multiple showings. In the store, the salesperson bringing out two or more pairs of similar styles to show in response to the style the customer has requested.

Munson last. A broad-toe last designed for army wear by Brigadier General Munson during World War I. After several later modifications, it was replaced by new lasts.

muscle. Elastic tissue that stretches and contracts with movement. Attached to bones, it is responsible for all body motion. The ends of muscles attached to bones are called tendons.

museum heel. See *heel*.

musical shoe. See *kroupeza*.

muted. Subdued or toned down, such as with colors.

mycosis. Any disease caused by a fungus, such as athlete's foot.

mystique. An elusive but magnetic quality related to a person or fashion, with sensuous undertones.

N

N. A loose designation or symbol for a narrow shoe width. In men's shoes, approximately B-C; in women's approximately A-B.

nailed construction. See *shoe construction*.

nailhead. A small metal or plastic piece like a nailhead, of various shapes, sizes, or colors, used in clusters as ornamental trim on some footwear.

nail shoe. An open-toed, flat, heelless Arabian sandal. Also known as "nails."

naked shoe. A very opened-up women's shoe that exposes most of the foot; also, a transparent vinyl-upper shoe. Both are in the "sexy shoe" category.

namrog welt. See *shoe construction*.

nap. The buffed surface of leather or other material to create a fuzzy-wooly surface texture. It can be a fine nap (suede) or a coarse nap (brushed). Also, the reversed (as opposed to grain) side of leather. See also *reversed leather*.

napa leather. See *leather*.

Napoleon boot. See *boot*.

Napoleon tap. A sole placed on top of the original sole but cut smaller than the original. Used like a platform sole. Worn by the short-statured Napoleon.

Napolitain. Name given by the French for a blucher-style shoe.

native cows. See *light native cows*.

native steers. See *light native steers*.

national brand. Any branded product nationally advertised and which establishes a national name recognition; as opposed to a regional brand or private label.

national advertising. Advertising done on a national scale in contrast to more limited regional or local advertising.

national shoe show. A large trade show or convention in a major metropolitan center, designed to attract nationwide trade attendance. National shows are usually sponsored by national trade associations.

naumkeaging. Smoothing the bottom of a shoe by means of a rubber buffing disc before finishing.

navicular. One of the seven tarsal bones, situated at the top of the long inner arch and an important structural element of that arch. Also known as the "keystone bone" and the "scaphoid bone."

navy shoe. Technically, any footwear worn by navy, coastguard, or marine military personnel as regulation footgear. Also refers to a standard, plain-toe, black blucher oxford used for dress uniform wear.

needle heel. See *heel*.

needle toe. An extremely pointed, long toe on a shoe.

negative heel. See *heel*.

net gain. A broad, general term referring to a net gain on any operation of a business—sales, revenues, profits, customers, traffic—after all related operating costs for each, or the business costs in total, are deducted. Also used as a gauge against a previous comparable period, such as net sales gain of one year compared to the previous year. Not to be confused with gross gain.

net margin. The difference remaining on the selling price after all costs and expenses, plus markdowns, are accounted for. Distinguished from gross margin. See also *gross margin*.

net profit. The profit remaining after all operating costs and expenses are accounted for.

net sales. The gross sales minus the amount of merchandise returned by customers, or pilfered, plus allowances or credits made to customers. In computing operating ratios, net sales volume is the base or 100 percent.

net worth. The collateral value of a business, including inventory, equipment, fixtures, accounts receivable, property, good will, and other assets, after all debts are deducted.

neutral. See *color*.

niche retailing. Targeting a specialized segment of a specialized market, then providing the merchandise, pricing, services, brands, and store image appealing to that market and its customers. E.g., prescription footwear, work and outdoor boots, athletic footwear, and western boots.

night opening. Store hours after 6 PM.

night splint. An orthopedic device used to correct a foot or gait deformity by altering the position of the foot and leg. The device is worn at night during sleeping hours and is applied to special shoes. Usually worn by infants and children.

nipple sole. A rubber-type sole whose surface is covered with tiny nipple-like nodules for traction or added resilience.

nitrite rubber. Chemically treated rubber to improve oil and grease resistance of rubber soles on work boots; sometimes compounded with polyvinyl-chloride (PVC).

NN. A loose size marking or symbol for extra-narrow width, ranging from AAA to A in women's shoes, and about A in men's.

non-aligned eyelets. Eyelets set in a zig-zag pattern along the lace row instead of on a straight line. Designed for better fit of the forefoot and more support by drawing the upper more snugly to the foot.

non-rubber footwear. An official trade classification for footwear not involving rubber or rubber-like materials as a primary element. E.g., shoes made mostly of leather or man-made materials or fabric uppers. The opposite would be rubber/canvas footwear, including sneakers and most athleisure footwear.

non-slip. See *heel stay*.

non-woven fabric. Fabrics in which the fibers are usually held together with resins. A fabric made directly from a web of fibers without the yarn preparation necessary for knitting or weaving. Commonly used in some shoe components such as linings.

normal foot. A foot that functions with adequate efficiency, without distress or limited capacity. In a structural or anatomical sense, however, there is no established standard for a "normal" foot because feet come in a wide range of sizes, shapes and proportions, any or all of which may be functionally normal, including some flat feet.

Norwegian moccasin. Essentially a loafer style.

nose of the quarter. The front of the quarter covering the instep.

notched collar. A V-shape or notched wedge cut into the back of the shoe rim or collar to prevent rubbing against the Achilles tendon.

notched heel. See *notched collar*.

notched storm welt. A storm welt strip whose ridge is notched as a decorative feature.

novelty fabric. See *fabrics*.

novelty shoe. A term or classification used commonly in the 1920s and 1930s referring to popular-priced footwear, in contrast to more classic styling.

nubuck. Cattlehide upper or side leather buffed on the grain side and having a light, velvety feel and appearance. Sometimes used to simulate buckskin.

nuclear sole. A generic term sometimes used for synthetic soling materials of various rubber or plastic compounds.

nude shoe. See *naked shoe*.

nullifier. A shoe with a high vamp and quarter, dropping low at the sides where a U-shaped elastic goring is inserted. Such shoes are deliberately made to be loose fitting and are generally used for house slippers or indoor wear.

nurse's shoe. See *duty shoe*.

nylon. A proprietary name for a synthetic fiber derived from coal, air, water, polymeric amides, and other substances. It makes a very tough, strong fiber, washable, quick drying, and elastic. Used in footwear for threads, meshes, etc.

nylon mesh. Nylon threads woven in mesh form and used in footwear mostly as vamp uppers, and commonly in athletic footwear because of its lightness and strength.

O

oak sole. Sole leather produced from heavy, vegetable-tanned hides.

oak tannage. See *tannage*.

oblique toe. A shoe toe shape with an off-center or oblique shape.

obsolescence. When a particular footwear fashion becomes outmoded. Also, when stock is no longer salable at regular or even markdown prices.

occupancy cost. See *rent*.

odd pricing. Prices set a few cents below a full dollar, such as $9.98 or $15.95.

odor. 1) Offensive foot odor stemming from foot perspiration with lack of evaporation and further accentuated when mixed with shoe chemicals. Medically known as *bromidrosis*. 2) Odors emanating from the shoe or boot when foot perspiration is mixed with chemicals in the shoe materials, especially when the shoe allows limited evaporation and accumulates inside the shoe.

odor resistance. Resistance to foot and shoe odors such as via the use of special powders or sprays, or the use of anti-odor insoles or linings.

oedema. See *edema*.

offal. Pieces trimmed from the less valuable parts of the hide, skin or leather. These are processed for use in cheaper outsoles, insoles, midsoles, counters, work gloves, etc.

offaly. A tanning term describing a skin that has an unusually large share of loose-grained parts such as flanks or bellies.

off-center. A design or pattern deliberately tailored to be off center, such as an off-center throatline; lacking symmetry.

official leather colors. The semi-annual or seasonal colors selected by the Textile Color Card Association. These become the "official" colors adapted by the apparel, textile, leather, and footwear industries so that the colors of their products are moving in a parallel direction rather than in diverse directions.

off-pricing. Below regular retail selling price; cut pricing. Stores specializing in off-pricing either sell at low margin and low prices but with large volume, or they purchase discontinued branded merchandise from manufacturers to sell at appreciably below regular prices.

offset heel. A combination of wedging and flaring to raise the heel seat area. The wedge is placed on the side where the support is most needed. Used chiefly as an adjustment or modification in prescription footwear.

offshore. Any foreign supply source or location outside the boundaries of a domestic country.

oil tannage. See *tannage*.

oil-tanned leather. A hide or skin which, during the operations of currying, has absorbed a considerable quantity of oil and grease.

old ladies' running shoe. A jocular trade term for an ultra-conservative or dowdy women's shoe.

ombre. (See *color*).

on the wood. Referring to a shoe on the last in the factory.

one-bar shoe. A women's shoe fastened over the instep by a strap attached to the inside quarter and buckled or buttoned on the outside quarter.

one-piece upper. The whole upper made in one piece rather than the usual group of pattern pieces stitched together.

one-price store. A store in which all the merchandise, such as footwear, is sold at one (possibly two) price.

onychocryptosis. Medical term for ingrown nail. See also *ingrown nail*.

ooze leather. A napped or sueded vegetable-tanned leather; also leather of other tannages napped on the grain side. See also *finish, nap*.

opanka. A native Greek, Balkan or Turkish shoe with turned-up toe and a large pom-pom on the toe tip or vamp. A slip-on shoe with low heel.

open-back shoe. A shoe, usually women's, with open back and no counter, held onto the foot with a narrow back strap. Also called a "slingback" and "halter strap."

open-to-buy. A retailer's inventory position in which, after he has made his basic purchases, he retains funds for closer-to-season purchases of special-item buys. The open-to-buy position is more flexible and volatile and less fixed than the basic buying position.

open grain. See *grain*.

open-shank shoe. A women's shoe, usually a pump with a medium to higher heel, with deep V-cuts at the side to give more foot exposure. See also *D'Orsay pump*.

open-stitched seam. See *seam*.

opening the sale. The initial procedure or strategy of the salesperson in the store from the point of greeting and seating the customer to taking the beginning steps of serving the customer and developing momentum for the sale.

open stock. See *in-stock*.

open-toe shoe. A shoe with a large cutout in the center (or off center) of the end of the toe, exposing toes of the foot.

opera pump. A pump cut from a single piece of leather or other material. Usually a plain, seamless, classic pump with a medium to higher heel.

opera slipper. See *slipper*.

operator. A person performing any of the hand or machine operations in the shoe factory.

operating costs. All costs or expenses involved in operating a business.

operating ratios. The ratio or relation between one cost and one or more other costs in a business, such as expenses to sales, net profit to net sales, etc. Such ratios allow the store to apply a more precise analysis of the overall operation.

operation. A general term for a retail business.

optimum stock level. The ideal inventory position of having neither too little or too much stock relative to demand or sales, and also the inventory being reasonably fresh and salable.

order writing. The process of the retailer filling in the order sheet of a vendor for purchases, or the shoe traveler doing the same for the retailer.

ordinary welt. A welt with a rectangular cross section.

Orlon. A trade or proprietary name for a synthetic fiber. Orlon threads are used in shoemaking because of their strength.

ortho. A Greek prefix meaning straight or normal.

orthodigita. A branch of podiatry dealing with toe deformities or lesions by either surgical or nonsurgical means.

orthograde. Walking upright on two feet with a stride. Only humans are capable of this.

orthopedics (or orthopaedics). The medical specialty dealing with the diagnosis and treatment of anatomical deformities, lesions, injuries or diseases of the bones, joints, and muscles. It originally dealt with children's bones and joint problems. Orthopedics involve both surgical and nonsurgical procedures of treatment.

orthopedic devices. Any of various mechanical devices applied to the foot, or inserted or incorporated in the shoe, to prevent or correct foot or gait disorders.

orthopedist. A medical practitioner specializing in orthopedics or orthopedic surgery.

orthopedic shoe. A shoe prescribed by a doctor or carried in stock in a store, to accommodate, control or help correct a disorder of the foot, lower limb or gait. It sometimes also refers to an ultra-conservative shoe.

orthopedic shoe technician. A shoe therapist specializing in making, modifying, or fitting footwear for problem feet.

orthopody. An earlier 19th-century term for orthopedics, now archaic.

orthoses. Procedures for designing and applying orthotic devices for the prevention, remedy, correction, or accommodation of foot and gait disorders.

orthotic. Any design or device, separate or inserted, or incorporated in the shoe for the accommodation, control, or correction of a foot or gait disorder. E.g., an arch support.

Orthotic.

orthotist. One specializing in orthoses.

os. Medical term for bone.

os calsis. The heel bone. See also *calcaneus*.

ossify. To harden and develop into bone, as the soft bone in an infant's foot gradually hardening into solid bone.

ostrich leather. See *leather*.

ounce. A measurement of the thickness of upper leathers; one ounce equals 1/64 inches or 4 mm.

outdoor boot. See *boot*.

outflare. A foot, last or shoe whose forepart swings or veers outward. Found in certain prescription shoes required for corresponding types of outflare feet.

EXTREME OUTFLARE—Used primarily as a follow-up for the open toe outflare shoe when the child starts walking.

outlet. A retail store selling merchandise directly to the consumer. Also applies to a factory or warehouse outlet store that serves as a retail establishment.

outseam. See *seam*.

outside counter. The part of the back of the upper quarters which enclose the heel of the foot. It may be an additional section or an imitation.

outside heel. See *heel*.

outside quarter. One of the two pieces (outside and inside quarters) which form the backpart of the upper and usually meet at the instep to close the shoe.

outsize. A shoe size larger or smaller than the standard size range, such as a men's 15 or a women's 3 1/2.

outsole (or outersole). The outermost sole of the shoe which is directly exposed to abrasion and wear. It can consist of any of a variety of materials: leather, rubber, plastic, cork, rope, crepe, wood, etc., plus differences in thicknesses or degrees of flexibility, and an infinite variety of surface designs.

oval heel. See *heel*.

overbuy. Merchandise purchased in excess of inventory needs or sales expectations.

overcast stitch. See *handsewn*.

over-the-calf hose. Long, over-the-calf height hose with elasticized top.

over-fit. A shoe fitted too long or too wide, or both.

overhead. The operating costs, fixed or variable, of a business, such as rent, utilities, advertising, insurance, etc.

overlapping lines. See *duplicating lines*.

overlapping toes. One toe overlapping another. Sometimes the cause is genetic or hereditary, and sometimes it is caused by the habitual wearing of ill-fitting or pointed-toe shoes, or outgrown shoes during childhood.

overlay. A piece of contrasting or harmonizing leather or other material attached to some part of the shoe (usually the vamp) for decorative purposes.

overseam. See *seam*.

overstocked. An inventory in excess of needs relative to sales or demand.

over-stored. In a given trading area, or mall, or on a national basis, an excess of particular kinds of stores, such as too many shoe stores for consumer demand.

oxford. A low, laced shoe in which the vamp overlays the quarters, meeting in front where they are laced. The style was first introduced in the 17th century and was made popular by students at Oxford University, England.

P

pac (or pack). See *boot*.

pacewalking. A brisk (4 miles an hour) walking pace with rhythmic arm swinging.

packable slipper. See *slipper*.

packaging. A box or wrapping of purchased merchandise. Also, in more liberal use, the way a product, idea, or plan is presented.

packer hides. 1) Big-packer hides derived from large meat-packing houses, usually better quality. 2) Small-packer hides derived from small meat-packing houses, sometimes of lesser quality.

packing room. In the shoe factory, the department where the final finishing and packing operations are done. Also known as the "treeing room," "shoe room," or "finishing room."

pad. 1) A cushioned layer or piece of material to prevent pressure or friction of the shoe against the foot. 2) A cushioned piece of material to serve as a support, such as an arch or metatarsal pad. 3) A padding between upper and lining, stitched together in a pattern to create a quilted effect on the outside.

padded collar. A cushioning of the back rim of the shoe to prevent rubbing against the Achilles tendon. Used mainly in sports footwear.

padded tongue. A cushioned layer on the under surface of the shoe's tongue to prevent irritation from tight lacing.

pailettes. Shiny, spangled bits of colored material affixed in clusters on women's dress or evening shoes.

painting. Applying a thick pigment finish to the shoe uppers or soles, done to conceal grain defects in the leather, or covering a poor finish.

pairage. The counting of pairs of shoes as a unit tally.

pairing up. Putting left and right shoes (or components such as uppers or soles) into matching pairs. Done either in the factory or the store.

palefoot. See *color*.

palmigrade. Walking with the palms or soles on the ground, heel raised. A manner of gait used by some apes (orang, gibbon) and some monkeys.

palm wax. See *canauba wax*.

pampootie. A soft-sole, moccasin-like laced shoe dating back over 2,000 years and still worn by natives of the Isle of Aran in Galway Bay, as well as in other rustic areas.

pancake heel. See *heel*.

panel. 1) A separate piece of an upper insert in a vamp or quarter or a boot shaft, usually of a different color and material for contrast. 2) A painted or embossed design on the bottom surface of the outsole.

pantoffles. 1) A wedged, mule shoe with cork sole and a heel about 1 1/2 inches high, the vamp ornately decorated and the heel often in contrasting color. Popular in 16th-century Europe. 2) Originally a backless slipper and today still worn as a slipper or indoor/outdoor shoe. 3) Originally worn as a protective cloth overshoe. From the French "pantofle" for slipper. See also *slipper*.

paper. Trade term referring to order writing for footwear purchases, such as "writing paper."

papyrus. Fibers from the papyrus plant, used to make plaited straw sandals which were among the earliest footwear of ancient Egypt.

parchment. Almost-tanned sheepskin, and the first suitable writing material (Dead Sea Scrolls, etc.) Developed by the ancient Egyptians, Hebrews, and others. The leather was pounded and beaten to paper thinness. The name "parchment" is from Pergamum, the country of origin. The finest parchment is made from calfskin and called "vellum." See also *vellum*.

Paris point. In the French or Continental shoe sizing system a Paris point is equal to two-thirds of a centimeter. Each Paris point is equivalent to a full shoe size (2/3 cm.). There are no half sizes in this system.

95

pasteboard. Paper layers laminated to form a thicker pasteboard, used as a substitute for fiberboard or leatherboard on cheaper footwear.

pastegrain. Thin leather, such as sheepskin, stiffened by one or more coats of paste.

pastel. See *color*.

pasting. A method of setting and drying leather whereby a mild paste solution is applied to the grain side and the leather is then stretched out over a smooth pasting board.

patch vamp. See *vamp*.

patella. The kneecap bone.

patent leather. Not, as often assumed, a particular kind of leather but a particular kind of gloss finish that can be applied to the surface of various leathers or other materials. See also *finish*.

patent colt leather. Made from chrome-tanned horsehide fronts and given a glossy, patent-like finish in the tanning process.

pathology. The branch of medicine dealing with the nature of the changes caused by diseases, such as those of the foot.

patten. A clog-like shoe attached to a raised metal (sometimes wood) platform sole to lift the foot off wet or muddy ground. A universal shoe, the platform portion is often detachable for indoor wear of the shoe itself.

pattern. A shape cut out of leather or other material to be fitted together with other pieces to form the shoe upper and linings in accord with the shoe's style and fitting requirements. Applied also to insoles and outsoles.

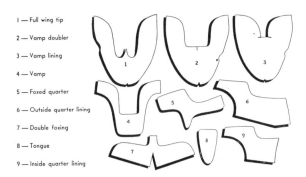

1 — Full wing tip
2 — Vamp doubler
3 — Vamp lining
4 — Vamp
5 — Foxed quarter
6 — Outside quarter lining
7 — Double foxing
8 — Tongue
9 — Inside quarter lining

Shoe patterns sewn together to form upper.

pattern department. The shoe factory room where the patterns are planned and designed.

pattern engineer. See *pattern maker*.

pattern maker. The skilled individual who converts the shoe's design into workable patterns for correct look and fit on the last.

patti. A leather legging worn by the soldiers of India in the 19th century. Patti is a Hindu name for a bandage or roll of cloth. The American word "puttee" is derived from this. See also *putti*.

peak season. The height or pinnacle of a selling season.

peaked toe. A pointed, turned-up toe design dating back to ancient Asia. Originally a shoe or boot worn by the aristocracy, priests, and other dignitaries. It is still used in some Asian cultures.

peaks and valleys. The highs and lows of sales activity in a business.

pearl finish. See *finish*.

peau de soie. See *fabrics*.

pebbled grain. See *grain*.

peccary leather. See *leather*.

ped. Latin prefix or suffix for foot, as in pedal and biped.

pediluvium. A foot bath.

pedicure. The cosmetic care of the foot.

pedicurist. A foot cosmetician.

pedile. A Greek term for a low or high sandal fastened to the foot with thongs or ribbon laces.

pedocosmetics. A coined word referring to the cosmetic grooming of the foot, or commercial products sold for that purpose.

pedometer. An instrument carried by a walker or runner to measure the distance covered by recording

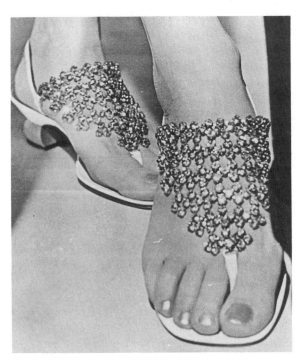

Pedocosmetic or ornamental foot jewelry.

96

the number of steps or strides. The pedometer is adjusted for stride length.

pedorthics. Therapy related to the design, construction, fit, or modification of footwear or related orthotics for persons with foot or gait or shoe problems.

pedorthist. A practitioner of pedorthics; a shoe therapist. The individual becomes a Certified Pedorthist (C. Ped.) when complying with the standard requirements specified by the Board of Certification in Pedorthics and accredited after testing and receiving a diploma of certification.

pedila. A simple sandal worn by the ancient Greeks. Of oriental origin where it was called the "sandalon," then becoming "sandalion" in Greek. Pedila was the Greek name for the sole tied onto the foot with thongs or ribbon laces.

peen heels. To repeatedly beat the edge or a sole and heel with the flat end of a face pane hammer.

peep toe. British term for an open-toe shoe.

peg. A wooden peg used like a nail or tack to attach soles to uppers. A common shoe construction in the 18th and 19th centuries, but rarely used today.

pegged process. See *shoe construction*.

pegged shoe. Any shoe or boot whose sole is attached by wooden pegs. Up to about 1870 there were 35 peg mills in the United States, producing about 75,000 bushels of shoe pegs a year. Pegged shoes virtually disappeared after 1880 because of the introduction of machine-sewn shoemaking.

pelt. A raw skin with the hair, fur or wool left on. Usually refers to skins of fur-bearing animals.

penny loafer. A loafer style of shoe with a bright penny inserted on the saddle over the instep. Also sometimes called a penny moccasin. The penny insert was a fad started by teenagers in the 1950s.

per capita. Literally meaning "per person" or "per head." Used as at statistical measure, such as the average number of pairs of footwear purchased per person per year.

perforations. Holes punched in shoe uppers for decorative effect. The holes are punched by machine in accord with pre-designed patterns, usually before the parts are stitched together.

performance. 1) The quality of work or productive results of an employee relative to some standard of output. 2) The quality of general wear satisfaction delivered to the consumer by a pair of shoes.

peribaride. A soft, boat-shaped slipper of plaited straw, worn by women of ancient Greece, Persia and Egypt.

permeability. The passage or transmission of liquid, gas or solid through a barrier without physically or chemically affecting the material, such as foot moisture through leather. In the shoe industry it is known as "breathability." See also *breathability*.

pero. A strong service boot of ancient Rome, made from semi-tanned leather and laced in front. Worn by peasants, laborers, and slaves.

perpetual inventory system. Maintaining the status of inventory by stock number or style via sizes in stock, sizes on order, sizes as sold. These numbers are constantly changed in accordance with inventory position in all three categories so that the store knows the stock status at any given time.

persaiki. A Persian shoe of 600 to 300 B.C.E. A fragile indoor shoe or slipper, sometimes worn outside with a covering sandal to protect the delicate white shoe, popular with women.

personal (or personal trade or P.T.). A trade term for a shoe store customer who requests or insists on being served by a favored salesperson.

personalized service. Service in the store that gives exclusive, one-on-one attention to the customer in fulfilling the selling process. This includes not only fitting service but counseling on fashion, product information, etc.

perspiration. Sweat. A saline body fluid that is 98 percent water and two percent salts and acids, secreted beneath the skin by sweat glands or ducts and emitted through the pores.

pes. Latin for foot.

pes cavus. Medical term for an abnormally high arch or humped instep.

pes planus. Medical term for flatfoot.

pes valgus. Medical term for a foot disorder in which the arch is low or flat and the forefoot everted or turned outward.

petal toe. See *almond toe*.

phaecasium. A soft shoe of wool, felt, or linen. Also a snug-fitting high boot of white leather, sometimes with embroidery, laced part way up the front. Worn

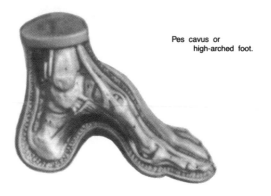

Pes cavus or high-arched foot.

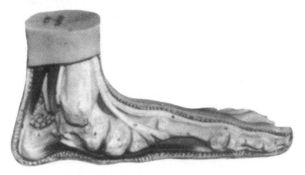

Pes planus or flat foot.

in ancient Greece and Alexandria by priests and philosophers to preserve silence in the temples and also to protect the marble and mosaic floors from scratches.

phalanges. The 14 toe bones.

phalanx. Any one of the toe bones.

pickling. A process of treating hides and skins in a solution of acid and salt to preserve and prepare them for tanning.

piece work. Work operations, such as in the shoe factory, in which the worker is paid on the basis of the number of pieces of work completed. A system common in years past in the apparel and footwear industries, but decreasing as a system of pay or work compensation.

pigeon toe. Slang term for a toeing-in stance or gait.

pigment. An inert coloring material used extensively in tanning for coloring leather with pigment dyes.

pigment finish. See *finish*.

pigment leather. Leather with a finish containing pigments.

pigskin leather. See *leather*.

piked shoe. See *poulaine*.

pike toe. The exaggerated long toe on a cracowe-type shoe popular in Europe in the 11th and 12th centuries. See also *poulaine*.

pile. A furry or velvety surface on a material produced by closely set filling yarns that form raised, even loops to give the surface a tufted feel and character.

pilferage. In a store, the stealing of small amounts of merchandise or money by customers or employees. Also called *shortages*.

Pilgrim shoe buckle. See *colonial buckle*.

pillow handbag. See *handbag*.

pilot order. An initial or test order from a vendor by a retailer, or from a supplier by a manufacturer.

pinafore heel. See *heel*.

pinch. A wrinkle in a vamp and/or lining which may rub and irritate the skin of the foot.

pinchbeck. A popular buckle for shoes and other apparel in the 18th century. Made from an alloy of copper and zinc, plated with gold or silver. Invented by London watchmaker Christopher Pinchbeck.

pinch pad. Any kind of pad applied inside the shoe to relieve pinch pressure on the foot from the shoe, such as on a prominent or bony cuboid or instep bone. Commonly applied in shoe stores when necessary.

pin grain. See *grain*.

pinking. 1) Notched or sawtoothed edge used as a decorative feature on shoe uppers. 2) A rounded braid sewn between seams to cover raw edges in the upper material. Essentially a fabric term.

pin seal. See *grain*.

pinson. Obsolete term for a fragile, thin-soled and thin-upper shoe or slipper.

pipe. A blister formed on the surface of some leathers, such as patent, wherein the coating separates from the leather beneath.

piped seam. See *seam*.

pipey grain. A very loose grain on finished leather, revealed especially on bending the grain inward, showing coarse wrinkles. Also known as "flanky."

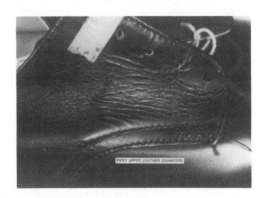

Pipey grain.

piping. A thin, narrow strip of leather or other material caught with a seam between larger pieces, or at the edge of an upper. Used to finish off upper seams and edges as a decorative effect.

piracy. The use of a shoe or other design without purchase or consent of the owner or originator. A practice common in the fashion apparel and footwear industries. See also *copy*.

piro. A laced dress boot in smooth leather.

pisnette. See *pantoffles*.

plain toe. Any shoe without a toe cap or tip or otherwise decorated, leaving a plain, smooth surface up front.

plaited leather. Braided leather strips used for shoe uppers or trims.

plantar. The sole surface of the foot.

plantar fascia. A wide, semi-elastic band of ligament-like tissue spanning the sole of the foot heel to ball. It serves both as a protective buffer zone against abrasion and shock, and also as a supplementary support for the long arch of the foot.

THE PLANTAR FASCIA

Plantar fascia stretched across sole of foot.

plantar fascitis. Inflammation of the plantar fascia.

plantar flexion. A downward movement or position of the toes and forefoot.

plantar reflex. The stroking of the sole of the foot with the fingertip to test for a reflex response relative to the foot's nerve system. Normally, in the adult, the toes will plantar flex with this test. In the infant the norm is opposite, with the toes and forefoot dorsiflexed or pointing upward.

plantar wart. A painful, ingrown wart on the sole of the foot.

plantation crepe. Crude natural rubber from cultivated rubber trees in contrast to wild rubber trees. Processed plantation crepe has a distinct beige color in contrast to the viscous white of latex. Crepe rubber soles are used for casual and sport footwear. Imitations of plantation crepe are also used.

plantigrade. Walking on the full sole of the foot, heel to toe, typical of human walking.

plastic. One of the many high-polymeric substances included in both natural and synthetic products, but usually excluding rubber. At some point, every plastic is capable of liquid or viscous form and flowing, under heat and pressure, into the desired shape and form via a mold. Plastics or plastic materials have numerous applications in footwear.

plastic patent. A derogatory name for nonleather materials, such as man-mades, using a patent finish to simulate genuine patent leather.

plasticizer. Any added substance that increases the flexibility and extensibility of a material.

plastizote. A proprietary name for closed-cell polyethelene foam used in any of several densities. Extremely light in weight, it is commonly used for prescription footwear and shoe modification applications.

platform shoe. A shoe attached to a sole whose thickness may vary from one-half inch to eight or more inches in height. The soles can be cork, wood or other material, usually light in weight. Platform shoes date back about 2,500 years.

Examples of platform shoes.

Oriental-type platforms. Ancient origins.

plating. Pressing leather with a smooth, heated metal plate under high pressure to give it a smooth surface.

playshoe. A somewhat obsolete term common from the 1930s to 1950s for a low-heel, inexpensive, casual shoe.

pleather. A coined term for a material combining

99

leather fibers with impregnations or bindings of various resins or adhesives. A hybrid mix of leather and plastic.

pleating. Making folds in leather or cloth by doubling the material over onto itself. Used on some women's fashion shoes.

plimsole. British name for a vulcanized rubber-sole, canvas-upper shoe. A sneaker or tennis shoe.

plow boot. See *boot*.

plug. A separate piece of leather or other material inserted in the upper as part of the upper pattern. It can be used as a vamp plug, as in a moccasin, as an eyelet stay, or as a quarter plug.

plug oxford. An oxford with a circular vamp.

plug vamp. See *vamp*.

plumping. The softening and swelling of leather fibers which contain little water. When the hide or skin is immersed in certain solutions, the protein matter expands and becomes soft and plump by absorbing some of the solution. Glove-type shoe leathers are formed in this manner.

ply. 1) The number of single yarns twisted together to form a plied yard, or the number of plied yarns entwined to form a cord. 2) One or several layers of the same fabric.

PM. 1) An acronym for "push money" or "premium money" paid to the retail salesperson by a vendor to push the vendor's merchandise in preference to other merchandise or brands. This practice, of questionable legal status, is in little use today. 2) Remaining inventory from broken lots or discontinued merchandise in the store. 3) An extra commission paid as an incentive to the salesperson by the store on sales of broken-lot or discontinued merchandise. Also known in the trade as a "spiff."

pneumatic sole. A shoe sole filled with compressed air to either simulate a low platform sole or to serve as underfoot cushioning. See also *air sole*.

pocket. A small pouch on the outside or inside of a shoe or boot upper in which to carry small items such as coins. The packet may or may not have a flap.

pod. From the Greek "podos" or "pous" meaning foot.

podalgia. Any pain in the foot.

podema. Swelling of the foot.

podiatrist. One trained and licensed to practice podiatry.

podiatry. The branch of medicine dealing with the diagnosis and treatment of foot disorders by surgical, mechanical, or other means. Podiatrists have the degree of Doctor of Podiatric Medicine (D.P.M.)

Formerly known as chiropody, now an obsolete term.

podistry. The reading of one's fortune or future from one's sole prints, similar to palmistry. Podistry is practiced in countries as diverse as the West Indies and China.

pododermatology. A specialized branch of podiatry dealing with diagnosis and treatment of skin ills of the foot.

podoeroticism. Dealing with the erotic nature of the foot, or related to persons or cultures who derive erotic arousal from the feet of persons of the opposite sex. Podoeroticism is universal and has achieved enormous influence in some cultures such as China, where the bound female foot was an object of intense sexual interest for 1,000 years. See also *foot fetishism*.

podogenesis (or podogeny). The study of the evolution of the human foot.

podogeriartics. The specialized branch of podiatry dealing with the diagnosis and treatment of foot ills of the elderly.

podolinguistics. A coined term relating to the "body language" expressed by the foot, particularly under certain conditions such as emotional stress or sexual communication. See also *footsie*.

podology. An obsolete term for podiatry.

podomechanics. The science of biomechanics involving the foot.

podometrics. The study and application of measurements of the foot.

podonomy. The nomenclature dealing with the foot.

podotomy. The anatomy, dissection or surgery of the foot.

pointed toe shoe. A shoe whose toe tip forms a point, from moderate to extreme. Pointed-toe shoes tend to move in fashion cycles.

point-of-purchase. Display, advertising, promotion and marketing materials designed for in-store use to

Pointed toe.

100

stimulate impulse sales or to provide information about a product or brand.

polar boot. See *boot*.

police shoe. A standard service shoe or boot, usually a black, plain-toe blucher oxford, worn by police officers while on duty.

policy. A principle, plan or program applied to the operations, personnel or customers of a store of company for the conduct of the business.

polish. Wax or creams used to clean the surface of a shoe and also produce a gloss or polished surface when brushed.

Polish boot. See *boot*.

polydactylism. The presence of more than five toes on a foot. Usually a genetic or hereditary condition.

polyethylene. Thermoplastic materials composed of ethylene polymers. A waxy solid unaffected by water. Used for making lasts or injection molded parts such as plastic shankpieces or counters.

polyurethane (PU). A family of chemically produced resins widely used as a gloss or patent finish on leathers or other materials, and also for outsoles and heel lifts.

polyvinylchloride. (PVC). A thermoplastic material widely used for man-made shoe upper materials such as PVC-coated fabrics, designed to simulate leather in appearance. Also, in denser form, commonly used for durable outsoles, welting, plus linings.

pompadour heel. See *heel*.

pom-pom. A furry ball used as a decorative feature on the vamp of some shoes and slippers.

Native shoe with pom-pom.

poplin. See *fabrics*.

popular price. A loose term designating merchandise in the lower to middle price ranges which account for the majority of footwear sales.

pore. A tiny duct and opening in the hide or skin for the escape of body moisture.

poromeric. A breathable, man-made shoe upper material simulating the appearance and texture of leather. It consists of a fabric base coated with ure-

thane and reinforced with a polymer. The term was coined by DuPont in the early 1960s.

porpoise leather. See *leather*.

porosity. The quality of having pores in a material, though not necessarily synonymous with "breathability" or the capacity for moisture and air transmission.

porosis. The formation of a callus.

porous. Full of pores.

post. A wedge under or inside a shoe.

postoperative shoe. A soft, loose-fitting, foam-lined shoe with a light foam or rubber sole, and heelless. Worn temporarily, mostly indoors, by persons recovering from foot surgery.

pouch handbag. See *handbag*.

pouf. A tuft or pom-pom of fleece, fluff or feathers on the shoe vamp as a decorative feature.

poulaine. A grotesque shoe with an extremely long toe ranging from four to 18 inches in length, worn by European gentry between the 13th and 15th centuries. The toe had to be stuffed with cotton or pieces of cloth to keep it erect. The longer versions were attached to the knee with a small chain. With its erect, flapping motion in walking, it was a blatant phallic symbol. It originated in Poland, then spread through Europe. See also *cracowe*.

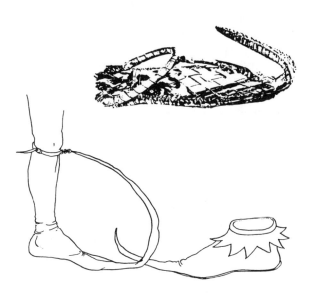

Various poulaine styles. The style dates back to ancient Egypt.

practipedist. A term coined by Dr. William Scholl around 1920. It designated a shoe salesperson in the store who had passed the Scholl Practipedics correspondence course in basic foot anatomy and foot problems, and who prescribed one or more of

Dr. Scholl's foot care items or arch supports for remedy. The term is now obsolete.

prefabrication. To manufacture parts or components which can be assembled with other parts to produce a finished product. The shoe manufacturer buys prefabricated soles, heels, insoles, etc., and assembles them to produce the finished shoe.

preforming. Molding an upper or part of an upper before lasting to facilitate the toe lasting operation.

prehensile. Adapted to grasping, such as finger-like toes capable of grasping and manipulating objects.

premolded. A shoe component (counter, box toe, contoured insole) delivered to the shoe manufacturer preshaped to conform to the last or shoe.

premium. Something extra given to or received by the customer as an incentive to make a purchase; also something of excellent quality.

prepack. An order for a given style or shoe but available only in prepackaged shipments of certain sizes and widths, in lots varying from 18 to 36 pairs. The buyer is not permitted to designate sizes of his own choice.

preppy look. A classic, semiconservative styling, usually related to somewhat uniform attire (apparel, footwear) worn by prep school boys and girls, and some adapted by men and women.

prepricing. Wherein the manufacturer sets the retail selling price, or the price is premarked on the merchandise, box or package by the manufacturer. Few retailers approve of this practice.

prescription shoe. Literally, a shoe prescribed for the customer or patient by a medical practitioner and fitted in the store in accord with the prescription instructions. More broadly, any orthopedic shoe stocked and sold by the retailer not necessarily by prescription; or a regular shoe adjusted to prescribed requirements via modifications. See also *modification.*

pressing. See *folding.*

prewalker shoe. Another name for a baby shoe worn before the infant starts to walk.

pretannage. A light, preliminary tannage which is followed by a complete tannage. Also known as "first tannage."

preteen shoe. A loose term for footwear for girls generally between ages 8 and 11. Not a standard or "official" classification.

prewelt. See *shoe construction.*

price bracket. The price range within which the merchandise is sold, usually related to the brand or quality of the merchandise.

pricing. The process of fixing a selling price to mer-

chandise after costs, expenses and profit are accounted for; or fixing the price at a level which will move the merchandise most effectively.

price leader. 1) A large or prestigious company whose pricing policy is often followed by other companies in the same field or market. 2) In a store, a particular popular item of merchandise marked at lower-than-usual price to attract customers into the store and who may purchase other merchandise.

price lining. Grouping similar types of merchandise into several price lines fixed at different price points, even though the retailer may have paid the same wholesale price for each. The customer chooses on the assumption that there is a difference in the quality or value among the lines. An unethical business practice.

price objection. The resistance or objection of the customer to the price asked.

price point. The preset selling price determined by the retailer and governing the merchandise he buys to fit those price points.

price promotion. An advertised promotion of merchandise based on lower or below regular price.

price range. See *price bracket.*

Prince Albert slipper. See *slipper.*

Prince of Wales. An oxford without a tongue, with fringes at both sides forming a lace adjustment by eyelets and loops. See also *ghillie.*

print. To make an artificial or simulated pattern on the grain side of leather by embossing. Also, a similar embossing process on man-made materials to imitate leather grains.

prison shoemaking. Shoes made by prison inmates in small shoemaking shops. Usually this footwear is not sold commercially but is used by prison inmates or personnel in other state or government institutions.

private label. Merchandise sold under a store's own brand name or label. Sometimes referred to as S.O.B. (store's own brand).

product knowledge. At the retail level, the salesperson's knowledge of or familiarity with the product (materials, crafting, etc.) being sold to the customer, and communicating that knowledge in selling.

production line. The sequence of assembly operations in the shoe factory.

production run. The preassigned number of pairs of a given stock number of footwear to be produced over a specified period.

productivity. A measure of output of work, product units, or sales per worker per hour, day, or week, gauged against wages paid. Applies at both the manufacturing and retailing levels as a measure of efficiency.

product mix. In a store, the assortment of merchandise in the inventory by brands, styles, categories, price lines, etc.

professional shoe fitting. *The process of fitting shoes based on training, skill, knowledge, and experience. Superior skill and ability in fitting shoes expertly.*

professional shoe. *Usually refers to somewhat standard or classic styles of footwear worn by business executives or those in advance-level professions. Examples: for men, a wing-tip brogue or straight-tip oxford; for women, a plain pump with medium heel. The term has only a loose or general meaning.*

profile. *The contour or outline of a last or shoe or any of its sections, such as the toe or heel or silhouette as seen in perspective.*

progression fitting. *During infant-to-tot stage, progressive changes in shoe design to conform to needs of growing and developing foot.*

promo. See *promotion*.

promotion. A marketing strategy using some unusual tactic or attractive incentive to draw attention to the product or store and hence stimulate sales and traffic. The strategy may involve special prices or a contest or a special premium or some other customer lure. Used by both manufacturers and retailers.

promotional calendar. A preplanned schedule of promotions by a store related to particular seasons, holidays, special events, etc.

pronation. On weight bearing, an outward rotation or twisting of the foot's heel accompanied by a depression and inward leaning of the long inner arch, plus

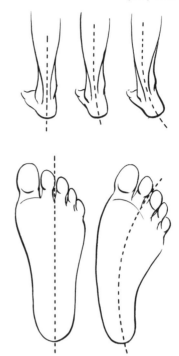

Top: left, foot without weightbearing; center, mild or normal pronation; right, extreme pronation. Bottom, foot at rest; right, outswing of forefoot and heel on severely pronated foot.

an eversion or outward swing of the forefoot. A mild degree of this is normal as a natural shock-absorbing action. When excessive it becomes abnormal and distressing and requires treatment.

pronation control. Any process or device designed to prevent or control excessive pronation.

pronograde. Walking with the body parallel to the ground, as with four-footed animals.

proportional grade. A last grading system in which the increments of sizes within a size range remain

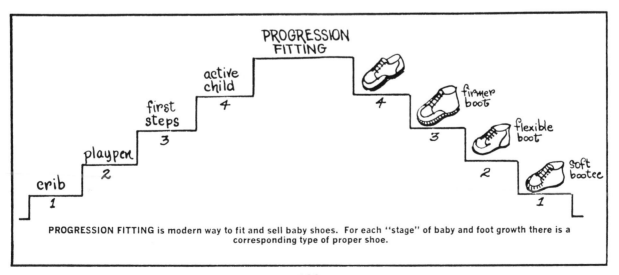

PROGRESSION FITTING is modern way to fit and sell baby shoes. For each "stage" of baby and foot growth there is a corresponding type of proper shoe.

in constant proportion. This retains control of the size/width combinations so that the fit of the last and/or shoe does not go out of proportion with the progressive size changes in feet, as can occur with standard last-grading systems.

proportional last. A last using geometric rather than arithmetic grading and conforming more precisely with the proportional dimensions of the foot with progressive size changes.

prosthetics. The medical branch dealing with the replacement of missing body parts with artificial or mechanical substitutes, such as toes or foot parts lost by accident or injury.

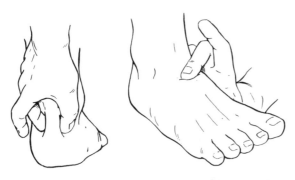

Foot pulses.   Left, in front of Achilles tendon; right, top behind instep bone.

protective footwear. 1) Rubber, waterproof, or storm footwear. 2) Safety shoes. See also *safety shoes*.

protein. A complex chemical substance and a major element of organic matter, and the key ingredient of all hides, skins and leather, contributing to leather's unique structure, texture, and performance.

proximal. Nearest to the central location of the body or a body part, such as the proximal end of a bone.

prunella shoes. A shoe with a wooly fabric upper of prune color. Popular with common folk of Britain and America in the 19th century, but shunned by upper-class women.

psychographics. An extension of demographics and dealing with the study of consumer attitudes, moods, or behavior. Used as a marketing tool to detect trends.

PU. See *polyurethane*.

publicity. Any information, activity or promotional effort that attracts attention to a product, business, person, or place.

public relations. Establishing a favorable company or store image via efforts or activities of public service not directly related to sales or profits. For a retail store the process operates on a local scale and is called "community relations."

puff. British term for box toe.

pulling the last. In the factory, pulling the last off the shoe.

pulling over. The factory operation of pulling the assembled upper over the last, done by lasting machines with finger-like pincers that grasp and firmly pull the upper over the last.

pullman slipper. See *slipper*.

pull-on boot. See *boot*.

pullover. A shoe upper pulled onto and over the last to show the style of the shoe without sole or bottoming; an unfinished shoe as a style sample.

pull strap. The short, looped back strap on a boot to pull the boot onto the foot. Also known as a "back strap."

pull-up. A test of leather quality and "depth." The finger knuckle pushes up from the underside of the leather to form a knob. The knob surface reflects a different tonal effect and the quality of this effect is known as pull-up.

pulse. The foot has two pulses: the dorsal pulse on the top surface just behind the instep bone, and the Achilles pulse just in front of the Achilles tendon. The foot pulses are taken in the same manner as the wrist pulse.

pump. A slip-on shoe not extending beyond or above the vamp and quarter top lines, held onto the foot without a fastening (button, buckles, lacing, etc.)

pump bump. A swelling, sometimes inflamed and often sore, over the Achilles heel tendon, resulting from repeated pressure and friction against the tendon from the back rim of the pump. Due to im-

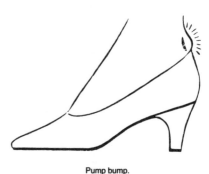

Pump bump.

proper fit or faulty heel curve on the last or shoe. Usually occurs with pumps on higher heels.

pump edge. A sole edge that does not protrude from the rim of the lasted upper. A close-edged sole.

pump shoe. Proprietary name for an athletic shoe

104

with a collar that can be inflated by a shoe-attached air pump for more snug ankle fit.

pump sole. A thin, single sole with beveled edge, used on women's or men's dress, formal, or dancing shoes.

punching. Perforations punched through the upper and lining in some shoe patterns for decorative purposes.

puncture resistance. The ability of a material such as leather to resist punctures from nails, tacks, or other sharp objects. A quality important for soles on work or utility shoes.

purchase discount. A discount on purchases by the retailer, given by the vendor for prompt payment; based on the vendor's prescribed terms, such as 3 percent for payment in 30 days.

purchasing power. The ability of the consumer to spend on goods and services, based on income and spending reserve.

push money. See *PM*.

puttee. A roll of wide, bandage-like cloth wrapped around the leg, worn by American and British soldiers during World War I. See also *patti* and *legging*.

PVC. See *polyvinylchloride*.

PX store. A commissary store on a military base or other government facility where merchandise, including footwear, is sold at low, untaxed prices to eligible personnel.

pyroxylin. A chemical substance used to manufacture adhesives for certain leather finishes; also known as cellulose nitrate.

Q

quality. The features of a product or service that give it its character, value and level of worth to a buyer. The word is from the Latin *qualitas*, meaning "what is it worth?"

quality circle. See *modular system*.

quality control. The maintenance of a predetermined standard of quality in the manufacture of a product or in the operation of a business. The application of a control system to achieve and sustain such standards.

quantity discount. A specified discount allowance on large quantity purchases, based on the quantity.

quantity pricing. See *quantity discount*.

quarter. The complete upper part of the shoe behind the vamp line and covering the sides and backpart. In boots, the quarter is also referred to as the "top."

quarter brogue. A bal or blucher pattern featuring a quarter wing tip extending about one inch beyond the normal tip line, trimmed with pinking, perforations, and stitching. See also *half brogue* and *full brogue*.

quarter corner. The front point or angle of the quarter where the side stitching ends and the tabs open.

quarter lining. See *lining*.

quarter over. The quarter portion overlapping the vamp at the vamp seam.

quarter round. An old trade term describing a round-toe shoe, the shape corresponding to the half circumference of a silver quarter.

quarter sizes. Measured in increments of 1/12 of an inch (versus 1/6 of an inch for a half size). First introduced by a few zealous manufacturers in the early 1920s, but soon discarded because of inventory cost problems for manufacturers and retailers.

quick response. See *just in time*.

quilted leather. Any upper leather stitched to a padded backing fabric. The stitching is done all over in some decorative pattern for a quilted look.

quilted lining. A mildly cushioned lining—tongue, quarter, or vamp lining, or all—with a quilted surface pattern for added comfort.

R

R&D. See *research and development*.

racing flats. A running shoe about 25 percent lighter and more flexible than an ordinary running or training shoe.

racewalking. A skilled sport of fast walking while observing rigid rules of racewalking technique. It involves a heel-to-toe step with vigorous arm swinging and alternate hip motion. Special racewalking shoes are used by professionals.

rack. 1) In the shoe factory, a piece of shelved equipment on wheels to hold semifinished pairs of shoes as the rack is moved from one operating station to the next. 2) In the store, either stationary or mobile shelving to hold stock or as a display unit such as for customer self-service or self-selection. 3) A shoe rack for closet use at home. See also *closet rack*.

rack jobber. A wholesaler or jobber who markets certain lines of merchandise to certain types of stores, providing the service of arranging, maintaining and stocking of shelves or display racks.

rack store. A shoe store, usually self-service or self-selection, whose merchandise is completely on display on open racks for self-selection. Usually a store selling lower-priced or cancellation merchandise.

racquetball shoe. See *sports shoe*.

raffia. Straw made from strong palm fibers, used to make some shoes with straw uppers.

ram's horn toe. A very long, turned-up and curled shoe toe popular in some European footwear of the 11th and 12th centuries. Also called a "scorpion toe."

rand. A beveled strip of leather or other material shaped like a horseshoe and fitting around the top edge of the heel in the crevice between upper and heel.

ratios. The numerical relation between associated things; a proportion. Ratios are commonly used in retailing to measure operating performance. E.g., the ratio of profits to sales, expenses to sales, selling cost to overall operating costs, etc.

raw edge. The unfinished edge of a shoe upper. It may be finished by folding, or may be deliberately left unfinished as in some casual or sport footwear.

Shoe rack in shoe factory.

raw eyelet. An eyelet that is simply a hole through the lace stay, without a metal or plastic eyelet. Actually a "raw eyelet" is not a true eyelet but simply a hole in a material.

rawhide. Cattlehide leather that has been dehaired and limed but not tanned. Used for lacings and small leather goods.

raw stock. Hides and skins before tanning.

ray. Sometimes used medically for a metatarsal bone.

rayon. See *fabrics*.

ready-made shoes. Shoes not custom-made. A term common in 18th-century America when shoes were custom-made entirely by hand. In their spare time shoemakers also made pairs of various sizes available to persons with corresponding sizes but not made to order. Also known as "sale shoes."

ready-to-wear. In the garment trade, ready-made apparel in contrast to custom-made or custom-fitted.

rearfoot. The tarsal section of the foot.

rearfoot control. Controlling or stabilizing excessive or faulty motion of the rearfoot, as in pronation, via orthotics or special shoe design such as in some sports footwear.

recede toe. A shoe toe shape slanted downward and forward or tapered. A style feature on some shoes, often men's.

Recede toe with slanting front and sides.

receipts. Monies received for services or merchandise sales.

receiving. The department or section of a factory or store where all incoming merchandise from vendors enters.

reconstituted leather. A material composed of collegen fibers derived from hide or leather scrap and reconstituted into sheets of leather.

recreational footwear. Colorful, casual, low-heel footwear for recreational wear.

recruiting. For a store, the process or strategies of attracting new personnel for employment.

recovery. See *regain*.

rectus. Straight, as in a straight-axis foot versus a valgus or varus foot.

referral. Usually relates to prescription footwear or to stores where the customer or patient is referred by a medical practitioner. Such a customer is called a referral.

reflective footwear. Shoes with specially treated stripe designs or other pieces that reflect the lights of oncoming cars. Used as a safety measure by some walkers and runners on roads at night.

reflex. The automatic or involuntary jerk or other physical reaction of a body part when tapped or stroked, such as knee jerk or plantar reflex. Used as a test for nerve response.

regain. The quality of a material to quickly or repeatedly regain its original shape and dimensions after stretching. Also known as "recovery."

regent pump. A pump style with a circular vamp and full quarter. A narrow collar extends from the front of the quarter around the throat of the vamp. The collar, which is part of the quarter, may extend around without a seam to the opposite quarter, wherein the two quarters are cut from a single piece. This is a "full" regent pump. See also *full regent pump*, *three-quarter regent pump*, and *split regent pump*.

reindeer leather. See *leather, buckskin*.

reinforcement rows. Extra stitching to reinforce a shoe in some particular section to resist undue stress with wear.

regular price. The selling price with full or regular markon.

reject. 1) In the factory, a damaged shoe rejected from the production line. 2) In the store, a damaged shoe returned to the factory for a credit.

relasting. A second lasting of a turn shoe. After the shoe is lasted inside out, the last is removed and the shoe turned right side out. A last is again inserted and the shoemaking process is continued.

reminder card. A form postcard sent to the parent of a young child two to four months after the shoes have been purchased, reminding the parent to bring the child into the store for a size checkup.

removable insert. Any removable shoe component, such as a contoured insole in a sports shoe, or an orthotic insert.

removable ornament. A clip-on or similar type of shoe ornament that enables the shoe to be worn with or without the ornament.

repair. During manufacturing, any repair made on a shoe to cover a blemish such as a scratch or burn or wrinkle in the leather.

repairing. The repair or replacement of a worn part of the shoe, such as the toplift or sole. Also known as "shoe remodeling."

repeat business. Repeated or steady purchases from the same store by customers, based on product, value, service and other satisfactions.

reptile leathers. Leathers from the skins of reptiles. See also *leather: alligator, lizard, snakeskin*.

research and development (R&D). That department or activity of a manufacturing company, or a laboratory, involved in technical research leading to the development of new or improved products.

resident buyer. An agent who specializes in buying, on a fee or commission basis, merchandise for one or several large retailers.

resident buying office (or R.B.O.). The office of the resident buyer for a department store, large specialty store, or a chain.

resin rubber. A blend of rubber and plastic commonly used for shoe soles.

resole. Replacing the old worn sole with a new one.

resort footwear. A trade term for footwear worn at summer or winter resorts, or styles seen at the more prestigious resorts and later adopted in popular-priced lines.

resource. A supplier or vendor for a manufacturer or retailer. A source of merchandise supply.

retail. The purchase of merchandise at wholesale for resale to the consumer by the store at a profit.

retailing. The complete range of functions in the operation of a retail store or business.

retan. A modifying second tannage following the primary tannage.

retanned leather. A leather that has been tanned first by one process, the retanned by another to produce leather with qualities not obtainable with only one of the processes.

reticule. See *handbag*.

return on inventory (ROI). Derived by dividing earnings by total assets. Used by retailers as another method of determining profitability.

returns. 1) In manufacturing, shoes returned to the vendor by the retailer, usually due to a defect or some other fault. 2) In retailing, shoes returned to the store by the customer for credit or refund, due to some fault in the shoe or some other dissatisfaction with the purchase.

reversed calf. See *leather*.

reversed side leather. See *leather*.

reversed split. See *leather*.

rhinestone. Colored or colorless lustrous stone made of paste or glass in imitation of ruby, diamond, emerald, and other gems. Used in various sizes on some shoes, especially evening shoes, and some handbags.

rib. A strip of canvas at the underside edge of the insole, forming a raised wall or surface to which stitching can be attached, usually on a Goodyear welt shoe.

rib sole. A serrated design on a rubber-type outsole to give a ribbed effect on the sole surface for more resilience and traction.

ribbed hose. Hose with ribbed vertical lines that are part of the hose pattern.

ribbon tie. A women's dress shoe with two half straps across the instep and connected through strap loops by a wide ribbon, such as grosgrain tied in a bow.

riding boot. See *boot*.

riding heel. See *heel*.

rigid foot. A foot incapable of using normal motions such as flexing, usually due to adhesions or stiffening of the joints caused by arthritis or other debilitating conditions. More common in the advanced years.

rigid shank. A shoe with a metal or other inflexible shankpiece that keeps the shoe's shank rigid, ostensibly for arch support.

rink system. See *modular system*.

ripple sole. A proprietary trademark for a ribbed rubber sole and heel whose resilient ribs are inclined rearward to add shock absorption in walking.

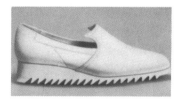

Ripple sole.

Ritz stick. A foot measuring device like a ruler for ascertaining foot length and ball width in shoe fitting. It has one length scale for adults, another for children.

riveted shoe. British term for a nailed shoe.

roan. See *leather*.

robotics. The science of designing, building and applying mechanical robots to performing specific tasks in industrial operations, plus numerous other applications. It has some applications in shoe manufacturing.

rocker bar. See *bar*.

rocker bottom. A longitudinal curve of the bottom of a last or sole, heel to toe, with exaggerated toe

Rocker bottom.

spring, enabling the foot to "rock" forward with each step without full use of the foot's natural flexing action at the ball. The design is essential on clog or platform-type footwear where sole flexibility is absent. It is also used on some prescription footwear for persons with rigid, inflexible feet and where the shoe must "do the walking" for the foot.

rocker sole. See *rocker bottom*.

rocket heel. See *heel*.

Roman sandal. A variation of the Greek sandal, but more innovative in styling treatments and more ornate in decorative features.

Romeo slipper. See *slipper*.

rope sole. Hemp or fiber braids coiled and shaped to form a shoe sole, fastened with adhesive.

Rope sole.

rope stitching. Heavy corded stitching used for decorative effect on the edges of the sole or elsewhere.

rosette. A ribbon decoration in the shape of a small rose, used for ornamental effect on some women's and girls' shoes.

rotation. The movement of a body part on an axis or pivot, such as the circular motion of the foot on the ankle joint.

roughing. The sanding or abrading of the lasting margin of the upper and the top surface of the sole edge to create a roughened surface for better adhesion when the two surfaces are cemented and bonded.

rough rounding. Rounding the edge of the outsole to the shape of the last by machine. The outline is later smoothed by edge trimming and finishing.

royalty system. A royalty paid by the user to the owner of the patent or copyright. In the footwear industry it usually refers to shoe machinery. The royalty system was started in the 1860s by Colonel Gordon McKay who leased his new, revolutionary McKay Sewing Machine to shoe manufacturers instead of selling it outright. He charged a per-pair royalty to shoe manufacturers. The royalty system was later adopted by other shoe machinery producers, especially the huge conglomerate called United Shoe Machinery Corporation, and the system became almost universal in the footwear industry between 1870 and 1954, after which the court decreed that shoe manufacturers would have the choice of buying or leasing shoe machines.

rubber. An elastic, resilient material made from liquid latex derived from the rubber tree. Rubber can be compounded to assume any of a broad range of densities and other characteristics. In both natural and synthetic forms, it has long had extensive uses in the footwear industry for soles, heels, cushioning, protective footwear, etc.

rubber/canvas footwear. A trade classification for sneaker-type footwear with rubber bottom and canvas or other cloth upper.

rubber footwear. Includes all-rubber footwear such as rubber boots, overshoes, or galoshes, low-cut rubbers.

rubberized fabrics. Fabrics coated with rubber and used for shoe linings and some stretchable shoe uppers. Also used as cover cloths to protect light-colored shoes while being processed in the factory.

rubbers. Low-cut, over-the-shoe protective rubber footwear for use in inclement weather. The *full* rubber covers most of the shoe. The *storm* rubber has a high tongue to also cover the instep. The *half* rubber covers only the forepart of the shoe, with a stretchable halter strap in back to hold the rubber onto the foot and also allow the rubber to be worn with any heel height.

rubber thong. A rubber or plastic thong slipper or sandal worn in locker rooms or at poolside. Sometimes called a "thong."

rullion. Scottish term for a kind of shoe or sandal made of untanned leather.

run around. The stitching for bringing the shoe's upper and lining together.

runner. A section included in the shoe bottom assem-

bly in the factory to add thickness to the sole, sometimes covered with a decorative edge. Similar to a midsole.

running shoe. See *sports shoe*.

runner's toe. See *turf toe*.

rush shoe. Made of woven straw or rushes, worn by European peasants of the 15th and 16th centuries.

russet. A standard or classic brown-tone color common in footwear.

russet leather. See *leather*.

Russian boot. See *boot*.

Russia calf. See *leather*.

S

sabot. An all-wooden, clog shoe dating back to the pre-Christian era. Sabot is the French and klompen the Dutch term for this universal shoe. The sabot is unpadded for those accustomed to wearing it, but padded for others. The sabot, usually boat-shaped, can be hollowed out by hand, the traditional way, or by machine tools.

sabot strap. See *strap shoe*.

sabotine. A makeshift shoe with wooden sole and coarse leather upper, worn by some European soldiers during World War I.

sac. A small body pouch filled with fluid, such as a bursa sac, to protect a part beneath from pressure or injury.

Sach heel. See *heel*.

saddle. A wide band of leather or other material stitched across both sides of the shoe's waist and instep, running from shank to lace rows, and usually in a contrasting color.

saddle finish. Leather colored and finished to resemble genuine saddle leather with its distinctive tan shade.

saddle oxford. An oxford with a wide piece of leather cradling the shoe's waist and instep, usually in contrasting color to the toe and quarter part of the shoe. Originally designed in 1906 by A. G. Spaulding as a gym shoe, with the saddle portion added to provide extra support for the arch and foot.

saddle seam. See *seam*.

saddle soap. A special soap used to clean, lubricate, and renew leather.

saddle stitch. A wide stitching with heavy thread, giving a hand-stitched effect; used for decoration on some footwear.

saddle welt. A strip of welting over the front of the vamp, to to vamp, used as a decorative treatment.

safety insole. A lightweight but strong metal plate used as a supplementary insole to prevent nail or spike punctures. One version was used by American troops during the Vietnam War as protection against lethal spikes hidden on jungle paths.

Saddle oxford.

Metal safety insole on military boot
to protect against planted spikes or "pungee sticks."

Plastic or metal shield on instep for protection.

safety shoe. Any shoe or boot with safety features to protect against injury at work or elsewhere, such as a safety toe, instep shield, puncture-resistant or non-slip soles, etc.

safety toe. The most common feature on a safety shoe or boot, consisting of a metal or hard plastic toe cap capable of resisting heavy falling objects.

Metal or plastic safety toe.

saffian leather. See *leather*.

sagittal plane. A hypothetical flat, vertical plane passing through the center of the body, back to front, dividing the body into right and left halves. A foot that moves on a sagittal plane would dorsiflex and plantarflex.

sailor tie. A two-eyelet tie shoe with lacing, usually a women's shoe with ribbon-type lacing.

Saint Amien. Said to be the original saint of shoemakers. He lived 200 years before St. Crispin and St. Crispianus.

Saint Crispianus. The brother of St. Crispin who together became the patron saints of shoemakers. The brothers, themselves shoemakers, were martyred November 8, in the year 288, in France.

Saint Crispin. With his brother Crispianus, one of the two best-known saints of shoemakers.

Saint Hugh. Also a patron saint of shoemakers, though lesser known than Crispin and Crispianus.

Saint Hugh's bones. The name for shoemakers' tools, especially in England. St. Hugh, of noble birth, after a long period of self-imposed penance, became a shoemaker. He became religiously martyred, hanged by decree of Roman emperor Diocletian. His bones, according to legend, were exhumed from his grave by fellow shoemakers and made into shoemaker's tools.

sale shoes. 1) Markdown or clearance footwear. 2) In early America when most shoes were custom-made, shoemakers in their spare time produced some ready-made shoes known as "sale shoes." See also *ready-made shoes*.

sales forecast. An estimated or budgeted anticipation of sales in dollars or units for a given forward period. The forecast may be made for given lines or categories of merchandise, or for all sales combined.

sales management. The planning, direction and control of sales and sales personnel in a business.

sales manager. The executive or other person responsible for a company's sales and sales management.

salesmanship. The skilled process of making the sale to the fullest extent of its sales potential in the quickest time with quality service and the whole process to the satisfaction of the customer.

sales per square foot. The store's sales for a given line of merchandise, or for all merchandise combined, relative to the selling floor space. It is sometimes reckoned on the basis of total floor space, including stockroom and other areas, though this method is less commonly used.

salesperson. An individual directly involved in serving the customers and completing the sale.

sales promotion. All special marketing activities other than personal selling designed to stimulate consumer buying and dealer effectiveness, including advertising, publicity, displays, demonstrations, contests, etc., not in the store's day-to-day operating routine. It is usually focused on some unusual theme or event. Not the same as a seasonal markdown or clearance sale.

sales psychology. The process of the salesperson attuning to the customer's anticipated needs and wants, and the use of subtle strategies to fill those wants and needs.

sales record. A record of an individual sale, or of sales by lines or brands, or of all merchandise combined.

sales slip. A slip in duplicate or multiple form on which is recorded the stock number, price, and other essential details of the merchandise sold to the customer.

sales sheet. A store's record of sales by style, stock number, size, etc., indicating the movement of each segment of the inventory, and a guide for fill-ins and reorders.

salon. French word for a drawing room or reception room. Also a showroom for exhibit purposes. The term is usually associated with stores selling upper-priced fashion merchandise, such as a shoe salon.

salt stain. 1) A discoloration from salt on the surface of hides and skins, and sometimes, due to faulty processing in tanning, on leather. 2) A stain accumulated on the shoe from salt on streets, such as used in snow removal.

sample. A model shoe used by the manufacturer's sales representative to show the style, construction, material, color, etc. of the shoe being offered to the retailer.

sample size. A standard model shoe size, such as a 6B women's, on which the manufacturer's samples are made, or which are shown in the store windows.

sample room. The vendor's showroom where all current samples are on display; or the vendor's showroom during a shoe trade show.

sandal. One of the oldest forms of footwear known. Originally a slab of leather sole attached to the foot by thongs. Today, any open shoe whose upper consists of any decorative or functional arrangement of straps. A sandal can be foot-low to knee-high, or with any heel height, designed for simple utility or casual wear or as a fashion shoe.

sandal bar. In some stores, a display or rack holding sandals, usually for self-service, or sometimes prepackaged.

sandalia. A slipper-like shoe developed by the ancient Persians and later adopted by the Greeks and Romans. Made of soft, light goatskin and lined with white flannel or lambskin, held onto the foot with thongs. An elegant shoe mostly worn indoors or for formal occasions.

sandalion (or sandalium). Of Persian origin, a women's elegant mule-style slipper with thin leather sole and luxurious upper fabrics embroided with gold or silver threads. The red and purple slippers of the medieval popes derived from this shoe.

sandalthique. A carpetbag containing various pairs of sandals, carried by the maids of wealthy women of ancient Greece, allowing the women to change into different sandals as the occasion required.

sanis. The Persian name for sandal. Sanis means a slab or board, referring to the leather sole of the sandal.

sanitized shoe. Shoes whose linings especially have been chemically treated to diminish or eliminate foot and shoe odors.

sartor. Latin for tailor, and originally a humorous term for one who mends or patches; later associated with fine tailoring or an artisan tailor.

sartorial. From the word sartor, referring to a person impeccably tailored, particularly in regard to men's clothing.

sasquatch. An American Indian term for the legendary character known as Big Foot. See *Big Foot*.

satchel handbag. See *handbag*.

sateen. See *fabrics*.

satin. See *fabrics*.

satin calf. See *leather*.

satin finish. See *finish*.

SATRA. An acronym for Shoe and Allied Trades Research Association, the prestigious British shoe research organization and the largest of its kind in the world.

savate. 1) French word for a coarse, rustic shoe with wooden sole of centuries past. 2) A sabot or all-wooden shoe. 3) A form of boxing with hands and feet.

Sbicca-Del Mac process. See *shoe construction*.

scallop. A curve or partial circle usually made in a series along an edge; used as a decorative effect in toplines or other locations on women's shoes.

scaphoid. See *navicular*.

scaphoid pad. See *cookie*.

Scarpa. The Italian physician, Antonio Scarpa, was the first to give a detailed description of clubfoot, in 1802, and to design a clubfoot shoe which has since been used with little change.

scarpetti. A rope-sole shoe used for climbing rocks.

scarpine. A very wide-toe shoe with slots or "pockets" for each toe, popular in 15th-century Europe. Also known as a "bear's paw."

sceo. Old Anglo-Saxon name for shoe, now obsolete.

Schaeffer's foot. A condition wherein the muscles, tendons and fascia on the sole of the foot are permanently contracted, resulting in an abnormally high arch and instep and a severe depression of the metatarsal arch at the ball, with the toes drawn back claw-like. Not quite the same as pes cavus. Usually congenital.

schlock. A trade term for an overcharge. Also, Yiddish term for cheap or junk.

schuh. Teutonic word from which we derive our word "shoe."

117

scoot shop. A shoe industry term common in 17th- and 18th-century New England referring to a shoe-making shop or small factory where small groups of temporarily hired shoemakers were rushed in to produce shoes as quickly as possible under the simplest constructions to meet an urgent order. See also *gang*.

scored sole. An outsole deliberately scored with a knife to make "scars" on the surface to prevent skidding and slipping in walking.

scorpion toe. See *ram's horn toe*.

scotch edge. A wide extensive of the shoe sole. The term "scotch outside" means a wider extension on the outside and a closer edge or trim on the inner side; and the reverse with a "scotch inside."

scotch inside. See *scotch edge*.

scotch outside. See *scotch edge*.

scotch grain. See *grain*.

scrap leather. Small, leftover pieces from cutting patterns, linings, insoles, outsoles, etc. from larger pieces of leather. The scraps are recycled into leatherboard or reconstituted leather.

scuff. 1) To scratch, gouge or abrade the surface of leather, or the mark left by scuffing. 2) A kind of slipper. See also *slipper*.

scuffer. A children's playshoe.

scuff resistance. The ability of a material or component or shoe to resist scuffing or scuff marks.

sculponae. A sandal-like or clog-like shoe with thick wooden sole and coarse leather straps, worn by slaves of ancient Egypt.

sculptone. A clog-like wooden shoe worn by peasants and slaves of ancient Rome.

seal of approval. A document or insignia of acceptance or approval given to a commercial product or service by an institution, business, or professional organization for meeting certain quality or performance standards. The recipient of the seal sometimes is expected to make some "contribution" financially to the seal source, and in turn often uses the seal for advertising, promotion, or publicity.

sealskin leather. See *leather*.

seam. The line formed by the butted edges of two pieces of material and the series of stitches holding the pieces together. In footwear and shoemaking there are a variety of seams used, as follows:

  back. The seam joining the two quarters at the back of the counter.

  butt. A flat seam in which the sections are placed edge to edge, with the thread passing from one surface through the surface of the next piece

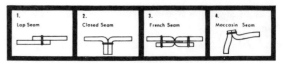

Examples of four types of shoe seams.

without passing through the opposite side of the material. Also known as a "jockey seam."

  closed. Made by facing together the edges of two pieces of material and running a row of stitches to join them. After the seam is made the seam and joined pieces are pressed flat for smoothness. Used mostly for decorative effect.

  cobbler's. Made by stitching through the edges of two joined pieces, similar to a saddle seam.

  French. A closed seam, but with more material left along the edge from the line of stitching. The extra-wide edges are separated, folded and cemented back against the side of the upper. They are then stitched through the upper with rows of stitches parallel with the closed seamline. Commonly used on fabric shoe uppers.

  gypsy. A closed seam usually extending from the toe tip to the vamp throat; also used as a side seam. Usually piped for ornamental effect.

  hand. Formed by two threads (or opposite ends of the same thread) passing in opposite directions through the same hole in a material, and then returning to the next hole. Used in sole sewing and welt sewing by hand. Also called an "overcast" seam or stitch.

  inseam. The hidden seam of a Goodyear welt shoe, holding together the welt, upper, insole, and lining. The seam is made by a curved needle making a chain stitch.

  jockey. See *butt seam*.

  lap. The simplest of all seams, with one edge overlapping the other and stitched through. The edges are then skived to produce a smooth, flat surface.

  moccasin. Made by joining two pieces of leather or other material whose edges are faced outward and then are stitched close to the edges to create a raised seam of rough, decorative effect. On a genuine moccasin this is a hand-stitched seam.

  open. The two sections are placed edge to edge and grain to grain, then stitched. This closed seam is then opened and flattened, then reinforced by stitching a tape over it on the flesh side with two parallel rows of stitching.

  outseam. Made with two separate waxed threads, one drawn up through the outsole, the other through the welt, with the threads locked tightly

118

around each other. Both raw edges appear on the right side of the upper.

overcast. See *hand seam.*

overseam. Made by butting two pieces of material and the seam covered with a strap or decorative trim, then finished with a zigzag stitch across the edges of both parts.

piped. A seam with a narrow bias binding inserted so that a strip of contrasting material is seen between the two edges of the leather or fabric which are being joined.

saddle. Formed by placing two pieces of material together with the edges faced outward, then stitched closed to the edges. Similar to a moccasin seam.

welt. One of the most difficult and costly seams. A narrow strip of leather or folded fabric is stitched between two pieces of material to be closed or attached. Used chiefly as a back seam for heavier shoes or boots. Sometimes a substitute seam is used by reinforcing a closed seam on the inside with a strip of sealing tape.

zigzag. A seam in which the pieces are placed edge to edge or surface to surface and joined by a seam passing side to side across the edges.

seam allowance. An extra measurement allowance on shoe patterns at all seam lines so that there is sufficient material for seaming.

seamless pump. A pump cut from a single piece of leather and seamless from toe to heel.

seamless quarter. The entire quarter made in one rather than the usual two or more pieces.

seamless shoe. Any shoe made with one upper piece rather than in pattern pieces joined together.

season. 1) In the footwear industry it refers to the peak retail selling period for any given season, usually several weeks before the actual weather season officially begins and continuing into the peak of the weather season. 2) In the fashion business a season can be divided or subdivided, such as early spring or early fall, or combined such as spring-summer or fall-winter, depending upon the nature of the merchandise.

seasonal buying. Buying seasonally-oriented merchandise in advance of season to be sold during the seasonal selling period.

seating. 1) The seating fixtures used in the store. 2) The arrangement or layout of the seats.

seat lift. A leveling piece (horsehoe shape or lift) placed between the heel seat and the heel to provide a level surface for the heel and blending in with the welt or sole.

seat sock. A piece of leather or other material stuck over the seat of the insole in certain types of footwear.

sebaceuous gland. A sweat gland or duct.

secque. A clog similar to the sabotine.

seed corn. See *heloma.*

self-selection. An in-store arrangement in which a pair (or single shoe) of each style in stock is on

Self-selection display.

119

open display, allowing the customer to browse and select, at which time a salesperson gets the requested shoe in the needed size from stock, then fits and serves the customer.

self-service. An in-store arrangement in which all the available merchandise in all available sizes is on open display, usually on racks, allowing the customer to browse and select, and also to try on the shoes in the needed size without the assistance from store personnel. The customer then takes the selected shoes to the cashier for wrapping and payment.

selection. In a shoe store or department, the range and depth of the merchandise or inventory in styles, sizes, colors, etc. made available to the customers.

selling costs. All costs of store personnel directly involved in selling to the customers, including wages, commissions, bonuses, and fringe benefits. It does not include indirect selling costs such as advertising, displays, special promotions, etc.

selling floor. In a store, the area or section where the selling and buying between salespeople and customers take place.

selling points. The features of the product or merchandise highlighted to the customer by the salesperson in the selling/service process.

selling price. The posted price of the merchandise which the customer is asked to pay.

sell-through. In shoe retailing, a measure of the amount of merchandise units sold as a percentage of the merchandise units available to sell, measured over a selected period such as three or six months.

semi-annual sale. In footwear retailing semi-annual sales usually occur in January and June/July, and the hiatus between closing out the prior season and the beginning of the new season when last season's remaining merchandise is advertised at markdown or clearance prices. Actual timing of a semi-annual sale varies by geographical region.

seminar. A gathering of people with common interests assembled at an educational meeting to hear speakers or lectures or participate in workshops on topics related to their interests.

sensible heel. See *heel*.

sensible shoe. A loose, arbitrary designation for an oxford-type shoe with broad toe and low heel, usually women's shoes.

sensor. An electronic device that feeds back impulses when pressure is applied. The impulses are recorded on a dial or other indicator. The sensor itself is often a wired wafer. Sensors are used for testing pressure points on the foot, or to track gait patterns.

sensory response. A nerve sensation response when the nerve or nerves are stimulated. E.g., foot tickling.

serge. See *fabrics*.

service. See *customer service*.

service shoe. Any shoe or boot designed for comfort and serviceability for particular occupations, such as a women's duty shoe or a policeman's shoe; also, some military shoes.

service shoe store. One offering personal customer services such as fitting, in contrast to self-service stores.

sesamoid. One of the two pea-sized bones under the great toe joint, between which passes a toe tendon. These two bones are not usually included with the other 26 bones of the foot.

setback heel. See *heel*.

sewn shoe. Any shoe or construction in which the sole is attached to the upper by sewing or stitching. Examples: Goodyear welt, stitchdown, McKay.

sewn seat. A flat, extended heel, vertical or sloping outward, with the heel breast usually rectangular.

sewn through. A method of sole attachment in which the last is withdrawn from the shoe and then the sole is stitched through the insole.

sexy shoe. Any shoe with a sensuous design, character or intent. Usually refers to women's shoes but can include some men's. The women's shoes are generally more open, such as a strippy, high-heel sandal. A men's shoe in this category would be sleek, with close-edge sole, narrow toe, soft, and snug-fitting.

shade. See *color*.

shadow box. In a store, a box-type or framed display with lighting inside.

shaft. 1) The leg portion of a boot above the ankle. 2) The middle or narrowed section, especially in a higher heel, between the toplift and the heel seat.

shagreen leather. See *leather*.

shank. The bridged portion of the sole between the heel breast and the ball tread area.

shank curve. The contour of the shank on the last or shoe, determined by heel height.

shankpiece. The flat, fingerlike slab of material inserted between outsole and insole in the center of the shank to reinforce the raised shank area against body weight and stress. The shankpiece may be metal, wood, fiberglass, plastic or other material. Sometimes cited as an "arch support," which it is not.

shank's mare. A plain, flat-heel women's shoe introduced by the fashionable I. Miller shoe stores dur-

Shankpiece under shank of shoe between insole and outsole.

Sexy shoes.

ing World War II to economize on frills in footwear. It became widely popular.

shantung. See *fabrics*.

shape. The shape character of the last or shoe as a basic element in all footwear fashion. Shape can refer to the last or shoe overall (profile or silhou-ette), or to a particular part such as the toe or heel. Shoe shape is influenced by fashion trends.

shape retention. The ability of a shoe to retain its original shape with wear.

sharkskin. See *leather*.

shawl tongue. See *tongue*.

shearing force. The abrasive torque action of one part or surface against another, such as the sole of the foot against the insole or the outsole against the ground. When excessive it can create friction, heat and distress to the foot or high abrasion or distortion of the shoe.

shearling. See *leather*.

sheepskin. See *leather*.

sheet material. A term used for leatherboard or fiberboard that comes in sheet form.

shelf life. The time period of merchandise on the store shelves from time of delivery to time of sale.

shell. 1) An unfinished base or framework of a foot mold, such as plastic, for making a shoe or orthotic. 2) The broad outline of a shoe pattern, made to conform to the size and shape of the last, and from which other patterns of the shoe are made.

shell cordovan. See *leather*.

shelled out. See *shell vamp*.

shell pump. A plain, low-cut pump with low topline.

shell sole. A unit sole with foxing sides molded to the shoe bottom. Also known as a "cup sole" or "dish sole."

shell vamp. On a pump, a low-cut vamp to expose toe cleavage. Also called "shelled out."

shewis. Old Anglo-Saxon term for "shoe." Archaic.

shield tip. See *tip*.

shin splint. A tiny hairline fracture or surface damage to a bone, mainly a leg bone, when the tendon is pulled away from its attachment to the bone, with consequent pain and inflammation. Common with runners and other athletes.

shock. Traumatic impact, normal or abnormal, as in step shock.

shock absorption. The natural ability of a body part, such as the foot, to absorb a normal amount of shock as in walking or running; or the use of special

121

shoe components or materials, such as cushioning, to aid in the absorption of step shock.

shock heel. See *heel*.

shoe. A protective and/or decorative foot covering. It designates chiefly low-cut footwear versus hightops or boots. The word "shoe" evolves from a series of ancient Anglo-Saxon terms: "sceo," then "shewis," followed by "shooeys" or "shoon," and finally "shoe." There is also some derivation from the Teutonic "schuh."

shoe box. The box or carton containing a pair of shoes or boots.

shoe care. The process or products involved in maintaining the serviceable and cosmetic condition of footwear.

shoe climate. The thermal conditions (heat, cold, humidity) inside the shoe during wear.

shoe chain. 1) A light metal chain attached to the sole of a shoe or boot for traction when walking on ice, snow, or rocky-slippery surfaces. 2) a group or organization of 11 or more shoe stores under one ownership.

shoe chemist. A chemist specializing in the chemical elements involved in footwear or its components and materials.

shoe chemistry. The study and applications of chemicals involved in footwear or its components and materials.

shoe club. An arrangement or agreement offered by a shoe retailer to customers or others to get their friends, relatives or work associates to buy shoes or other merchandise at the store. The customer organizer receives a "credit" for a purchase made by a referred friend and is compensated with free merchandise or cash in proportion to the sales accounted for. The participants in such a plan expand to become a group called a "shoe club."

shoe construction. The particular method or process used for constructing or assembling a shoe. Essentially the manner in which the sole is attached to the upper. There are scores of known ways to "construct" a shoe, though only a few are used commercially. Many are simply variations or combinations of others. The most common shoe constructions are as follows:

American welt. See *prewelt*.

bonwelt. A variation of the cement construction. Its distinguishing feature is a strip of welting attached by stitching or cementing to the top edge of the insole. The shoe is then flat-lasted. It is not a true welt construction wherein the welt is attached to the rib of the insole.

California. See *slip-lasted*.

cement. The outsole is attached to the upper by an adhesive rather than by stitching or other bonding methods. Also known as the Compo process, first introduced in 1929 and the first commercially practical and successful method of cement-bonding soles to uppers. There have since been numerous variations of the cement process.

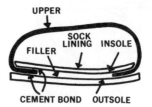

Cement construction.

Compo. See *cement*.

Del-Mac. See *skeleton insole process*.

Del-Mac sewed. See *skeleton insole process*.

Del-welt. See *skeleton insole process*.

Duo. Assembling the shoe upper by cementing rather than stitching the edges.

Goodyear welt. This is distinguished by a raised insole rib to which both the welt and insole are attached and secured by a strong, flexible chain stitch. This is supplemented but a lockstitch outseam bonding the welt and outsole. The process is regarded as the sturdiest of all shoe constructions.

imitation moccasin. Any variation or simulation of a genuine moccasin construction. The imitation is either entirely or partially machine-made.

imitation welt. A shoe that has a strip of welting

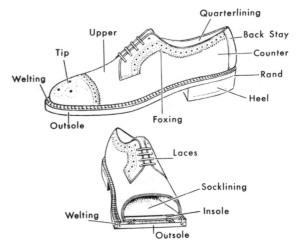

Anatomy of a men's Goodyear welt shoe.

around the top edge of the sole but is not part of the actual construction. Used to imitate the look of a genuine Goodyear welt construction.

injection molding. A plastic (PVC, urethane, etc.) is preheated then forced by a plunger through a nozzle into a closed mold, forming the outsole which is then heat-sealed to the upper. When the plastic material in the mold is cooled, the sole-upper bonding is completed.

Littleway. A flat-lasted shoe construction using a lockstitch to fasten the insole to the upper and midsole or outsole. Known also as UCO and Littleway lockstitch processes. See also *lockstitch*.

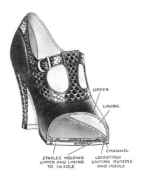

Littleway lockstitch construction.

lockstitch. The outsole, insole and upper are bonded by a lockstitch seam which is usually imbedded in a channel or open groove on the tread surface of the outsole. The shoe is flat-lasted. On some shoes an outsole is cemented to a midsole containing the lockstitch seam.

McKay. A sewn process wherein the upper is tacked, stapled, or cemented and the outsole attached with a chain stitch. Rarely used today.

moccasin. In a genuine moccasin construction a single piece of leather is wrapped around the last to form the bottom, sides and upper of the shoe, held onto the foot with thongs, rawhide lacings, or drawstrings. The sole may be the same soft material as the upper or a firm sole may be attached. Also, a plug may be inserted at the vamp, held on with handsewn, puckered seams. The moccasin is perhaps the oldest shoe construction. The plug was a later innovation of the American Indians, who also decorated the shoe with colored beads and fringed collar. The imitation moccasin, very common, has the visual appearance of a moccasin but does not have the wrap-around construction of the genuine moccasin.

nailed. Attaching the sole to the insole and upper by nailing. In this category are variations such as "loose-nailed," "standard screw," and "pegged." The nailed process is rarely used today.

namrog welt. An imitation welt shoe in which the sole is attached by cement.

pegged. Attaching the sole to the upper by means of wooden pegs, a common method of the 18th and 19th centuries. The process is now outmoded, first replaced by nailing, later replaced by stitching and cementing.

prewelt. This features a welt stitched to the edge of the upper before the upper is formed on the last. During this stage it may have both an outsole and insole, or only an outsole with a filler. The outsole is permanently fastened to the extended edge of the welt with a Goodyear lockstitch. The process is also called a "mock welt." Shoes of this construction are used chiefly for slippers, infants' and children's shoes.

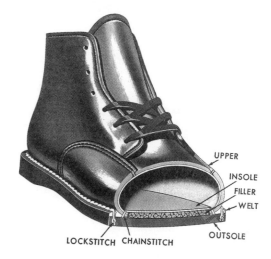

Prewelt construction.

Sbicca Del-Mac. Similar to a turn construction, resulting in a shoe with a smooth insole and high flexibility. See also *skeleton insole*.

silhouwelt. A welt-type shoe with outsole and upper attached by cement. Constructed like a Goodyear welt up to the point of sole-attaching.

skeleton insole. A sole blank of suitable thickness is split to produce and outsole and insole. The insole has a rand (slightly raised portion) or skeleton piece at the center of the forepart, and the outsole has the thickness of the original outsole at the center of the forepart. After preparation of the bottom stock the skeleton insole is tacked to the last. The soles may be attached by lockstitch, chainstitch or cement. The process is also known as a Sbicca Del-Mac, Del-welt, Del-Mac sewed, and a single-sole shoe.

slip-lasted. The upper is stitched to a light, flexible insole to make a kind of bag into which the last is forced (the process is sometimes known as "force lasting"). The construction produces a comfortable, cushioned effect created by a mid-sole or platform. Also known as California process, it is used most commonly in casual footwear.

standard screw. The sole is attached by a "standard screw" cut from a coil of threaded wire. Used mostly in heavy work boots. See also *nailed*.

stitchdown. The bottom edge of the upper is flanged or flared outward and stitched to the sole. Sometimes an overlay welt or rand may be attached to the top edge of the sole for better shaping and security. The construction may have single, double, or triple soles. In some countries it is known as "veldt" and "veldtschoen." The stitchdown process is used for lower-priced footwear.

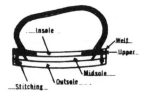

Stitchdown construction.

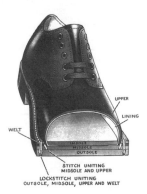

Three-sole stitchdown construction.

turn. A single-sole, flexible shoe in which the sole and upper are stitched together with a chainstitch while the shoe is inside out on the last. Later, the upper is turned right side out and the shoe is completed. Also known as "hand-turned" process, it is in little use today.

UCO. See *Littleway*.

welt. Any construction using a welting, either as an integral part of the construction or simply for imitative effect.

shoe cover. A covering material or mitten to keep white or other light-colored shoes protected and clean during shoemaking.

shoe dermatitis. An irritation and inflammation of the skin of the foot caused by rubber compounds and shoe and leather chemicals, affecting those persons allergic to such substances when mixed with perspiration. Wearing rubber-free shoes with vegetable-tanned leather is usually remedial. The condition is also known as "contact dermatitis."

shoe doctor. A tongue-in-cheek term for a shoe repairman.

shoe dog. Trade term for a retail shoe salesperson.

shoe fitter. One who fits shoes to customers in a store.

shoe fabrics. See *fabrics*.

shoe factory departments. Any of the "rooms" or departments specializing in a group of operations in the sequence of assembling and manufacturing shoes. The main departments or rooms are: cutting, stitching, lasting, bottoming, making, finishing, treeing, and packing.

shoe form. See *display form*.

shoe freak. A colloquial term for a person who constantly buys and owns excessive amounts of footwear, or who has a collection obsession about shoes.

shoe horn. A simple, contoured instrument slipped between the back of the shoe and the back of the heel of the foot to ease the foot into the shoe.

shoe-in. See *Appendix I*.

shoe lining. See *lining*.

shoe mitten. A loose cloth or plastic covering for shoes while stored in a closet or while traveling.

shoemaker. A craftsman who makes shoes start to finish, usually by hand. Also, one who attends to only one or a few specialized operations in the shoemaking process.

shoemaking. The art, skill or technology of making footwear.

shoe manufacturing. The industrial process of assembling components and materials in a factory for the mass production of footwear.

shoemobile. See *mobile shoe store*.

shoe modification. The skilled process of incorporating adjustments in ready-made footwear in accord with a particular foot or gait need of the customer. An essential part of a prescription footwear or custom shoemaking business.

shoepack (or shoepac). Similar to a genuine Indian

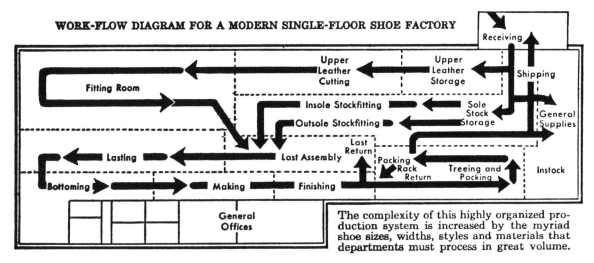

WORK-FLOW DIAGRAM FOR A MODERN SINGLE-FLOOR SHOE FACTORY

The complexity of this highly organized production system is increased by the myriad shoe sizes, widths, styles and materials that departments must process in great volume.

moccasin with or without separate sole attached; ankle high, usually of white, water-resistant, oil-tanned upper leather. Worn by settlers in early America. The modern version is a heavy half boot worn by loggers, known as a "pac" or "shoepac."

shoe rash. See *shoe dermatitis*.

shoe rebuilder. Essentially a shoe repairman.

shoe remodeling. Remaking a finished shoe longer or wider.

shoe repairer. A mender, repairer or rebuilder of worn shoes.

shoe room. British term for the treeing and packing room in the factory. See also *packing room*.

shoe rose. A rose-shaped ornament made of cloth, ribbon or leather (or sometimes an actual rose), varying from small to as much as 10 inches in diameter. Popular in 17th-century Europe, it was worn on the vamp of the shoe, of matching or contrasting color with the shoe or garter, worn by men and women. Some of the more ornate roses cost more than the shoes.

shoe serviceman. See *shoe repairer*.

shoe size. Essentially the shoe's length measurement corresponding to the length of the foot. It also includes ball width. But on the last where the shoe

size measurements are determined, additional measurements are used, such as heel width, heel-to-ball, waist and instep girth, etc. These are all part of shoe "size" essential to the fit of the shoe. However, for more simplified measuring the foot and fitting shoes in the store, shoe size consists mainly of two measurements: overall length and ball width.

There are various shoe sizing systems throughout the world. In the American system size increments are designated as follows: 1/3 inch for each full size increase, 1/6 inch for each half size, and 1/4 inch for each width change. In most other countries the metric rather than the arithmetic system is used, but with a different size progression plan (See Table 1 and Chart 1). The world's first "official" system for standard shoe sizes and widths was introduced by Edwin B. Simpson of New York in 1880. His standardized sizes were designated separately for men's, women's and juvenile lasts and shoes, and prevailing, with a few minor changes, to the present day.

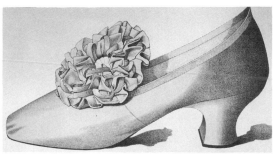

Shoe rose.

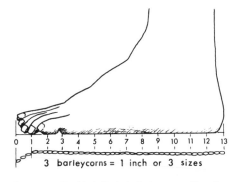

3 barleycorns = 1 inch or 3 sizes

Shoe sizes supposedly originated by laying barleycorns end to end, each barleycorn equal to one-third inch and hence representing one full shoe size, and three barleycorns equalling one inch. The "system" was introduced in 1324 by King Edward II to establish the first official measurements for inch and foot. The system was adopted by shoemakers to apply to shoe sizing, which up to then had no "standard" measurements.

Shoe Size Classification

The chart of Size Classifications below is commonly used by shoe manufacturers. For pictorial presentation the various runs of sizes are shown in inches in relation to the basic last lengths.

Variations in size runs sometimes made in these groups are indicated by the extreme sizes within the shaded areas.

Such names as Big Boys—Junior Misses—Babies—Tots, and others, are not shown but fall within the "Extremes" or shaded areas in the several classifications.

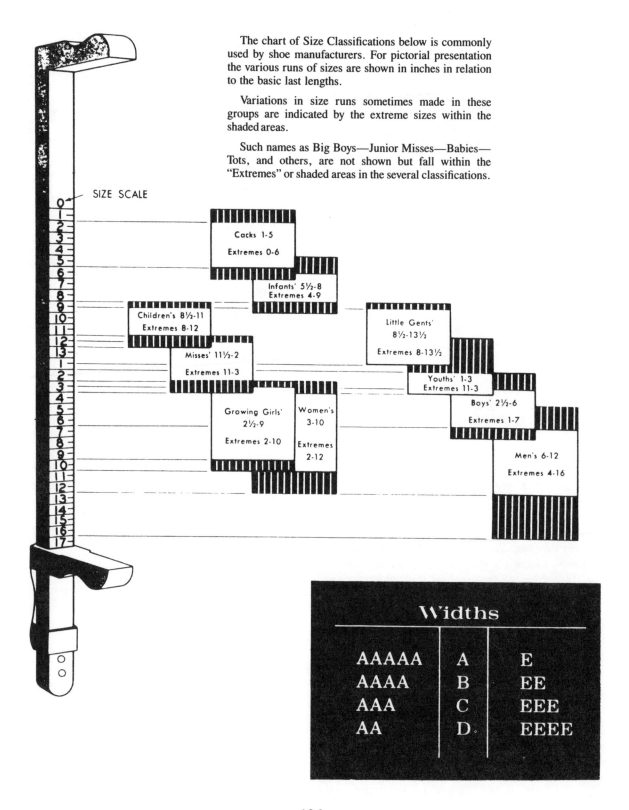

SIZE SCALE

Cacks 1-5
Extremes 0-6

Infants' 5½-8
Extremes 4-9

Children's 8½-11
Extremes 8-12

Little Gents'
8½-13½
Extremes 8-13½

Misses' 11½-2
Extremes 11-3

Youths' 1-3
Extremes 11-3

Boys' 2½-6
Extremes 1-7

Growing Girls'
2½-9
Extremes 2-10

Women's
3-10
Extremes
2-12

Men's 6-12
Extremes 4-16

Widths

AAAAA	A	E
AAAA	B	EE
AAA	C	EEE
AA	D	EEEE

126

Table 1   Comparisons of Men's Shoe Sizes:
             American, Continental, British, Japanese

AMERICAN	CONTINENTAL	BRITISH	JAPANESE
5 1/2			23.5
6	39	5 1/2	24
6 1/2	39 1/2	6	24.5
7	40	6 1/2	25
7 1/2	41	7	25.5
8	41 1/2	7 1/2	26
8 1/2	42	8	26.5
9	43	8 1/2	27
9 1/2	43 1/2	9	27.5
10	44	9 1/2	28
10 1/2	44 1/2	10	28.5
11	45	10 1/2	29
11 1/2	45 1/2	11	29.5
12	46	11 1/2	30
12 1/2	47	12	
13	48	12 1/2	
14	49	13	
15	50	14	

shoe size classifications. American footwear is classified by particular consumer groups, each of which falls into a shoe size range category. The size ranges are divided into regular and "extremes" (extending a bit beyond the regular range). The "official" sizes by classifications are as follow:

  cacks: 1 to 5 (extremes 0 to 6).
  infants': 5 1/2 to 8 (extremes 4 to 9).
  children's: 8 1/2 to 11 (extremes 8 to 12).
  little gents': 8 1/2 to 13 (extremes 8 to 13 1/2).
  misses': 11 1/2 to 2 (extremes 11 to 3).
  youths': 1 to 3 (extremes 11 to 3).
  growing girls': 2 1/2 to 9 (extremes 2 to 10).
  boys': 2 1/2 to 6 (extremes 1 to 7).
  women's: 3 to 10 (extremes 2 to 12).
  men's: 6 to 12 (extremes 4 to 16).

shoe size codes. Any code system that substitutes for the actual size marking, making it difficult or impossible for the consumer/customer to read or know the true size. These deliberately concealing or deceptive systems are in decreasing use. Following are a few typical size codes selected from the many used (also see chart: Sample Shoe Size Code Systems):

Shoe size comparisons:
arithmetic vs. metric.

127

American (or Standard) System
The first number in the code indicates the width (1 = A, 2 = B, etc.). The second number followed by a zero denotes a whole size; if the second number is followed by a 5 it indicates a half size. Examples:

Code No.	Width	Length
0080 = 8AAA	00 = AAA	80 = 8
080 = 8AA	0 = AA	80 = 8
185 = 8 1/2A	1 = A	85 = 8 1/2
280 = 8B	2 = B	80 = 8
385 = 8 1/2C	3 = C	85 = 8 1/2
590 = 9E	5 = E	90 = 9
	6 = EE	

French (or Dash) System
In this system 32 is the key number and is subtracted from the first two numbers to obtain length. The last figure indicates width. The dash between figures indicates a half size. For multiple As zeros are used (0 = AA, 00 = AAA, etc.) For multiple Es the numbers simply continue forward (6 = EE, 7 = EEE, etc.) Examples:

40-00 = 8 1/2AA
39 1 = 7A
41-3 = 9 1/2C
43 6 = 11EE
44 7 = 12EEE

shoe show. An exhibit of new seasonal lines of vendors presented at a central exhibit location and visited by retailers and buyers for viewing or purchasing. Shoe shows may be national or regional and are organized and presented by trade associations or private organizations.

shoestring. A cord, string, or ribbon for fastening a shoe.

shoe talc. See *dusting powder*.

shoe traveler. A sales representative employed by a shoe manufacturer, importer, distributor, or other vendor, who travels a prescribed territory selling his or her lines of merchandise to retailers. The traveler is usually in the exclusive employ of one company.

shoe therapist. One who practices shoe therapy, usually in a store.

shoe therapy. The designing, prescribing, fitting, or modifying of footwear for persons with foot or gait disorders and requiring special shoes, or shoes with special adjustments, to accommodate or help to remedy such disorders. See also *pedorthics* and *prescription footwear*.

shoe tree. A foot-shaped, last-like form of plastic, wood, metal, or other material used as a shoe insert to retain the shoe's form and condition while the shoe is not in use.

shoetrician. A coined term for a shoe repairman. The term was first used in 1940 by the Texas-Southwestern Association of Shoetricians.

shoe width. Representing both the linear and girth measurements at the ball, determined by the last. In the shoe store, only the linear measurement is used. American or arithmetic standard width measurements range from AAAAA to EEEEE (or even more in extreme widths). Widths change in increments of 1/4 inch per width progression. A looser width measurement system is designated N (narrow), M (medium) and W (wide), and sometimes XN for extra-narrow or XW or WW for extra-wide. However, the latter system lacks the dimensional precision and standardization of the A-B-C-D-etc. system.

shooey. Obsolete Anglo-Saxon term for shoe.

shoon. Obsolete Anglo-Saxon term for shoe.

shooting boot. See *boot*.

shortage. A delivery whose units fall short of the original order. Also, missing merchandise from the inventory. See also *pilferage*.

shortback last. A last designed to make the foot look smaller and shorter without altering the size. Used especially for women's shoes, it is achieved by shortening the distance of shank area between the heel breast and ball. Also known as a "short-coupled" last.

Left, regular pump; right, same pump on short couple last.

short boot. See *boot*.

short-coupled last. See *shortback last*.

short heel girth. A girth measurement taken on the last from the bottom back end of the heel to the top of the instep.

shortened calf muscles. A contraction or shortening of the calf muscles due chiefly to the habitual wearing of high heels. When flat heels are worn, the shortened muscles stretch and ache. Exercises to stretch the muscles can usually remedy the condition.

shortened first metatarsal. See *Morton's foot*.

shoulder. The forepart of the hide in front of the forward spine point, and with the belly and head part

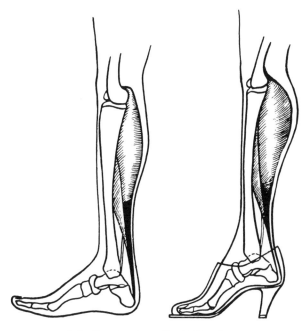

Left, calf muscles of normal length without shoes; right, shortened muscles with high heel.

of the hide cut off. Leather made from this portion is of poorer quality.

shoulder strap handbag. See *handbag*.

shower clog. A wooden clog or plastic platform shoe worn in a locker room or shower.

show-me. A trade term for the shoe store customer who repeatedly says, "show me this" or "show me that."

showroom. 1) At a shoe show, an exhibitor's room or booth where the merchandise is on display. 2) A vendor's permanent sample room, such as in the factory or an office building. See also *sample room*.

show-and-suggest. A primary principle or practice in retail selling wherein the salesperson, during or after the sale, shows and suggests additional merchandise to the customer. Also called "suggestion selling."

shrinkage. 1) A decrease in the size, weight or value of a material, such as a hide or skin, due to excessive climatic or thermal exposure. 2) At retail, the loss of merchandise from in-store pilferage. See also *pilferage*.

shrunken grain. See *grain*.

shrunken leather. Leather specially treated during the tanning process to shrink the grain side and hence accentuate the grain.

side. Either half of the hide cut along the spine line to create two sides for easier handling of large hides.

side gore. See *goring*.

side laced. A shoe laced at the side instead of at the front.

side lasting. Lasting the shoe at its sides for snug conformity to the last, done by side lasting machines.

side leather. See *leather*.

side line. A secondary line carried by a manufacturer's sales representative, or a second occupation.

side seam. See *seam*.

side strap. See *strap*.

side upper leather. See *leather*.

side wall last. A last with a straight-up edge or rim on the forepart upper, forming a walled side. A design feature on some shoes.

signing. The use of any signs inside or outside the store.

silhouette. In footwear, the outline, profile or contour of a shoe. A fashion term.

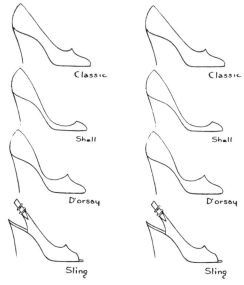

Silhouettes of different pump styles.

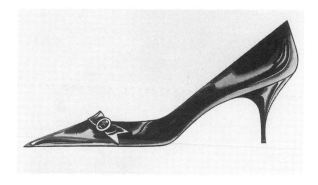

Silhouette or profile of women's pump.

129

silhouwelt. See *shoe construction*.

silicone. A polymeric material resistant to heat and moisture, used for shoe molds, or for waterproofing and insulating footwear.

silk. See *fabrics*.

single. One shoe of a pair.

single sole shoe. See *shoe construction, skeleton*.

sisal. Smooth, fine straw sometimes used for shoe uppers.

size. (See *shoe size*).

size codes. Blind or coded sizes marked inside the shoe to conceal the true size from the customer. The coded size enables the salesperson to tell the customer, sometimes untruthfully, that the shoe is the needed or requested size if the needed size is missing. A means of customer deception. Code markings today are in rapidly declining use. See also *shoe size codes*.

size fill-ins. Reordering missing or needed sizes in the retailer's stock.

size markings. The printed marking of size and/or width on the shoe's quarter lining, heel pad or tongue.

size range. From smallest to largest sizes and width in a given footwear category (men's, women's, children's); also, the available size range in a vendor's line or the retailer's inventory.

size stick. A measuring stick like a ruler for measuring the foot, heel to toe, or heel to ball, or ball width. The stick has a stationary heel rest and a movable or adjustable wedge for determining foot and shoe size. The size stick dates back at least 3,000 years.

sizeup. See *size fill-ins*.

size writing. Writing in needed or wanted sizes on the vendor's order blank, done by the retailer or the vendor's sales representative.

sizing. The retailer, ordering shoes from the vendor, filling in the order blank with the wanted sizes in the given stock numbers.

skating shoe. See *sports shoe*.

skeleton insole. See *shoe construction*.

skeleton lining. A strip of leather around the edge of a fabric quarter lining on a low shoe. Usually used on men's shoes where a lighter lining is wanted.

skeletonized shoe. A light, trim, airy, opened-up shoe usually made of fragile materials with a myriad of cutouts, or an arrangement of narrow straps, plus thin soles, designed to give the shoe a "naked" look.

ski boot. See *boot*.

skimmer. A plain, flat-heel, slipper-like shoe with light upper and thin sole.

skip. A retail shoe trade term for a customer who leaves the store with merchandise not paid for, or leaves a bad check in payment.

skin. The continuous layer of tissue covering the body surface, and consisting of two layers, epidermis and dermis, plus sweat glands, pores, and hair follicles. The largest organ of the body.

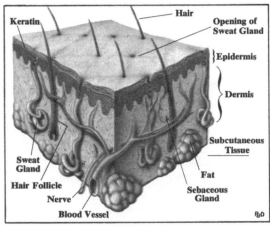

Skin, magnified cross-section.

skin fit. A nylon tricot shoe lining material bonded to foam and usually in color, sometimes patterned.

skin hose. A leg-hugging leather stocking worn in medieval times.

skirts. The rim or less valuable portions of the hide, such as shanks, belly, neck, etc. Usually trimmed off before the hide is tanned; or it may be tanned with the rest of the hide, then the skits trimmed for

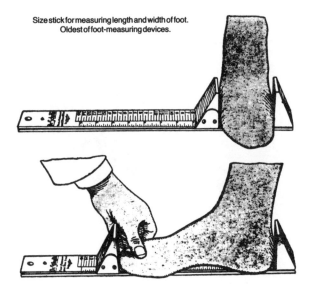

Size stick for measuring length and width of foot. Oldest of foot-measuring devices.

leather shoe components other than uppers and soles.

skitty boot. See *boot*.

skiver. 1) The grain side of a vegetable-tanned split sheepskin, sometimes used for inexpensive shoe linings. 2) A thin slipsole inserted inside a shoe as a filler for shoe size adjustment.

skiving. Cutting a beveled scarf or edge of leather or other materials to thin the edges and prevent ridges on the finished shoe. Used in such components as counters, box toes, insoles, linings.

SKU. See *stockkeeping units*.

slab rubber. A sheet of rubber from which shoe soles, midsoles, or top-lifts are cut.

slack tannage. See *tannage*.

slap sole. A flat, removable layer of sole (leather or wood) worn over the regular sole and heel to protect the shoe above from soil and mud. The sole "slaps" the mud to the sides and prevents the shoe from sinking into it. Introduced in the 17th century. The term is derived from the sound made by the sole in walking.

slashings. Decorative cuts or slips made in the leather or fabric upper of the shoe, usually on the vamp.

sleeve gore. See *goring*.

slew foot. Colloquial term for a toeing-in gait.

slide fastener. Any zipper fastener, as used on some footwear.

slim. A loose designation for a narrow width. A common footwear term of the 18th and 19th centuries.

slingback. An open-back, mule on a medium to higher heel with a halter or back strap.

Slingback shoe.

slingback strap. See *strap*.

sling pump. See *slingback*.

sliplasted. See *shoe construction*.

slipon. A plain but dressy pump without lacings or other fastenings, worn by either men or women. Any shoe without fastenings.

slipper. 1) A dressy evening shoe, usually for formal wear, for either men or women, such as a dancing slipper. 2) A soft, lightweight, flexible shoe de-signed chiefly for indoor wear and which can be any of numerous designs in a wide range of patterns, color and, materials. The common types of indoor slippers are as follows:

ballet. A lightweight, soft-sole, heelless cloth-upper slipper with padded or reinforced toe, held onto the foot with long strings or ribbon lacings, worn by ballet dancers.

bed. A light, soft-sole, heelless, warm fabric slipper worn to bed by persons with cold feet.

bedroom. A soft-sole, heelless slipper, usually with fabric upper, for bedroom wear.

boudoir. Dressier than a bedroom slipper, some-times like a mule in design, sometimes with a low heel.

Cambridge. A cloth-upper slipper with elastic gus-set sides, low heel, soft or firm sole, worn by men and women.

dowie. A drawstring pulled around the top rim of the slipper for snug fit, soft sole and upper, with or without heel. Derived from early moccasin de-sign.

elasticized. A slipper with an elasticized fabric up-per that clings to the foot and requires no fasten-ing.

Everett. A men's slipper with high front or tongue and low backpart.

Faust. Men's high-cut slipper with V-cuts at the sides but without elastic gusset or goring.

folding. A soft-sole, heelless, featherweight slipper that can be folded and packed for traveling. Simi-lar to a Pullman slipper.

fuzzy-wuzzy (or fuzzies). A colloquial term for any slipper lined with fleece or shearling. Usu-ally heelless.

hostess. A dressy, colorful indoor slipper/shoe, usu-ally with colorful fabric upper, low heel, some-times backless. Worn at home for informal entertaining.

house. A loose term for a comfortable, often felted upper and heelless slipper worn around the house.

Juliet. A women's loose-fitting house slipper with high back and front and goring at the U-shaped sides.

knight's. A heavy fabric sock formerly worn inside metal boots centuries ago by armored knights in combat. The sole slipper-socks were sometimes worn indoors.

leisure. Similar to the hostess slipper.

lounge. Similar to the hostess slipper.

opera. A women's dress or evening pump, sometime backless, with medium to high heel, usually with jeweled ornament. Also a men's house slipper, usually with leather upper.

packable. See *folding slipper*.

pantoffle. A backless shoe originally (and still) used as a slipper. Introduced in 16th-century France. From the French word for slipper.

Prince Albert. A men's low-cut house slipper with elastic goring at the sides and a raised seam at the center of the vamp, toe to throat-line.

Pullman. See *folding slipper*.

Romeo. A men's slipper with either cloth or leather upper, cut high in back and front, with low-cut sides.

scuff. A backless, heelless house slipper.

slip-on. A plain slipper with elasticized topline, heelless, with soft or firm sole.

slipper socks. An ankle- or calf-high cloth upper with soft leather sole, worn for warmth indoors.

slipshoe. An obsolete term for slipper.

slipsole. 1) A thin insole inserted into the shoe for a needed fitting adjustment or for added warmth. 2) Another name for a half sole from the toe to the front of the shank on a repaired shoe.

slush molding. A method of casting rubber and thermoplastics poured in liquid form into a hot mold and the molded bottom stripped out. Used for molded waterproof rubber or polyvinylchloride (PVC) footwear in which no lasting is required.

slunk. The skin of an unborn or prematurely born calf. Tanned slunks (with hair on) are sometimes used for uppers on women's fashion shoes, or for expensive handbags.

small leather goods. Small leather items such as wallets, belts, key or comb cases, etc.

smoked elk. See *leather*.

smooth leather. See *grain*.

smooth plating. A tannery finishing operation performed on most light, smooth-finish leathers. After glazing and dry staking, the skins are subjected to high pressure under a heated metal plate, creating a glass-smooth surface.

snakeskin leather. See *leather*.

snap fastener. A metal or plastic device in two pieces, one with a hole, the other with a small knob, clasping together for a secure hold. Used as a fastener on some footwear.

sneaker. Footwear with a rubber sole and upper of canvas or other materials, constructed on the vulcanized process. The first sneakers, called "croquet shoes," were produced in 1867. The term "sneaker"

came from street kids because the rubber soles allowed them to "sneak up" on one another.

snowshoe. Shaped like a large tennis racquet, a special shoe for walking on soft snow. A lightweight frame with woven, mesh-like center, worn with a boot. It originated with the Eskimos.

snuffed finish. See *corrected grain*.

snuffed leather. The same as "corrected grain."

S.O.B. Acronym for store's own brand.

soccae. A soft, light, slipper-like shoe with flat heel and soft sole, worn as an indoor shoe in ancient Greece.

soccer shoe. See *sports shoe*.

soccus. A sandal with flat sole and two side straps converging forward in a V-shape between the first and second toes, worn with a tabi-like white linen sock with divided toes to accommodate the strap between the toes. Worn by both men and women of ancient Rome, and also known as a "udone" shoe. Our word "sock" is derived from it.

sock. See *hose*.

sock lining. See *lining*.

soft goods. Merchandise of soft texture such as apparel and footwear, in contrast to "hard goods" such as furniture, household appliances, etc.

soft sell. A restrained, nonaggressive approach to selling strategy in contrast to the more pushy "hard sell."

soft-sole shoe. Any footwear without a firm sole, such as a soft-sole slipper or moccasin.

soft-sole moccasin. A moccasin without a firm slab of soling, and whose sole is either a continuous part of the leather upper, or an extra soft, reinforcing layer of sole sewn to the upper.

soft support. A soft arch cushion or a cushioned, semi-flexible orthotic in contrast to a rigid support.

soft tip. A shoe having no box toe, or a very soft box toe, under the toe tip. Also known as a soft-toe shoe.

soft-toe shoe. See *soft tip*.

sole. Derived from the Latin "solea," meaning soil or ground. See also *outsole*.

solea (or soleae). A simple sandal with a slab leather sole, worn mostly indoors in ancient Rome.

sole laying. Temporarily attaching the outsole to the shoe with an adhesive after bottom filling and prior to sewing. Done by a machine that holds the sole in place until permanently attached.

sole leather. Any heavy leather, usually cattlehide leather, dry-finished and used for shoe soles. The leather can be produced from any of several tannages, though generally vegetable tannage, or can be impregnated with other substances such as rubber compounds to increase durability.

soleret. See *scarpine*.

soleus. The smaller of the two calf muscles, the other being the gastrocnemius.

sorting. The tannery process of sorting hides and skins according to quality or grade, or doing the same with leather to detect blemishes or defects.

sourcing. 1) For a manufacturer, seeking out sources or locations for a manufacturing plant, domestic, or overseas, or seeking out suppliers. 2) For a retailer, seeking out resources, domestic or foreign, to provide footwear, particularly in the case of large or volume buyers.

soutache. A narrow braid used in making shoe decorations such as rosettes or for shoe trims.

southern tie. A women's two-eyelet, ribbon-tie shoe.

space shoe. See *custom-molded shoe*.

spade last. A last or shoe with a wide flare or swing on the outer side, tapering forward toward the toe, and an extended sole corresponding with it.

Spade last.

spade sole. See *spade last*.

Spanish boot. See *boot*.

Spanish heel. See *heel*.

spat. A low-cut spatterdash. See also *spatterdash*.

spat boot. See *boot*.

spatterdash. A cloth gaiter over ankle and calf, buttoned, zippered, or laced at the side, held on with a strap under the shoe's shank. Originally worn by soldiers to protect the shoes, hose or, pant leg from mud splashings. Popular with civilians up to the 1930s. See also *spat*.

spectator heel. See *heel*.

spectator pump. See *spectator sport shoe*.

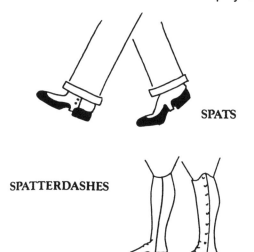

SPATS

SPATTERDASHES

spectator sport shoe. In women's, a brown/write or black/white pump with perforated toe and foxing, usually with pinked edges, and medium to high stacked heel. The same color combinations in men's shoes, only in oxford style.

special order. An order placed with a vendor by a retailer, usually for a single pair in a particular size for a customer.

specialty store. A store specializing in one or a few related merchandise categories, such as apparel plus accessories. For a shoe store, one specializing in a particular category of footwear such as men's, women's, or children's, in contrast to a family or multiple-category store.

speed lacing. A shoe or boot lacing method using D-ring hook eyelets instead of hole eyelets, enabling the shoe or boot to be laced faster and easier than by inserting lace tips through holes.

speed walking. Walking one or more miles at a sustained fast pace averaging five or more miles per hour.

spew (or spue). A white exudation sometimes appearing on leather. It consists of crystals of fatty acids and sometimes accumulates on shoes or boots kept in damp places at low temperatures.

spiff. See *PM*.

spike. A short, sharp metal piece protruding from the bottom of the shoe sole, used for traction on track shoes. Also used on some shoes or boots for mountain climbing or walking on slippery surfaces.

spike heel. See *heel*.

spike last. An inflare last. See also *inflare*.

spliced heel. In hose, a heel of double thickness.

splay foot. A loosely jointed, flabby, spready foot. See also *flaccid foot*.

133

splint. See *counter splint*.

split leather. See *leather*.

split regent pump. Similar to a three-quarter regent pump except that both inside and outside quarters have collar extensions that meet and are seamed at the center of the vamp throat. See also *three-quarter regent pump*.

split vamp. See *vamp*.

spool heel. See *heel*.

sportive look. Women's apparel and footwear with an outdoorish, sporty (though not athletic) motif for casual wear.

sports medicine. The branch of medicine dealing with the diagnosis and treatment of sports injuries, including those of the foot.

sporthotic. A coined term for an orthotic insert used in athletic shoes.

sport shoe. A sportive, casual shoe for nonathletic wear. A semi-dressy classification, not to be confused with a sports shoe.

sports shoe. An athletic shoe designed for any particular kind of active sport. Each sport usually has its own shoe design requirements. Many sports shoes are variations of others, usually with one or more additional features to adapt to the special needs of the particular sport. Also known as an "athletic shoe." The main types of sports shoes are as follows:

    baseball. An oxford with lightweight upper of kangaroo or quality cowhide leather, though sometimes combining nylon/leather uppers. Soft or semi-soft toe cap, firm counter, padded collar, round toe, shawl tongue overlapping the laces, the sole with cleats. Usually a cement construction. Some professional players now use hightops.

    basketball. The shoe may be either hightop or low-cut, with upper of canvas, nylon/canvas, or leather/canvas, laced to toe, reinforced toe tip, padded collar, cushioned insoles, or sometimes a removable orthotic insole insert. The traction sole is either rubber or polyurethane. Air holes are in the upper for added ventilation.

    bowling. An oxford laced to toe, upper of leather or leather and nylon mesh, round toe, firm counter, man-made soling with relatively smooth surface.

    boxing. A hightop with soft leather, laced to toe, lightweight with thin sole and moderate traction, firm counter, padded collar and arch cushion.

    cycling. For race cycling these shoes are made on special lasts with semi-pointed toe, wide ball, narrow waist and heel, high toe box, and extra toe spring. Uppers are light leathers perforated for ventilation. U-throat with lace-to-toe design, or with velcro closure, unlined, padded collar and tongue, cushion insole. The sole is rigid (reinforced with wood or steel shank), cleated for traction. Shoes for tour or distance cycling are uncleated and more flexible.

    football. The style can be low-cut, demi-boot or full boot, depending on playing position. Uppers of leather or leather/nylon mesh, rigid counter and box toe, studded rubber soles, padded collar and tongue. Styling and other features vary depending on type of playing turf.

    golf. An oxford with cleated sole for traction. Styles, patterns and upper leathers vary widely, depending on personal choice.

    gymnastic. Usually little more than a simple ballet slipper with elasticized topline.

    ice hockey. Hightop leather or leather/nylon upper with reinforcement at the counter and lace stay. Raised hard box toe, padded collar and tongue, broad last.

    ice skating. Deep-cut U-throat pattern with lace-to-toe design, ankle-high boot, rigid counter with extra medial length, padded collar, lightweight leather upper. Designs vary a bit, such as for race skating and figure skating.

    racewalking. Lightweight with thin outsole, firm midsole and heel, EVA-type wedge, upper of light leather, rigid counter extended forward on the outer side, extra toe spring, U-throat upper design.

    racquetball. Lightweight, with either leather or canvas upper with ventilation holes, a thin rubber or polyurethane sole with good traction design, firm counter, padded collar and tongue, cushion insole. Essentially the same shoe is used for squash and handball.

    roller skating. Very similar to the ice skating shoe, but with the boot design cut a bit higher.

    rugby. The same basic design or construction as either football or soccer shoes, with variations depending upon the playing surface and the player's position.

    running. For distance running, a lightweight shoe with leather or leather/nylon mesh upper, cushioned midsole or insole and heel, flexible forepart, rigid counter, traction sole, motion control throughout for stability, padded collar and tongue, lace-to-toe, ample toe spring.

    soccer. Snug fitting, lowcut, narrow toe, soft-thin

upper leather, padded collar and high, padded tongue. Traction sole with supplementary studs or cleats, midsole wedge for added support and cushioning.

tennis. Canvas or leather/nylon mesh upper with ventilation holes, upper cut a bit higher than ordinary low-cut shoe; firm counter, under-foot cushioning, padded collar and tongue, lace-to-toe, protective toe tip. Sole design depends on playing surface (grass, clay) and can vary from moderate to high traction.

track and field sports. These include sprints, jumping, shot put, javelin, hammer and discus throw, pole vaulting, etc. Shoes for each of these events vary a bit, also depending on indoor or outdoor track. Soles may have spikes, as in sprint shoes, but other traction design for others. In common features are light weight, firm counter support, little or no underfoot cushioning, firm support around waist and instep.

wrestling. A lightweight, hightop shoe with leather or canvas upper, traction sole, padded collar and tongue, criss-cross reinforcement bands for added instep and ankle support.

sprain. See *ankle sprain*.

spring. See *toe spring* and *heel spring*.

spring heel. See *heel*.

spue. See *spew*.

spur. See *heel spur*.

square edge. A sole finished with sharp edges top and bottom as a decorative feature.

square heel. See *heel*.

squeaky shoes. Shoes that emit a squeaking sound in walking, due to the rubbing and friction between leather outsole and leather insole, or outsole and insole rubbing against the shankpiece between. This is much less common today than in years past because of shoe construction improvements.

stability. The normal balance of the foot inside the shoe without excessive or abnormal motion during walking or running.

stabilizer. A design feature or orthotic insert to help stabilize the foot and shoe during vigorous foot action such as in sports activities. Used mostly in sports footwear.

stabilizer cup. See *heel cup*.

stacked heel. See *heel*.

stadium boot. See *boot*.

staining. Applying a stain to a shoe part such as a sole or heel edge or the bottom surface of the sole. Also called "inking."

stain resistance. The ability of a material or component to resist staining, usually by incorporating a chemical or coating, such as with shoe upper, insole or lining materials.

stamping. Imprinting sizes, stock numbers, brands or other markings on sock or quarter linings, heel pads, etc.

stance. The angle made by the two feet when positioned side by side in standing or walking, such as in-toeing or out-toeing or pointing straight ahead.

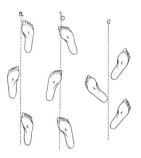

Stance: a) toes straight ahead stance; b) in-toeing; c) out-toeing.

stand. A store display fixture for holding shoes or other merchandise.

standard screw process. See *shoe construction*.

standardization. Any system of sizes, weights, shapes, dimensions, etc. adopted and accepted by an industry, trade, profession or science as a standard for use of a product or process. For example, standard measurements for lasts, or shoe sizes, or certain shoe components, or leather weights. While such standards exist in footwear and the shoe industry, certain liberties are sometimes taken to veer from the fixed standards.

standard last. See *universal last*.

standard mark-on. The generally accepted, contemporary level of retail markon for any given category of footwear or other merchandise. Also called "full markon."

staple. 1) A small piece of U-shape metal wire or brad driven into the shoe by machine as a fastener for sole attaching. 2) At retail, a basic shoe not usually vulnerable to markdowns or seasonal change in style or demand. A moderate but steady seller.

starting inventory. The quantity, makeup and value of the store's inventory at the beginning of the month. See also *beginning of month*.

startup. A kind of buskin worn by country folk in Europe during the 16th and 17th centuries. In more stylistic form, footwear popular with the gentry or upper classes of 16th-century England. It consisted of a combination of shoe and legging. When the lower classes adopted it the gentry was displeased with this social impostering, and from this rose our term "upstart" for a pretender or parvenu. See also Appendix II.

statement stuffer. A piece of advertising or promotional literature enclosed with an invoice or bill sent to the customer.

steerhide. See *leather*.

step shock. The jolt effect occurring with each step or stride when walking on a nonresilient surface with shoes lacking shock absorption.

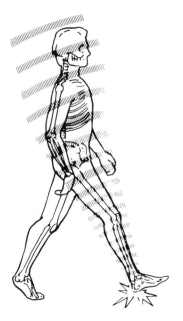

Step shock. Shock waves travel from foot up through body column.

step-in. A shoe with a vamp front higher than an ordinary pump, held onto the foot without any visible fastener, but often with a concealed vamp or side goring. See *slip-on*.

stick length. The overall length of the last measured with a last size stick.

stiffener. Any component or material used to reinforce some part of the shoe, such as a counter or box toe.

stiletto heel. See *heel*.

stitch count. The number of stitches per inch on a shoe sole or upper. Usually the greater the number and the finer the thread, the better the quality of the stitching or shoe.

stitchdown process. See *shoe construction*.

stitched aloft. A sole stitched in a groove. Sole attaching when no channel has been made in the sole and the thread shows through on the bottom of the shoe.

stitching. Refers mainly to the sewing operations of shoe uppers, and particularly to decorative stitching called "fancy stitching."

stitching room. The department in the shoe factory in which the various parts of the shoe upper are sewn together. Also called the "fitting room." It is the costliest department because stitching is a labor-intensive operation requiring skills.

stitch pattern. Usually applies to western boots in which various standard stitching designs are used on the shaft and vamp of the boot. It also applies to the "fancy stitching" on some dress and fashion shoes.

stock. Merchandise in inventory.

stock boy. A person assigned to gathering and returning shoes from the selling floor to the stockroom and keeping the stock and stockroom in order.

stock control. See *inventory control*.

stock fitting. In the factory, preparing the various parts of the shoe bottom for assembly, lasting and making.

stocking. Long hose. The word first appeared in the 16th century and derives from the Anglo-Saxon *prican*, meaning to stick. The hose was "stock" or "stuck" with sticking pins (knitting needles). Hose eventually became known as "stocken" and finally "stocking." See also *hose*.

stockkeeping. Maintaining the stock or inventory in an orderly manner in the stockroom, and also recording daily or weekly changes in the inventory.

stockkeeping units (or SKU). An inventory system of counting the number of units or pairs of shoes in stock.

stock manager. A retail trade term for a salesperson or store manager to whom another salesperson passes on a customer when a sale is stalemated or appears to be lost.

stockmanship. The art and skill of sound inventory management.

stock number. The number assigned to a given model in the manufacturer's line to facilitate identifying and ordering by the retailer.

stockout. Out of stock.

stock room. In a factory or store, the area in which the stock is arranged and stored.

stocking up. Adding to inventory up to required level or needs.

stock-to-sales ratio. The rate or percentage of sales movement relative to the amount of stock on hand. A measure of stock turnover rate.

stogie. A heavy, coarse work shoe of the brogan type, worn by American slaves and farmers in the 18th and 19th centuries. See also Appendix II.

stomper. A large, heavy boot or shoe, so called because of the heavy tread sound when walked on.

stoning. Smoothing leather by repeatedly rubbing a smooth stone over the surface. Now an obsolete practice.

storage cost. The value depreciation of the shoes on the shelf while they remain unsold past their peak salability time. The cost or value is based on rent, utilities and other fixed costs, part of which is affixed to the storage expense.

store brand. See *private label*.

store front. The outside front facing if the store, including windows, entry, signs.

store layout. See *layout*.

store hours. The hours of the day or evening when the store is open.

store manager. The person in charge of day-to-day store operations and personnel.

store's own brand. Merchandise manufactured exclusively for a chain of stores or a large store under the brand name of the store or stores.

store traffic. See *traffic*.

storm boot. See *boot*.

storm rubbers. See *rubbers*.

storm welt. A welt with a ridge running along the inner top edge to fill the crevice between sole and upper. The welt can be plain or notched.

stouts. Trade name for a comfortable women's shoe worn by stout women or women with large or puffy ankles.

straight inner border. A shoe, usually orthopedic, with a straight inner border from ball joint forward, and wide inflare of the shoe's forepart.

straight last. 1) A last whose shoe has neither right nor left and can be worn on either foot. A common last design for men, women and children until the beginning of the 20th century. 2) A last whose long axis is drawn through the exact longitudinal center of the foot, heel to center ball and exiting between the second and third toes, dividing the last into two equal longitudinal halves. Most feet have this straight-axis design, but most lasts do not because of shoemaking "tradition."

straights. An outmoded term for shoes made on old-fashioned straight lasts without lefts and rights.

straight tip. See *tip*.

strapping. The use of lengths of adhesive tape, one inch or more in width, to strap the foot as treatment for weak arches, ankle sprains, or other foot disorders, to correct, stabilize, or temporarily immobilize the foot. Various patterns of foot strapping are used by podiatrists and other foot therapists.

strap shoe. Any shoe held onto the foot by means of one or more straps of any of various widths or design arrangements. The common types of strap shoes are:

ankle. One or more straps extending from the vamp or quarter, wrapping around the ankle and fastened with a small buckle.

back. 1) Used with an open-back shoe, with the strap extending from one side of the quarter, extending around the back of the heel and buckled at the other side of the quarter. 2) A wide looped strap attached to the back rim of the boot shaft and used to pull the boot onto the foot. Also called a "pull strap."

buckle. A strap attached with a buckle.

button. A strap attached with a button.

cross. Straps criss-crossing over the instep in an X design, one or both fastened to the side of the shoe with a buckle or button.

front. 1) A shoe having one or more straps extending down in front of the instep to the throatline of the vamp. 2) A single strap across the front of the instep and buckled at the side. Also known as an "instep strap."

halter. See *slingback strap*.

instep. See *front strap*.

monk. A wide strap across the shoe's instep or tongue, buckled at the side. Also called a "sabot strap." A men's shoe style.

Various styles of strap shoes of 1920s.

137

sabot. See *monk strap*.

side. Used on a closed-front shoe, the strap extending from vamp to quarter on the outside.

slingback. A backless shoe except for a back strap attached in front of the ankle or instep to hold the shoe onto the foot. Also known as a "halter strap."

T-strap. An ankle strap met at the top of the instep by a strap extending up from the vamp and meeting the ankle strap to form a "T" design on the instep.

wishbone. A V-shaped strap, the V starting at the vamp and extending up to the quarter.

straw. A fabric made by braiding, plaiting or weaving natural fibers (straw, stalks, grass, bark) or artificial straw fibers. Used for making uppers for summer or warm-weather footwear, plus handbags.

strawfoot. Union army slang for a raw rural recruit during the Civil War, coined by drill sergeants who taught these men to march. Many of the young men were illiterate, not knowing left foot from right. So the drill instructors had them tie hay to the left foot and straw to the right, then shouting the march cadence "Hayfoot! Strawfoot!" rather than "Left! Right!" Another version of the word's origin is that it referred to lads who still had farm straw in their boots when they reported to the army.

streaking. Uneven surface color finished on leather due to faulty application of dyes or a fault in the dye itself.

street shoe. A loose designation for a plainer, more tailored women's shoe than a dress shoe for daytime wear.

stress. Pressure, tension or pull on the body or a body part.

stress fracture. The sudden or gradual pulling away of a tendon from its bone attachment, leaving one or more tiny cracks or "fractures" on the bone surface, such as on the foot or leg. A distressing condition common with runners and other athletes.

stretch fabric. A fabric with interwoven elastic threads, allowing the fabric to stretch.

stretch (foot). A measure of extension of the foot on weightbearing; the difference in foot length between the foot at rest and on weightbearing.

stretch hose. Hose made from elasticized fabric and allowing one size of hose to accomodate several foot sizes by virtue of the hose stretch.

stretch shoe laces. Made on the same principle as a stretch fabric, allowing the laces to yield rather than bind over the instep.

stretch slipper. See *slippers*.

stride. The full but natural extension of each leg in successive motions in walking or running. Longer than a step. Natural stride lengths vary, depending on body height, lower limb length, male or female.

string lasting. A lasting method in which two strings are attached to the upper by a zigzag seam, one for the forepart and one for the backpart, enabling the upper to be gathered in drawstring fashion and fastened over the insole.

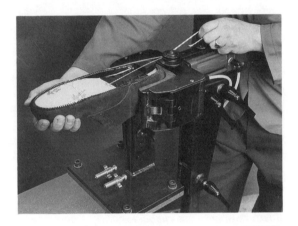

String lasting.

strip center. A very small, open shopping center with a few stores located side by side in a row; a convenience shopping area.

stripes. The bands of leather, usually in one or more contrasting colors, forming a saddle-like effect on the quarter around the instep and waist. Used for functional reinforcement, brand identity or for decorative effect. Found mostly on athleisure footwear.

strippy sandal. A women's sexy, high-heel sandal with multiple narrow straps comprising the upper to expose the foot.

stuck-on. British term for a cement shoe construction.

studs. 1) cleat-like knobs on the shoe's sole for added traction, such as on some sports shoes. 2) Sometimes used like nailheads on the soles or sides of some heavy outdoor or mountain boots for added durability, or for ornamental effect.

structured shoe. Any shoe construction with firm body and shape (counter, toe, upper) and conforming to the last. The opposite of an unstructured shoe.

stuffed leather. Leather tanned with wax or grease worked into the leather to give it a plump, soft texture and waxy surface. See also *glove leather*.

style. The particular and distinctive cut or design character of an article, such as a shoe or dress, that distinguishes it from any other style. Style is from the Latin "stylus," an instrument for drawing or tracing an outline or profile. Style is not to be confused with fashion. Style is basic, permanent, a one-of-a-kind, while fashion is constantly evolving, changing in according with contemporary lifestyles and trends. Fashion is any variation of a basic style. A pump is a basic style, but its many variations are adaptations to suit contemporary fashion.

styleman. In footwear, the individual employed by the manufacturer and responsible for developing or styling each new season's line for his company. A shoe designer or line builder.

stylist. 1) A person who conceives and creates the original models in a line of footwear. Sometimes known as a modelist. More creative or innovative than the styleman, the stylist may work for a single manufacturer or may free-lance. 2) A professional observer and evaluator of fashion trends who reports on these trends to his or her clients.

subcontracting. See *contract shoe manufacturer*.

subleasing. An arrangement between retailers wherein one leases a store from another who holds the original lease.

subluxation. An incomplete or partial dislocation of a joint, as in the foot or a foot joint.

subtalar joint. The joint just below the ankle between the talus and calcaneus bones.

suction cups. Indentations on the outsole surface to provide traction on smooth surfaces. Used on some running shoes.

suede. See *finish*.

suedine. A suede or napped finish on a man-made or fabric material to imitate suede-finished leather.

suerer. An archaic French term for a tanner or shoemaker or one who workers with leather. Used in the Middle Ages, the word means "sweater" and refers to the process of sweating raw skins in the preparation of leather-making.

suggestion selling. See *show and suggest*.

sultan toe. A shoe or slipper with a curled or turned-up toe, usually decorated with a pom-pom.

Sunday opening. Sunday open hours for a retail store.

super-mall. A huge shopping mall with several hundred stores, plus restaurants, theatres and other features.

supernumerary toes. A foot with six or more toes; extra toes beyond the norm. See also *polydactylism*.

supination. A foot stance or condition in which the foot's sole turns inward and upward while the heel, ankle, and forepart move in the opposite direction while standing, walking or running.

supinator shoe. An orthopedic shoes designed to help correct a supinated foot, usually in children.

supplier. One who produces or distributes the needed products or merchandise to a manufacturer or retailer.

support. 1) The foot's natural support system which includes the bones and joints, muscles and tendons, ligaments, arches, and plantar fascia. 2) Any supplementary components or design built into the shoe and offering support to the foot's own support system, or to a foot whose support system is weakened or in disorder.

support hose. A fabric with spandex or elasticized weave to create leg-hugging hose for added leg support and comfort.

surf shoe. A rubber or plastic shoe worn in the water or for water sports.

surgical boot. 1) A special boot for postoperative comfort and care of the foot. See also *postoperative shoe*. 2) A specially designed shoe to serve as an adjunct in correction of a foot deformity after surgery. 3) A boot specially designed to accommodate or help correct a foot deformity by mechanical means.

survey. 1) A poll of customers taken by a store to ascertain the footwear needs and wants of customers, or customer attitudes concerning the store and its merchandise, prices, services, personnel, etc. 2) A company-sponsored poll or study of consumer opinions and attitudes concerning a company, brand, product, buying habits, preferences, etc., based on a questionnaire or personal interviews. The responses are used to guide marketing strategies based on the response data.

sustained mark-on. Sustaining the original markon or full price, and not resorting to markdowns.

sustentaculum tall. The small shelf of bone on the inner-upper surface of the heel bone, which helps to support the long arch and maintain proper foot balance and function.

suwarrow boot. See *boot*.

swagger handbag. See *handbag*.

swatch. A small sample piece of leather, fabric or other material used for sampling purposes.

sweat gland. See *sebaceous gland*.

sweat socks. Socks with material of high sweat-absorbing capacity, used by runners, athletes and others with foot perspiration problems.

swing. The curvature of the outer rim of the outsole, or on a last.

swing cycle. In a walking or running gait, the time period or cycle of the stride movement of each leg start to finish in the stride sequence.

syconia. A shoe originally from Sicyon in ancient Greece, later adopted by the young dandies of Rome. Made of light-colored leather with an open, sandalized design covering the foot and leg.

sykhos. A soft, low leather boot of oriental design and origin. It later evolved into the Roman "soccus,"

essentially the same shoe worn with a sock during the colder months.

syndactylism. The medical term for web toes.

synovial fluid. The viscid fluid in the membrane of a joint cavity or synoivial sac, for lubrication of the joint.

synovial sac. The lining membrane inside a joint and holding the synovial fluid.

syntan. A synthetic organic tanning material.

synthetic. Any of a variety of man-made materials used for shoe uppers, linings and components.

T

tabi. A Japanese, mitten-like sock with a separate slot for the big toe and a slightly thickened sole. Usually in white cotton and worn with the *gēta* thonged sandal.

table run. Leather which is sold by tanners without being sorted or graded. Also called "factory run" and "tannery run."

tack hole. A tiny hole made by the assembling tack during the lasting operation, near the top of the back seam. The upper in some constructions is tacked to the last to prevent slippage during lasting.

tacking. A tannery operation in which skins of light leather are stretched over a board and tacked to it to preserve the smooth condition of the leather and prevent it from shrinking and wrinkling during drying.

tailored shoe. A women's shoe with simple, classic lines and minimum trim, for daytime wear.

tailor's bunion. A protrusion of swollen or inflamed flesh at the midfoot or "cuboid" area of the outer border of the foot, caused by pressure and friction, such as from a shoe. It derives its name from the old-time tailors who sat cross-legged at their work, their feet resting on the outer border while seated on a table or floor.

talaria. The symbolic winged shoes or sandals fastened at the ankle, as seen with the Greek and Roman gods Hermes and Mercury; also wings on the ankles.

talipes. Disorder affecting the foot and ankle together. A combination of the words "tali" (ankle) and "pes" (foot).

talipes equinovarus. Medical term for clubfoot.

tamancos. Portuguese name for platform shoes.

tannage. The particular method used for tanning leather. There are various tannages, each producing leathers of different properties. The more common tannages are:

alum. The use of alum combined with other materials. This was one of the first forms of mineral tannage, but is little used today.

bark. The use of vegetable tannins found in bark, wood, or other plant derivatives.

chrome. The use of chrome substances as the main ingredient in this mineral tannage. It is distinguished from other tannages by the greenish color at the cut stage. It is the most common of all tannages for upper leathers, its origins dating back to the 1850s.

combination. Using a combination of tanning agents such as several vegetable tanning extracts or the combination of vegetable and mineral agents. The combinations are determined by the type and quality of leather desired.

formaldehyde. A special tannage used particularly for white or washable glove leathers.

iron. Leather tanned with the salts of iron.

oak. Originally a tannage used mainly with oak bark and chestnut wood extracts to produce heavy leathers such as sole leather. Now it generally refers to vegetable tannage for all heavy leathers.

oil. Tanning with oils, chiefly marine oils. One of the earliest tannages dating back to prehistoric times.

slack. A light, incomplete, preliminary tannage.

union. The use of a combination of vegetable tannins, chiefly oak and hemlock, to produce sole and other heavy leathers.

vegetable. Any tannage using extracts from a wide variety of plants, trees, shrubs, bark, etc. Seldom used today for upper leathers, and used chiefly for sole and heavy leathers.

tannery run. See *table run*.

tannin. An astringent substance found in various parts of plants, leaves, bark, wood, roots, etc., used in tanning leather. Over recent decades synthetic tannins (syntans) have replaced vegetable tannins.

tanning. The complex chemical and mechanical process of converting raw hides and skins into leather by use of tanning agents. The process involves an extensive series of operations.

tanyard. A section of the tannery that houses the wooden vats in which leathers are vegetable tanned.

tap. A new half sole replacing and old or worn one, or a new sole placed on top of the old one.

tape. A narrow strip of fabric included in the folded edge of the quarters, toplines or other parts of the upper for reinforcement or to prevent stretching.

tapered toe. A toe of any shape that tapers down on a slant toward the tip and sides of the shoe's toe. See also *recede toe*.

tapestry. See *fabrics*.

tap shoe. A shoe with a metal piece on the toe tip of the sole and on the heel, for tap dancing.

tariff. 1) A system of taxes and duties imposed on imported goods or products. 2) The arrangement of shoe size/width combinations offered by the manufacturer or retailer and capable of fitting feet within those size ranges.

tarsal arch. See *arch, transverse*.

tarsal bone. Any of the seven bones comprising the tarsal section of the foot. They are: navicular, cuboid, talus, calcaneus, and the internal, medial and external cunieforms.

tarsometatarsal joint. Any joint formed by the base of a metatarsal bone and one or more of the tarsal bones.

tarsus. The rear skeletal section of the foot composed of the seven tarsal bones.

tassel. A dangling ornament with threaded cords or strips of leather or fabric hanging in a loose fringe

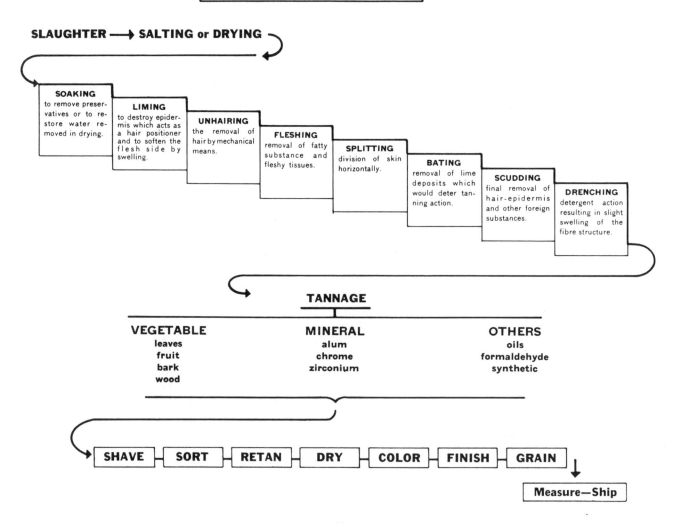

TYPICAL TANNING FLOW CHART

SLAUGHTER → SALTING or DRYING

SOAKING to remove preservatives or to restore water removed in drying.

LIMING to destroy epidermis which acts as a hair positioner and to soften the flesh side by swelling.

UNHAIRING the removal of hair by mechanical means.

FLESHING removal of fatty substance and fleshy tissues.

SPLITTING division of skin horizontally.

BATING removal of lime deposits which would deter tanning action.

SCUDDING final removal of hair-epidermis and other foreign substances.

DRENCHING detergent action resulting in slight swelling of the fibre structure.

TANNAGE

VEGETABLE	MINERAL	OTHERS
leaves	alum	oils
fruit	chrome	formaldehyde
bark	zirconium	synthetic
wood		

SHAVE — SORT — RETAN — DRY — COLOR — FINISH — GRAIN

Measure—Ship

Sorting hides in the tannery.

Tassel shoe.

or knotted at the ends. Usually an instep decoration on men's and women's sports and casual shoes.

taste. In reference to apparel and footwear, the ability to notice, discern, appreciate, and judge what is beautiful, appropriate, and harmonious.

tawed leather. Leather which has been alum tanned.

tawing. An outmoded term for the process of tanning leather with alum by various methods. Formerly used to distinguish between alum tanning and vegetable tanning.

tear strength. A measure or test of the ability of a material to resist a pull or pressure force, measured in pounds or equivalent units. A standard applied to leathers, man-mades or other materials for footwear, testing the pounds pulled before the material tears or ruptures.

technology. The science or study of the practical or industrial arts in the design and production of industrial or commercial products.

teenage shoes. A general designation for footwear for the market embracing ages about 12 to 17, and catering to the volatile tastes of this market.

telemarketing. Selling products or services to consumers via telephone.

temperature. The temperature of the surface of the foot, normally about 90 degrees Fahrenheit. The ideal temperature for the foot surface both inside and outside the shoe.

tendon. The narrowing elastic end of a muscles which attaches to a bone or joint and is responsible for the movement of that bone or joint.

tendo Achilles. See Achilles tendon.

tendonitis. Inflammation of a tendon.

tendosynovitis. Inflammation of a tendon sheath.

ten-footer. A tiny 10-by-10-foot shoemaking shop common in New England towns up until about 1860. Usually one shoemaker worked in each shop, making the shoe start to finish by hand.

tennies. British term for tennis shoes or sneakers.

tennis shoe. 1) A plain, white canvas-upper, rubber-sole oxford. 2) A specially designed high-tech shoe worn by serious or professional tennis players. See *sports shoe*.

tennis toe. See *turf toe*.

tensile strength. See *tear strength*.

tequa. A buckskin sandal worn by Indians of New Mexico.

TARSUS

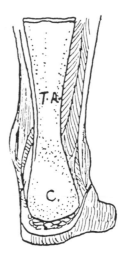

The Achilles tendon.

143

terrycloth. See *fabrics*.

test marketing. Testing a new product or service in a particular, selected marketplace prior to bringing it to a broader, full-scale market.

texture. The distinctive surface appearance and feel or touch response to a material such as leather, fabric or man-made materials.

thank-you note. A note or postcard sent to a customer by the store, expressing thanks or appreciation for a recent purchase. A customer-relations strategy.

theatre boot. See *deer foot*.

theatrical shoe. Any special-function shoe used by a performer in a theatrical act. Usually associated with dancing such as tap, ballet, chorus line, etc.

theo tie. A pump-like shoe with an open front, held onto the foot at the instep with a ribbon, cord or lacing through one or two eyelets.

therapeutic. Any medical or mechanical application that is part of the therapy in the treatment of a bodily disorder.

therapy. 1) The treatment of a foot disease, injury, or disorder by medical or mechanical means, usually excluding surgery. 2) The use of special footwear or shoe modifications as an adjunct in the treatment of a foot or gait disorder.

thermal. Having to do with heat.

thermoplastic. A material that will repeatedly soften when heated and harden when cooled. While soft it can be molded and cast under heat and pressure. Various shoe materials and components (counters, box toes, some soles) are thermoplastic.

thermoset. Any material subject to a chemical reaction from heat or ultraviolet light so that the material cannot be fused or melted. Some such materials are used in shoe components.

thirty-four. A retail trade term meaning "go away." Said by one salesperson to another who is interfering with the customer or sale.

Thomas bar. See *bar*.

Thomas heel. See *heel*.

thong. A strip or cord of leather or rawhide used as a sandal or shoe fastening.

thread. A fine twist of fibrous filaments, smoother, stronger, and more pliable than yarn, hence more suitable for sewing. A variety of threads are used in footwear—cotton, silk, linen, nylon, orlon, rayon, etc.

three-quarter regent pump. A regent pump made with two separate quarters, having the collar piece extending from the forepart to the outside collar. The latter is seamed to a shorter extension from the

Thong sandal.

forepart to the inside quarter at the side of the vamp throat.

three-quarter vamp. See *vamp*.

throat. The central part of the shoe's vamp on top just behind the toes. The entrance area for the forepart of the foot.

throatline. The edge or rim of the vamp throat. It is subject to a variety of design treatments. On a pump, for example, the throatline can be round, square, V-shaped, offsided, etc.

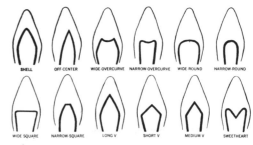
Different types of throatlines.

through sole. British term for midsole.

throwout. A retail trade term for a customer to whom it seems impossible to please or sell anything.

thumbpoint toe. See *almond toe*.

Thursday room. In a shoe store or department, a permanent, self-service clearance section with merchandise on racks or in bins.

tibia. The shin bone, and the larger of the two leg bones, the other being the fibula.

tibilia. A medieval term referring to hose made of leather, silk, or other cloth.

ticket. 1) A ticket affixed to a shoe and providing information about size, price, color, stock number, etc. 2) A ticket affixed to a shoe on display, providing price or other information. 3) A ticket affixed to a shoe being processed in the factory, designating stock number, lot number, date, shipment, etc.

tie shoe. An oxford with not more than three eyelets, usually laced with ribbon. Designated as a one-, two-, or three-eyelet tie.

tight line. A shoe that fits tightly onto the last at the topline.

tight to toe. Describing the right way to cut upper materials or components, with the grain direction of the material stretched perpendicular to the direction of the greatest lasting tension—that is, perpendicular to the direction of the stretch.

tinea pedis. Medical term for athlete's foot.

tingling. A foot sensation occasionally experienced when leg or foot circulation is temporarily impeded, or with mild pressure on a nerve, such as when the knees are crossed for a prolonged period, or when the foot "goes asleep."

tint. See *color*.

tinting. The coloring of a fabric with use of dyes. Untinted shoes are usually purchased in white fabric, then tinted to match a gown or dress such as a bride's or bridesmaid's gown.

tip. This term usually applies to men's shoes. A toe tip is an important design or decorative feature. Also known as a "toe cap." The common toe tip designs are as follows:

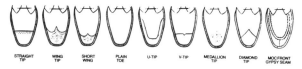

Examples of toe tip styles.

diamond. A triangular upper half of a diamond shape. It can be a plain diamond seam or line, or perforated.

imitation. The illusion of a tip made by one or more rows of stitching across the vamp and made up of the same piece of vamp material.

medallion. A design in perforations on the tip.

moccasin front. A long U-curve covering the vamp and giving the impression of a plug within the U-area. Often used with a gypsy seam at the bottom of the U-curve and continuing forward down the center to the sole.

mudguard. A leather tip covering the rim of the

toe box but not extending further over the toe. Also known as a "moccasin toe box."

plain. An undecorated toe with no tip design.

shield. A modified wing tip which appears to shield the toe rather than being parallel to the end line of the toe. There is only a slight sweep from the center point to the sole.

short wing. The same as a full wing tip only shorter and lower. Usually perforated at the toe tip.

straight. A straight line across the center of the toe tip, perpendicular to the toes. It can have a stitched, ridged or other design.

U-tip. A horseshoe-shape or U-shape design. The U can be low, medium or high on the toe.

V-tip. A straight tip with a small, short V-cut in the center.

wing. A tip with an upside down V-cut in the center and the end of the toe fully perforated. Sometimes the wing design has pinked edges.

tip stitching. Seaming the tip and vamp of a shoe upper together.

toe box. The firm, reinforced toe area of a shoe. See also *box toe*.

toe cap. An extra piece sewn to the vamp and covering the toe area. See also *tip*.

toe expression. The shape of the last or shoe at the toe. A term common with last makers and shoe designers.

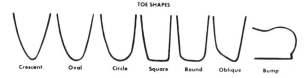

Various toe shapes or "toe expressions."

toeing in. The feet angulated or pointed inward toward each other. It is either a generic condition or sometimes due to a malpositioning of the foetus before birth. This manner of gait is usually outgrown or self-corrected in early childhood, but it is not unusual for it to continue into adulthood with one or both feet.

toeing out. The feet angulated with the forepart pointed outward. Usually generic or inherited. A mild degree (up to about 15 degrees) is normal and very common. But when extreme it generally indicates a serious foot disorder, such as excessive pronation, that requires treatment or correction.

toe lasting. Lasting the shoe at the toe with a special toe-lasting machine.

toeless shoe. See *open-toe shoe*.

145

toenail polish. A cosmetic item the same as fingernail polish, available in colors. Used on toenails by some women when sandals or open-toe shoes are worn.

toe-off. The pushoff from the toes with the step.

toe pitch. See *toe spring*.

toe point. The foremost point of the last at the toe.

toe post. A knob-like piece of leather or other material projecting up from the top surface of the sole and fitting between the first and second toes, as on some sandals.

toe puff. British term for a box toe.

toe ring. One or more ornamental rings worn on one or more toes when barefoot, or when wearing sandals or open-toe shoes. The custom, still in use today, dates back to ancient Persia.

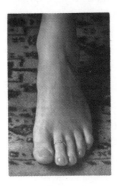

Toe ring.

toe rubbers. A short rubber covering only the forepart of the shoe and held on with a stretchable rubber strap around the shoe's back. Worn by women with high heel shoes in inclement weather. See also *rubbers*.

toe shape. See *toe expression*.

toe shield. See *safety toe*.

toe separator. A small rubber or foam piece inserted between two toes to relieve pressure or friction between the toes, as in the case of a soft corn, or as an orthotic device to help straighten crooked toes.

toe spring. The elevation of the under surface of the sole at the toe to give the sole a slight rocker effect for an easier step. The amount of toe spring (built

Toe spring.

into the last) depends of shoe style, sole thickness, heel height, etc. The heel also has a mild spring design.

toe walking. Sometimes occurs with infants during the beginning stages of walking, with the infant walking on ball and toes only and not using the heel. Within a few months the child usually assumes a normal heel-to-toe gait, though occasionally the condition persists due to some neuromuscular disorder. Also known as "equinus."

toggling. A tannery operation whereby skins of light leather are stretched smoothly over perforated metal frames and attached to them by toggles or metal clamps. The method is now largely outmoded.

tonality. A general color scheme, or the collective color tones of an apparel and footwear ensemble, such as a tonality of blues or browns.

tone. See *color*.

tongue. The flap part of the shoe's upper, or a section affixed to the vamp and extending rearward and upward to cover the instep or beyond. Functionally it protects the instep, serving as a buffer layer against the lacings of an oxford shoe. It is sometimes used in more elaborate form as a decorative treatment on a shoe. There are various styles of shoe tongues, as follows:

From left to right: plain tongue, bellows tongue, fringed tongue and apron tongue.

apron. A fringed tongue that extends upward from the vamp and folds back over the instep to the vamp throat again. Aprons are sometimes secured in this folded position by a strap stitched to the quarter and fastened across the tongue.

bellows. A broad, accordian-fold tongue stitched to the sides of the quarter or a blucher shoe or boot to make it watertight. Used in some work and outdoor boots.

colonial. Extends and flares out above the instep instead of lying flat on the instep. Stitched to the vamp throat and placed under the lacing of a Colonial tie, or extended above the vamp line on a Colonial pump. It is frequently ornamented with a large buckle or bow.

fringe. A broad tongue having a fringed top edge, often perforated for decoration.

high front. A high, flared, unornamented tongue on a men's slip-on shoe or a women's pump.

146

High-tongue styles of 18th century.

Shawl tongue.

shawl. A slashed tongue that folds back and down over the instep to concealing the eyelets and lacing. Originated in 1640 in England and was introduced to modern fashion by the Prince of Wales in 1925.

slashed. Similar to the shawl and apron tongue, with lengthwise slits for half or three-fourths the length of the tongue.

tongue guide. A tag or slit in the tongue through which the lacings are slotted to hold the tongue in place. Also called a "lace keeper."

tongue lining. See *lining*.

tongue pad. An extra tongue lining composed of light, foam-type material as a protective buffer against the lacings. Usually used on some athletic footwear.

toothpick toe. A 19th-century term for American shoes with extremely pointed toes.

top. All parts of the shoe above the vamp and quarter, as in a "boot top." Now somewhat obsolete.

top boot. See *boot, jockey*.

top coat. The final coat of finish on leather or a man-made material.

top edge. The top rim of the shoe's upper, including the exposed edge of the upper and the eyelet edge.

top facing. A binding or lining which is sewn around the inner part of the upper at the top. It serves to finish off the lining and reinforce the shoe at this section. It is sometimes stamped with a marking of the shoe size or brand.

top grain. The first or upper cut from the grain side of a split hide, from which hair and other surface matter is removed, leaving a clean grain surface. A term referring to better quality leather. Also known as "full grain."

top lift. The bottom layer of a built-up heel and the part to which the top piece is attached. Sometimes used synonymously with "top piece," though they are not exactly the same.

top piece. The hard-wearing bottom layer of heel material in direct contact with the ground, and the piece replaced when worn down.

top stay. A facing of leather or other material stitched to the outside of the upper at the top. When contrasting material is used, the top stay is called a "cuff." See also *cuff*.

torque. A twisting or rotary force, such as the foot action inside the shoe.

torsion. A stress caused by twisting a material or part of a unit, such as a foot or shoe.

total look. A designer or fashion term referring to the harmony of color, material, or design of the combined ensemble of apparel and accessories.

tote bag. See *handbag*.

track shoe. See *sports shoe*.

traction. The pulling or drawing of a load against the ground surface, and the leverage action resulting

Traction soles.

147

from the friction between the moving and the stationary parts.

traction sole. An outsole with a special ground-gripping design and material to improve traction.

trade association. An industry or business organization composed of member firms with the same common business interests.

trademark. A registered logo, symbol, or name identified with a product or service and protected by law against infringement.

trade press. The specialized media or publications serving a particular category of industry, business, trade, or profession. Also known as the "business press."

trade show. A convention or exhibit of companies and products convened in one place to display their merchandise or services for buyers to examine and purchase. Such shows may be national, regional or local.

trading area. In retailing, the geographical radius from which the customers are drawn to buy at a local store.

trading up. Getting the customer to make a higher priced or better quality purchase.

traditional. Handed down by custom or convention; classic or changing little with time, as in traditional or classic fashion.

traffic. In retailing, the number and movement of customers within a store at a given time or over a period of time. A measure of the store's sales volume.

traffic flow. The pattern of customer movement within the store, usually determined by the store layout or floor plan.

tragic cothornus. See *cothornus*.

training. In retailing, a store program for training new sales personnel, or the continuing education of experienced personnel, by the use of a manual or other literature, plus in-store meetings, demonstrations, etc.

training shoe. See *sports shoe*.

transducer. A small, wafer-type device to convert an applied force into an electric signal. It is used in gait testing with the transducers attached to foot and leg, or used for testing foot or gait disorders, detecting where excessive pressures or imbalances are occurring.

transient. Temporary or passing through, such as a transient customer in contrast to regular or repeat customers.

transitional. In fashion, crossing over from one season to the next, or from one period in the fashion cycle to the next. The in-between period.

transluscent. Descriptive of a material that transmits some light but not clear enough to see through. Typical of some upper shoe materials.

transplant. In modern foot surgery, the use of toe or partial foot transplants to replace corresponding parts lost by injury or disease. Called transplant surgery.

transporter. See *conveyor*.

transverse arch. See *arch, transverse*.

transverse bar. See *bar*.

traveler. See *shoe traveler*.

tread. 1) To walk on, or the particular way the weight-bearing foot implants itself on the ground to create a tread pattern. 2) On the last, the widest section across the ball, and also the design of the last bottom so that the shoe will "walk" properly. 3) On a shoe, the areas of the sole and heel that are in primary contact with the ground in walking. Proper tread is important to the foot, last, and shoe.

treadmill. A mechanical apparatus with a wide movable band to walk or run on, adjusted for varying speeds so that the walker/runner is always in the same place though moving. Used for exercising, or for testing gait or footwear in gait laboratories or clinics.

treadpoint. The point at the bottom forepart of a last or shoe in contact with the base plane or ground surface.

treatment. The manner in which trims, ornamentation and other decorative effects are used on a shoe.

tree. See *shoe tree*.

treeing. A shoe factory operation consisting of shaping, smoothing and cleaning the shoe with finishing touches in the treeing or packing room.

treeing room. See *packing room*.

trench calf. British term for reversed calf.

trench foot. Similar to frostbite but resulting from longer exposure to dampness and cold. The term was common during World War I when soldiers spent long periods in cold, wet trenches.

trend. The prevailing direction or movement of current events, such as a fashion or business trend.

trials. In the shoe factory, testing new patterns or styles for look and fit; preliminary testing before approval.

trial-and-error fitting. In the shoe store, the repeated testing of each style or size brought out from the stockroom by the salesperson in a try-on for fit on the customer's foot. Because shoe sizes are not uniform, trial-and-error fitting is inevitable to arrive at the proper fit.

tricot. A knitted fabric (nylon, rayon, etc.) commonly used for linings in women's shoes.

trim. The ornamentation of a shoe via decorative effects such as underlays, overlays, binding, stripping, ornaments, etc. Also known as "treatments."

trimming. 1) Removing the portions of the raw hide (flesh, tail, shanks, etc.) not suitable for making leather. 2) During the tanning process, the removal of rough or scraggly edges on the hide or skin to provide a cleaner, more uniform appearance of the finished leather.

triple header. In the shoe store, a three-pairs sale to a customer.

tripod weight bearing. The three-point pattern of weight bearing on the foot—at the heel and the inner and outer ball. In modern foot mechanics theory this traditional pattern has been somewhat revised and refined.

trunk show. 1) The presentation of a company's complete seasonal line to managers and buyers at a retail store—usually a large or prestigious store. 2) A presentation of the manufacturer's line, usually a prominent brand or designer's label, in a store for the store's customers who have been previously notified by advertising or mail. The customers can buy from stock or sometimes can order, on a make-up basis for an extra service charge, a particular shoe in a color or material not available from stock.

try-on. 1) A retail trade term for trying on a shoe to the customer's foot for fit and style viewing. 2) A disposable sock provided free by the store to barefoot customers wanting to try on and buy shoes; a sanitary precaution.

T-strap. See *strap shoe*.

tuberosity. A small enlargement or growth on an otherwise smooth, normal bone. Sometimes occurs on foot bones.

tunnel wedge. See *heel*.

turf toe. And inflammation and soreness of one or more of the toes, frequently the result of repeated toe trauma against the end of the shoe during prolonged athletic activity such as tennis, running, or football on artificial turf. The cause can be a recede toe design of the shoe; or the sole's traction design that causes the foot to slide forward inside the shoe when the shoe abruptly "brakes." Also known as "tennis toe," "runner's toe" and "walker's toe."

turn shoe. See *shoe construction*.

Turkish leather. An obsolete term formerly applied to genuine morocco leather. See also *leather, morocco*.

turnover. 1) A retail trade term for a customer who is switched from one salesperson to another. 2) The change or departure of personnel in a store for any of various reasons. 3) The rate of sales and replacement movement of a line or the total inventory of a store relative to the shelf life of the stock. A measure of customer demand for the store's merchandise or for a given style or line.

tween-age. A coined trade term for a demographic group, usually girls, between the ages of eight and eleven, and the footwear styles designed to appeal to them.

twig store. A smaller branch store, usually of a large department store.

twill. See *fabrics*.

two-sole construction. See *shoe construction, stitchdown*.

two-tone. See *dual tone*.

two-way stretch. An elasticized material that stretches both lengthwise and sidewise.

tzanga. A knee-high boot of purple leather worn only by Roman emperors. For anyone else to wear it was a punishable crime.

U

UCO process. See *shoe construction, Littleway*.

udone. See *soccus*.

unborn calf. See *slunk*.

unconstructed shoe. See *unstructured shoe*.

underbuy. An over-cautious order by the retailer. A stock purchase that does not meet demand level and often results in lost sales.

underlapping toes. One or more toes that underlap others. It is sometimes hereditary, sometimes caused by habitual wearing of ill-fitting shoes. Usually the lesser toes are affected.

underlay. 1) A piece of leather of other material placed between the outside upper and the lining beneath a cutout, perforation or other opening. 2) An addition made to an upper section to permit another section to be attached to it. See also *seam, lap*.

undressed kid. Kidskin leather finished by a suede process on the flesh side. Very little such leather is now used.

unhairing. A tannery operation whereby the hair is removed from hides and skins with the aid of depilating agents and the use of mechanical equipment. The hide or skin is unhaired immediately after it has been fleshed.

uniform shoe. A service shoe worn by all persons in a uniformed occupation and working for the same company. Also, shoes worn by children in parochial or some private schools, boy and girl scouts, etc.

ungulate walking. The gait of hooved animals (deer, horse, etc.) whose hooves arc actually greatly enlarged and hardened toenails or claws which evolved into hooves.

unilateral. Affecting only one side, such as left or right, or medial or lateral.

union label. A marking on some manufactured products indicating that it was made by members of a labor union. Formerly used on some footwear, but rarely used today.

union tannage. See *tannage*.

unisex shoes. Any shoe style or pattern that can be worn by either sex. Examples: loafers, sneakers, athleisure footwear.

unisole. See *unit sole*.

unit bottom. See *unit sole*.

unit control. In a store, a system of recording stock on hand, on order, and sold for a given period, the data showing shifts in customer merchandise preferences. Done periodically.

unit cost. The cost per item or, in a shoe store, per pair.

units. 1) In footwear, pairs. 2) Number of stores under one ownership.

unit sole. A molded sole in which the sole and heel are molded as a single unit in predetermined sizes. The unit sole is attached to the shoe as a single unit, resulting in labor cost reduction and time saving.

universal last. A last or mold usually used by producers of sneakers and athleisure footwear on one width for all sizes.

unlined shoe. A shoe without any linings, as in some loafers or moccasins.

unordered shoes. See *sale shoes*.

unstructured shoe. A shoe whose upper section has no counter or box toe and often no lining, so that the upper has a deliberately "collapsed" look.

upper. All the parts or sections (vamp, quarters, linings, etc.) above the shoe's sole that are stitched or otherwise joined together to become a unit, and then attached to the insole and outsole.

upper cutting. See *cutting*.

upper fitting. In the shoe factory, fitting together and stitching or seaming the various parts of the upper.

upper leather. Any suitable leather used for footwear uppers, usually lighter leathers.

upscale. Refers to customers or markets with above-average incomes and education who buy or can afford to buy better quality, higher priced merchandise.

updated. A product, style or line that has been revised or revived to fit into contemporary trends, tastes or lifestyles.

upstanding counter. A counter extending vertically above the ankle bones and used for added ankle support in some boot-type orthopedic shoes.

urethane. A cellular elastomeric material combined with polyols to become polyurethane, a hard-wearing material used chiefly for shoe soles. It can also the chemically manipulated to become urethane foam for shoe cushioning.

urethane patent. A leather or man-made material finished and coated with urethane compounds for an improved glossy finish service to provide durable, crack-resistant, blister-resistant wear.

U-throat. A U-shape throatline on a shoe, such as a pump.

utility footwear. Any shoe or boot designed and used chiefly for service or utility wear.

U-tip. See *tip*.

V

valgus. A deformity or abnormality in which the anatomical part is turned or forced outward. Example: hallux valgus in which the great toe is bent outward toward the other toes.

valgus knees. Knock-knees.

value pricing. See *market pricing*.

vamp. The lower forward part of the shoe's upper, covering the forepart of the foot. There are various types of vamps:

choked-up. Cut high and closed up rather than a shelled-out silhouette.

circular. The vamp extending from the toe to the heel breast. Similar to a three-quarter vamp.

cutoff. Cut off at the toe slightly below the toe-tip line. The cut-away portion is completed by the toe tip which is seamed to the vamp.

gypsy. Split down the center from the throat to the toe with a closed seam, frequently piped.

moccasin. A vamp having a genuine or imitation moccasin seam.

ombre. Made of narrow strips of leather of graduated color shading.

patch. Made by stitching together leather patches of various colors into a complete vamp shape.

plug. A circular vamp with a plug insert at the throat, extending upward in a split piece to form the eyelet stays.

seamless. A whole vamp that extends from toe to heel on both sides without a seam.

split. A vamp that has been split into one or more parts which are seamed together with a closed seam and frequently piped. A combination of leathers or other materials are frequently used.

three-quarter. A whole vamp which extends from toe to heel on the outside only. The inside is cut off at the shank and a separate piece of foxing is seamed to complete the inside of the vamp.

whole. See *seamless vamp*.

woven. Made of narrow strips of leather or other

Woven vamp.

material which have been woven together. See also *huarache*.

Y-vamp. A vamp split into a Y-shape laced stay.

vamp (or vampay). A sock or short stocking worn in Colonial America.

vamp crease. 1) The deep or excessive crease or fold across the vamp of the shoe due to improper size or fit, or because the vamp has not been cut correctly. 2) The normal crease lines across the top of the vamp when the foot is flexed. 3) The crease deliberately designed into the vamp as a decorative feature, as on western boots.

vamping. Sewing the vamp to the quarter or other parts of the shoe.

vamp length. The length, toe rearward, of the vamp.

vamp over. A shoe having the vamp overlapping the quarter at the vamp seam.

vamp point. A point on top of the last at the intersection of the center line and the ball line across the last.

vamp stay. A reinforcement, sometimes circular, placed on an oxford where the vamp and quarters meet.

vamp throat. See *throat*.

vamp wing. Each of the two symmetrical sides or

153

"wings" of the vamp directed rearward toward the heel, which are stitched to the quarters.

vamp wrinkles. See *vamp creases*.

vanity handbag. See *handbag*.

variable width lacing. A design in which one pair of lacings is close together, the next farther apart, in a similar series. This is to allow more comfortable lacing for any width of foot.

varus. An abnormal turning inward of a body part, such as a foot. The opposite of valgus.

varus knees. Bow legs.

varus wedge. A wedge built into the shoe to prevent or correct a varus or rolling-in condition of the foot.

V-cut. In a high boot a small V-cut is made at the back and front of the top rim of the boot shaft to accommodate the calf of the leg and for ease in pulling off the boot.

veal. A large calfskin almost as large as a kipskin.

veal leather. See *leather*.

veau velours leather. See *leather*.

vee. Any part of a women's shoe using a V design (vamp trim, cutouts, throatline).

vegetable tannage. See *tannage*.

veiny leather. Leather whose flesh or under side reveals patches of visible blood vessels in the form of indentations.

Velcro. A proprietary name for a fastener consisting of two pieces with thorny-like surfaces which, when joined, form a secure bonding.

veldt. See *shoe construction, stitchdown*.

veldtschoen. See *shoe construction, stitchdown*.

vellum. See *parchment*.

velours. French for velvet. Also a proprietary name for a soft-finish, chrome-tanned calfskin.

velvet. See *fabrics*.

velveteen. See *fabrics*.

velvet finish. See *finish*.

vendor. A seller of merchandise. Usually refers to a manufacturer, importer, or distributor who sells to retailers.

venez-y-voir. In French it means "come hither." A term in 18th-century France for a women's shoe style opened up in the back, or with jeweled backpart.

vent. A punched or perforated opening in a shoe, sometimes eyeletted, for added inside-shoe ventilation.

ventilating eyelets. Eyelets stamped into the upper, usually at the inner side of the arch or waist area for added shoe ventilation.

ventilated shoe. Any shoe with "air holes" (special eyelets, punchings, perforations) to help ventilate the inside of the shoe.

verucca. Medical term for a wart. See also *planter wart*.

vertical retailing. In shoe business, a store specializing in one line or category of footwear. Also, a store that carries fewer styles but greater depth in sizes and widths.

vici kid. See *leather*.

Vienna cut. A shoe upper made with a single circular seam down the outside of the shoe's upper.

vinyl. Short for polyvinylchloride, a plastic coating or film used on a fabric-based material and commonly used for shoe uppers, mostly on women's and girls' shoes, and also for linings. In clear or transparent form it is sometimes used for uppers on women's shoes and known as "clear vinyl."

vogue. The mode or contemporary fashion.

volume. 1) The dimensions on the last that determine the amount and shape of the space inside the shoe to accommodate the foot, especially the forefoot. 2) A store's total dollar sales.

volume retailer. A store that sells in large amounts or volume.

V-tip. See *tip*.

vulcanizing. The process of treating crude rubber or latex by chemical means to improve such properties as hardness, durability, elasticity.

vulcanizing process. See *shoe construction*.

W

W. A loose symbol for a wide shoe width; roughly E in men's, D in women's.

wading boot. See *boot*.

wadloper. Dutch for "shallows walking"—slogging across shallow, muddy flats, a sport popular in the Netherlands.

waffle sole. A lug-type sole of rubber or polyurethane with a surface design similar to that of a waffle iron, used for traction and shock absorption on running shoes.

waist. The section around the foot, last or shoe between ball and instep.

waist girth. The girth measurement at the waist on a last.

walk. See *walkout*.

walk the chalk. As far back as the 17th century it was customary in the American Navy for a straight chalk line to be drawn along the deck of a ship as a test for drunkenness of sailors returning from liberty ashore. Sailors who failed to meet the chalk-line walking test were punished, often by flogging. The term "walk the chalk" was first used in 1823.

walker's toe. See *turf toe*.

walk-in. A transient customer who walks into the store from the street, usually after looking at and being attracted by merchandise in the window. It can also apply to a person seeking employment.

walking club. Any group or organization with a common interest in walking, especially exercise/fitness walking, whose members participate in walking together as a group.

walking heel. See *heel*.

walking shoe. Any shoe purchased and used primarily for walking. In a more precise sense, a shoe designed with high-tech features biomechanically structured exclusively for exercise/fitness walking.

walkout. A store customer who walks out without making a purchase.

wallaby leather. See *leather*.

wall last. A last with vertical rims or "walls" at the toe and sides of the forepart.

walrus leather. See *leather*.

wardrobe. The assortment of footwear owned by an individual consumer and selected for wear on appropriate occasions.

wart. See *planter wart*.

washable leather. Any leather specially tanned to make it washable without loss of color or dimension.

waterproofing. Any method of making leather impervious to water, such as with coatings or impregnations of oils, waxes, or chemical solutions. Used mainly on work and outdoor boots. Waterproof is not synonymous with water-resistant.

water-repellant. See *water-resistant*.

water-resistant. A material or product specially treated to resist entry or repel absorption of moisture, but not necessarily waterproof.

wave sole. A proprietary name for an outsole with a series of raised, wave-like, horizontal sections across a thick, rubber-type sole. Used on some casual and walking shoes.

waxed calf. See *leather*.

wax polish. Any shoe polish whose chief ingredient is a carnauba or other wax.

waxy finish. See *finish*.

weakfoot. A general, loose term for a foot lacking full

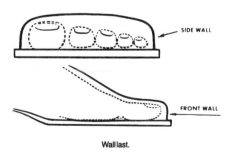

Wall last.

Wave sole.

strength or functional ability and subject to soreness and fatigue.

wear bar. A plug built into or applied to a shoe's outsole or heel to give added wear to the heaviest tread portion. Used on some running and walking shoes. Such plugs are replaceable.

wear pattern. The areas of wear on the shoe's outsole surface. The pattern is used for tread analysis on runners' shoes, or in the diagnosis of gait problems.

wear plug. See *wear bar*.

wear test. Any method of evaluating the durability or abrasion resistance of a material against wear conditions.

web toes. See *syndactylism*.

wedge. A piece of leather or other material tapered to a thin edge on one side, used to elevate some particular part of the sole or heel to correct a foot or gait imbalance or disorder. Used in shoe therapy and foot orthopedics.

Various wedges used on children's shoes.

wedge angle. The angle of the heel seat, back to heel breast, relative to the flat plane of the ground. An important measurement on lasts.

wedge heel. See *heel*.

wedgie. A shoe with a wedge heel.

wedging. The skilled process of designing, making, and applying wedges in footwear, often a custom procedure.

weight. The weight of a shoe, usually adapted to certain weight standards for particular types of footwear, such as running shoes.

weight bearing. The act of bearing weight on the foot in standing, walking or running.

weight distribution. The pattern in which the body weight is borne and distributed over the foot in standing, walking, or running.

weighted leather. Leather which has been filled and stuffed with any of various substances worked into the fibers to add to the plumpness and weight of the leather. Most frequently applied to some sole and other heavy leathers, and also glovey/waxy/oily shoe leathers.

wellies. A British or Australian term for Wellington boots.

wellie throwing. A contest or sport popular in Australia and Britain, the object being to see how far one can throw a Wellington or rubber boot. The records are listed in the *Guinness Book of Records*.

welt. A strip of leather or synthetic material between the edge or crevice of the upper and sole, lying flat on the sole edge, to which both the upper and sole are attached, as in a Goodyear welt shoe as a functional part of the construction. Some shoes use an imitation welt stitched around the top flat edge of the sole for decorative purposes, but is not a functional part of the shoe.

welt beating. The factory operation of lightly beating the welt by hand or machine into a smooth position

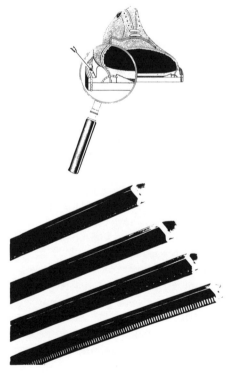

Welting on shoe (above). Different styles of welting (below).

156

around the edge of the shoe prior to attaching the sole.

welt seam. See *seam*.

welt shoe. See *shoe construction*.

wet look. A fashion term sometimes applied to apparel, shoes and boots worn as an ensemble and made of materials with a gloss or patent finish.

whang leather. Strong leather, such as rawhide, used for lacings, cords, or thongs.

wheeling. An ornamental ridging ir pattern stamped into the top, exposed edge of the outsole by means of a corrugated wheel.

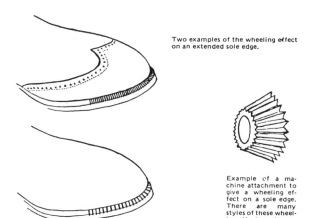

Two examples of the wheeling effect on an extended sole edge.

Example of a machine attachment to give a wheeling effect on a sole edge. There are many styles of these wheeling attachments.

Wheeling device pressed on shoe edge surface to produce decorative effect.

whipping the cat. An old shoemaker's term (1700–1850), referring to the itinerant shoemakers of early America who traveled on horseback, living briefly with farm families while making shoes for the family. The term related to the family cats who played with the shoemaker's dangling threads, requiring him to shoo or "whip" them away.

white leather. Leather tanned with alum and salt.

Whitman plate. A metal orthotic or arch support with a high inner flange. The plate extended heel to ball, inserted in the shoe, intended to correct or relieve severe arch or pronation problems. Perhaps the first arch support or foot orthotic, introduced in 1907 by orthopedist Dr. Royal Whitman. Now outmoded.

whole cut. A one-piece upper, or one-piece vamp or quarter, in contrast to the usual two or more pieces to a section.

whole length. A piece of thin leather or other material cut to the shape of the insole to give a visible insole surface a more finished appearance. Similar to a full-length sock lining.

wholesale price index. A government measure of the movement of manufacturer or raw materials prices on selected products, and a gauge of the related retail prices to follow.

wholesaler. A distributor or middleman who buys large lots from the manufacturer or importer and resells to the retailer, usually serving retailers in a more local or regional area. Most such shoes do not carry a manufacturer's brand name but may be given a "brand" or house name by the wholesaler.

whole vamp. See *vamp*.

wicking. The absorption or sucking up of moisture by a material, such as a lining or insole, to keep moisture away from the foot while evaporating.

width. A standard measurement of linear width across the ball of the foot, last or shoe and designated in standard width sizes such as A-B-C-D-etc., or the looser width markings of N-M-W. On standard widths the progression is one-fourth inch for each width change, the range for AAAAA to EEEEE, or 14 widths, with extreme widths (on special order) adding even more. Standard shoe widths were first introduced in 1880.

willow calf. See *leather*.

willow finish. See *leather, boarded*.

willow tanned. A term used in the sporting goods industry for well-oiled, supple, chrome-tanned cattlehide or horsehide leather used for baseball and other athletic gloves.

willow walk. In China of centuries past (1100 to 1920) the name for a fragile, delicate manner of gait of women with bound feet, which resembled the sinuous movement of a willow in the breeze.

Wilson. A trade code term among retail shoe salespeople, meaning "We've run out of the size." Spoken to another store person in front of the customer. Now somewhat obsolete.

window. In a chamois skin, a thin portion that transmits light when the skin is held up and viewed against a window or a lighted background.

window card. Any small sign in the store window.

window display. The arrangement of the merchandise in the store window.

window trimmer. One who specializes in store window displays or decorative arrangement. Also known as a "window decorator."

wing tip. See *tip*.

winklepicker toe. A British term for a long, extremely pointed-toe shoe.

wishbone strap. See *strap*.

women's shoe sizes. Classified as sizes 3 to 10 (extremes 2 to 12).

wooden shoe. Any shoe made entirely of wood whose

inside is carved out, or a shoe dominantly of wood such as some sabots. Worn by peasants and work-men for centuries in Europe and Asia. See also *sabot, clog, klompen*.

wood heel. Any heel made of wood, usually covered with a material matching or contrasting with the upper, and with a rubber or plastic toplift. The first wood heels were introduced in America in 1871. Today the wood heel has been largely replaced by stronger plastic heels which are less subject to breakage.

wooden sole shoe. Any shoe with a wooden sole and an upper of leather or other material, as in some clogs or platforms.

Wooden sole.

working capital. Cash reserves available for business operations.

workmen's compensation. A form of on-the-job accident or illness insurance paid for by the company or store, or by company/store and employee combined.

work shoe. A heavy, sturdy shoe or boot used by workers on rugged jobs such as building construc-tion. This laced footwear has heavy leather uppers and usually thick, lug-type rubber or synthetic soles, with firm counter and box toe.

woven shoe. A shoe whose upper consists of strips of leather, straw or other material woven in a pattern.

woven vamp. See *vamp*.

wrap. 1) To apply a piece of material over a shoe component as a covering for a heel or platform. See also *heel cover* and *mudguard*. 2) A retail trade term for an easily-sold customer or an easily-made sale.

wrap-up. See *wrap*.

wrestler heel. See *heel*.

wrinkle. 1) An indelible mark, crease, or furrow in the grain surface of a hide, skin, or leather. 2) An unnatural crease in a shoe such as excessive creas-ing across the vamp, or tension pull at the inner arch or waist of the shoe.

write paper. The process of writing a purchase order by a buyer or sales representative on a size order sheet.

write sizes. See write *paper*.

WW. A shoe size marking loosely designating an extra-wide shoe, roughly E to EEE in men's, E to EE in women's.

X

XN. A size marking and loose designation for an extra-narrow shoe size; roughly A for men, AA or AAA for women.

x-ray shoe fitting. An X-ray apparatus formerly used in shoe stores between the 1930s and 1950s. With the customer standing and shod feet inserted under the box-like equipment, the salesperson could look down through a fluroscopic viewing mirror and see the skeleton outline of the foot inside the shoe, and hence the actual inside-shoe fit. The device was outlawed in the 1950s by the Federal Trade Commission because of potential danger to customer and salesperson from exposure to X rays.

XW. A size marking loosely designating and extra-wide shoe size; approximately E to EEE in men's, E to EE in women's.

Y

yield. 1) Referring to leather, the amount of leather in pounces or square feet obtained from 100 pounds of raw stock weighed in at the time of purchase. 2) The proportion of material obtained in cutting an upper or sole pattern related to the waste generated.

youths' shoe. A shoe industry classification referring to sizes 1 to 3 (extremes 11 to 3) for younger boys.

Y-vamp. See *vamp*.

Z

zancae. An ornamented red leather boot worn by Roman emperors, and forbidden to be worn by persons of lesser rank.

zapatillas. A thin-sole, canvas-upper shoe popular with women in Argentina and other South American countries, worn as a casual shoe.

zapatos. A slipper-type shoe worn by Mexican women.

zig-zag seam. See *seam*.

zipper. A metal or plastic slide fastener. The term was coined in 1923 by B. F. Goodrich Co. for its rubber overshoe slide fastener. Goodrich failed to trademark the name and it became generic. The zipper itself was invented and patented in 1893 and went through a series of identifying names such as universal fastener, clasp locker or unlocker, C-Curity (the first zipper for men's trouser flies), and the hookless fastener. It was originally designed for footwear use, and today is still used on some footwear.

zone therapy. See *reflexology*.

zori (or zo-ri). A sandal native to Japan. It can be made of wood, straw or felt. For men, the zori has a low heel, but it is heelless for women. It is usually worn with a "tabi" or white cotton, mitten-like sock.

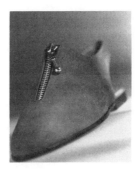

Zipper shoe.

APPENDIX I

Origin of Footwear-Related Words

Most footwear terms—words like pump, boot, mule, slipper, last, even shoe—are usually taken for granted. But the majority of them came into the language in strange and intriguing ways, eventually evolving into their current meanings. Here is a sampling of the etymology of some of our common footwear-related words.

bal. Bal is short for Balmoral Castle in Scotland, a favored retreat of Prince Albert and Queen Victoria. While there in 1840, a new shoe pattern, a variation of the oxford, was designed for him by J. Sparkes Hall, bootmaker to Queen Victoria. It was a shoe with a closed seam at the throatline or bottom of the lace row, and a much trimmer version of the prevailing oxford style. When he returned to London wearing it, it caught the eye of the gentlemen of the court. Soon the popular "balmoral" style became the "bal" and has remained a men's classic ever since.

blucher. This pattern was designed by Prussian Field Marshall Gebhardt Leberech von Blucher in 1810, who decreed the style for the shoes and boots of his officers. The tongue of the shoe is an extension of the vamp, rather than being a separate part stitched to the vamp. The two front ends of the quarter were open flaps, drawn together by lacing. The result was a dressy but more comfortable shoe. Like the bal, the blucher has become a perennial classic, especially in men's shoes.

bobby sox. The term emerged in the early 1920s when the new, emancipated breed of young women cut or "bobbed" their hair short. They also "bobbed" their hose by rolling them down to just below the knee, a daring innovation made visible by the scandalous short skirts of the Flapper Age. These were first called "bobby hose," which latter evolved into "bobby sox" when their height was reduced to just above the ankle. In the 1950s, these became widely popular when worn with saddle oxfords.

boot. The knee-high boot with wide-flared top was long popular with the cavalier men of France. The French had called the "butt" for water bucket, which they resembled. When the Normans crossed the English Channel into Britain in 1066, the soldiers wore such boots. The British eventually adopted the style, the word evolving to "boute" and finally "boot." The boot style itself dates back to

Mongolian horsemen around 600 B.C.E., worn to protect the legs while in the saddle.

brogue. The wing-tip brogue with perforated toe and pinked edges has became a classic men's style. It was originally a clog-like shoe with wooden bottom and crudely tanned leather upper, worn by Scottish peasants and shepherds as far back as 1200. It was later adopted by Irish farmers and laborers who changed the name to "brogan" and also altered the construction, using a heavy, nailed leather sole and coarsely tanned upper leather, fastened to the foot with lacings or buckles. It could be either a shoe or boot. A few centuries later in about 1800, London shoemakers redesigned it to give the shoe a dressier look for wear by gentlemen. Gradually special touches were added, such as the wing tip, perforations and pinking, plus the choice of bal or blucher patterns.

casual. The term "casual shoe" is an offshoot of Parisian designer Coco Chanel's revolutionary casual clothing first introduced in 1934. However, America and Europe weren't quite ready for it because most people lived in cities and there was little time or mood for "casual living." After World War II and the mass exodus to the suburbs, the lifestyle concept of casual living became a reality. So did casual clothing and footwear. Casual shoes (earlier known as "playshoes") became a major footwear category to supplement the traditional dress shoes. Casual footwear has since become a major and solidly established classification.

chukka boot. The word "chukka" refers to one of the time periods into which the game of polo is divided. It is derived from India where the British adopted the game of polo as a sport. The original chukka boot, preferred by the Indians, is actually a two-eyelet demi-boot. While the British preferred the jodhpur boot for polo, it is the original chukka style that has become a men's classic in both America and Europe.

clog. The word is from the Old English "clogge," meaning a lump of wood. Its origin as a shoe is lost in antiquity. The clog has long been a universal kind of shoe for peasants, farmers, laborers. In the 16th century it was used by the gentry as a kind of overshoe to protect the shoes from wet and muddy ground. It differs from the sabot in that it has a coarse leather upper or wide upper straps nailed to the thick wooden soles with studs at the sides. It made its entry as a "fashion" shoe in America in the late 1930s when dressy clogs hand-crafted by Oscar Auested became popular with University of Oregon coeds, and the style spread to other campuses. From time to time clog fashions enjoy periods of fashion popularity.

cordovan. Genuine shell cordovan is made from an oval-shape, ligament-like tissue under the butt hide of a horse (also zebra and mule). It is the only leather not made from a hide or skin. It is used mostly for expensive men's shoes, and only a very limited supply is available. The key word is "shell," which distinguishes the genuine from imitation cordovan which is made from cowhide. Genuine cordovan has a polished burgundy color, and the color is as often associated with cordovan as the leather itself. The name is derived from Cordova, Spain, which in the 12th and 13th centuries produced the world's finest leathers and shoe craftsmen, most of whom were Moorish artisans. From Cordova also comes our word "cordwainer," a fine craftsman.

galosh (or galoshes). Today we think of galoshes as rubber overshoes worn in inclement weather. But originally the galosh was a kind of clog with wooden sole whose bottom edge was rimmed with short spikes or sharp metal ridges to prevent slipping on ice or snow and also to protect the shoe resting on it. It was known by any of various names such as goloshes, galoe-shoes, gallage, galocke, gallosh, galoches. In modern times galoshes enjoyed their peak popularity in the 1920s and 1930s, when it was a rubber overshoe worn unbuckled by flappers of the day.

ghillie. This is a low-cut, laced sport shoe without a tongue, the corded lacings fringed at the ends, passing through loops crossing over the instep and usually wound around the ankle. It is of Scottish origin dating back to the 15th century. Its name is derived from "gillie," a boy attendant of the gentry while hunting, who wore such shoes in cruder form. The word "gillie" in Scottish means "gamekeeper." The Prince of Wales (later the Duke of Windsor) launched the style into general popularity when he wore a pair of ghillies during his visit to America in the 1920s.

jodhpur. In India, this was the name for the riding breeches worn by polo players. The native players of India used the shorter chukka boot. But the British preferred the higher, dressier boot to wear with their jodhpurs, and they dubbed it a jodhpur boot.

kangaroo. This exotic leather is highly desirable for comfort and athletic shoes, and even some quality dress shoes. But why do we call it "kangaroo"? In 1770, when Captain Cook discovered Australia and went ashore, he and his men saw a strange pouch-bellied animal jumping about with prodigious leaps. Cook asked the local chieftan, "What is that?" The chieftan, not understanding English replied, "kangaroo?" which in his native tongue meant "What did you say?" Cook thought he had been given the name of the animal—and kangaroo it has been ever since.

last. The last is the foot-like form over which the shoe is made, and is almost as old as shoemaking itself. The word is from the old Anglo-Saxon "laest," meaning a footprint—or, in broader context, a foot mold.

moccasin. This term is from the American Indian word "mok-sin," meaning a foot covering. The moccasin is the oldest known form of footwear, dating back at least 12,000 years. It probably originated with the Mongols who crossed the Bering Strait to what is now Alaska, then moved south. The moccasin had always been a simple piece of crudely tanned leather wrapped around the foot and held on with rawhide thongs. When it was later adopted by the American Indians it underwent much refinement. The Indians made their moccasins of soft deerskin. They also introduced the moccasin plug with its unique puckered edges on the vamp. Then they ornately decorated their moccasins with slashed fringes and colored beads. The beads were more than ornamentations. Their colors and arrangement designated one's tribal status—hunter, warrior, chieftan, medicine man, etc. Any violation of these status symbols was considered a serious infringement.

mule. The mule style was originally a heelless, backless slipper worn indoors. The word is from the ancient Sumerian "mulu," meaning an indoor shoe. The Egyptians adopted it and placed a heel under it, allowing it to be worn outdoors as a semi-dress shoe. Around the 17th century the French adopted it, calling it a "mulette," with higher heel and ornately embroidered fabric uppers, though still backless, to make it a sexy fashion shoe for both men and women.

oxford. Up until the early 17th century most shoes used straps or buckles as fasteners. In fact, Birmingham, England, was the world center of shoe buckles, employing a then huge labor force of 20,000 making shoe buckles exclusively. In 1640, a radical new style, low black shoes with laced fronts, was mass-adopted by the students of Oxford University. The style spread rapidly and the Birmingham shoe buckle industry was devastated, despite pleas to the king to prohibit the new laced shoes. Late in the century Thomas Jefferson was one of the first Americans to wear oxfords. He was chided by his peers for succumbing to "the foppish French fashion."

While rawhide cords and ribbons had been used as shoe fasteners many centuries earlier, shoe lacings and the oxford style as we know it today did not appear until the middle 17th century. Shoe lacings were later to become a small industry. In the latter part of the century an Englishman, Harvey Kennedy, made a fortune of $2.5 million (enormous in those days) after he patented and introduced the aglet, the metal tip at the end of the lacing to make it easier to lace the shoe. In the same century John Bunyan, when he was in prison for his controversial views (he was the author of *Pilgrim's Progress*), kept his family from starving by hand-fixing metal tips to shoe laces.

patent leather. Why do we call it "patent" leather? Actually, it isn't a kind of leather but a kind of special glossy finish that can be applied to almost any leather. Enamel coating of leather was a process developed in Europe about 150 years ago (though it had been used by the Chinese 2,000 years earlier on other materials). Bismarck quickly adopted it for his elite troops, providing them with shiny boots and helmets. The carriage horses of the rich were adorned with patent leather blinders and harness. But it was the British who gave it its name. They saw the glossy finish as something "patent"—meaning obvious, mirrored, as we refer to something being "patently clear." And so it has remained.

pump. The pump style has been with us for several centuries—a simple, sleek slip-on shoe with a heel of various heights and shapes. The pump style itself has been subject to thousands of fashion variations and treatments. The pump received great impetus with the invention of elasticized goring in 1837 by J. Sparkes Hall, bootmaker to Queen Victoria. The new hug fit of the pump without benefit of fastenings delighted the queen and the pump rose rapidly in popularity.

Why do we call it a "pump," and how did the style itself originate? Perhaps the most acceptable version is that the name was derived from the carriage footmen of England, who were called "pumps" (they pumped the carriage brakes with their feet). They wore a standard uniform shoe, a plain, simple slip-on. When the British gentry adopted the style, though in much more elaborate form, they retained the word "pump." In French, the word "pompe" means an ornament, though there seems to be no link with the pump shoe style. Also, there is the German "pumpsteifel" and "pumphosen"—boots and stockings as narrow as water pumps or hoses, though the relation to the pump seems remote. In 1921, a number of prominent American women's shoe manufacturers tried to change the name "pump" to something more exotic, suggesting "cameos" and "pynsons," neither of which made any lasting impression.

retailer. Why do we call a shoe merchant a "retailer"? The word is from the French "tailleur," meaning to cut into pieces. For example, a fabric store cuts a bolt of cloth to sell in smaller pieces; a tailor sews small pieces into a whole garment for resale. They deal in small segments of a whole or large lot. Thus the retailer buys in multiple lots from the whole or large lot from the wholesaler, then resells in small amounts of "pieces" to the consumer. Retailer has also been linked to "detail," a small part of the whole, and "tally," keeping score of the small parts of the whole or eventual total.

saddle oxford. This term dates back to 1906 when the style was first introduced by A. G. Spaulding as a "gym" shoe. He added a wide overlay band of leather around the sides of the upper's waist and instep for extra support for the arch and called it a "saddle." The saddle oxford eventually evolved into a popular classic as a casual or sport shoe for men and women. Thus, what started out as a kind of orthopedic shoe became an established fashion.

sandal. Next to the moccasin the sandal is the oldest known style of footwear, dating back perhaps 10,000 years. The root word for sandal is the Latin *sanis*, meaning a board. The "board" was a slab of leather sole held onto the foot with thongs. The ancient Persian word is "sandalon," and the Greek word "sandalion."

shoe. In English this term dates back many centuries, beginning with the Anglo-Saxon "sceo," meaning a foot covering, and evolving into "schewis," then "shooys," and finally "shoe." The German "schuh" has the same origin. Through the centuries the word "shoe" has evolved with at least 17 different spellings and some 36 variations of the plural.

slipper. This term has an obvious origin—a loose-fitting, heelless indoor shoe that "slips" easily onto the foot. Over the past century it was redesigned as a formal shoe worn at balls and ceremonial affairs by men and women alike, but essentially it remained an indoor type of footwear. Legend has it that the slipper was first used in China many centuries ago, worn indoors with padded soles so as not to disturb the silkworms bred in many homes. The same padded-sole, cloth-upper "slipper" is worn today in China as both and indoor and outdoor shoe by hundreds of millions of Chinese and other Orientals (in Korea, Vietnam, Thailand, etc.). Almost every nation has its own form of slipper.

sneaker. The first patent for attaching rubber soles to shoe uppers was granted to Wait Webster in 1832. The first rubber-soled footwear manufactured in the United States was produced in 1868 by the Candee Rubber Co. of New Haven, Connecticut, using what was then the new vulcanizing process to attach rubber soles to fabric (canvas) uppers. This footwear was originally called "croquet sandals," used by the rich to play croquet on their lawns. The new footwear quickly trickled down to the common folk. By 1873 it had acquired the name "sneakers," a name probably given by city children because the rubber soles allowed them to "sneak up" on each other. At the end of the century they were called "gym shoes," and in the early 1920s became known as "tennis shoes."

sole. The word is a spinoff from the Latin "solea" or shoe bottom, which in turn derives from "solum," meaning the soil or ground contacted by the solea. When the Romans invaded Britain, the word "solum" became "soil" and "solea" became "sole."

suede. Suede is not a kind of leather but a napped finish that can be applied to almost any leather by buffing. The buffing process was first developed in Sweden over a century ago and the unique leather quickly became popular in Europe. In France the leather had no identifying name, so the French called it "Swede" leather, which came out sounding like "suede." And so it has remained ever since.

tongue. The tongue of the shoe was first introduced by the ancient Romans who designed it to protect the instep from the pressure of the straps and thongs of their sandals and also to protect against injury in battle. They called it a "lingula," Latin for tongue, because it resembled the tongue of the mouth. It wasn't until centuries later that it was adopted by the Germans who called it "zunge," their word for tongue. In English, zunge evolved into "tongue."

wholesaler. This stems from two English words, "whole" and "sale," meaning the sale of goods or merchandise in large or "whole" (rather than small) amounts or lots. Thus the wholesaler (or manufacturer) is one who sells "whole" lots to retailers, who in turn resells them in small amounts (one or two pairs) to consumers. See also *retailer*.

APPENDIX II

English Words with Foot or Shoe Origins

With passing generations many words take on new spellings and sometimes altered meanings. A word born in one genre can gradually slip over into another. This has happened with some of our common words that began as foot and shoe words and have become woven into the English language with meanings quite different from the original. Here are examples:

blackguard. A scoundrel or villain, vulgar and abusive. The term originated in England about 1665 and was applied to lowly young men who worked in the scullery of inns and manors. Among their tasks was the blacking of boots. Many of these young men were lazy, unreliable, fond of drink, and frequently made self-serving advances and promises to the young, gullible scullery maids. The term "blackguard" (guardian of the shoe blacking closet and supplies) came to be associated with an untrustworthy, lying, cheating person.

bluestocking. Today this term refers to an elitist, learned woman of high social heritage, a kind of aristocratic snob. The term derives from 18th-century London when a group of upper-crust women formed an exclusive club to set themselves apart from other women who were less mannered or educated, or who succumbed to contemporary fashions. The elitist group dressed soberly and wore dark blue stockings to distinguish them from others.

boot. Today we assign this name to a young navy or marine recruit, or to a training area (boot camp). Why boot? Because it is closest to the ground or dirt. Thus a "boot" is the lowest order in any heirarchy. The term dates back to medieval England and to the lowly servants at inns who cleaned the boots of guests and travelers. They were known as "boots" (and also, later, as "blackguards"). Even today, in England's private clubs the youngest and newest members are known as "boots" who must serve a period of lowly apprenticeship status before rising to full acceptance. Our own military "boot camps" operate on the same principle.

bootlegger. One who makes, transports, or sells illegal or smuggled merchandise. In the early days of the American merchant navy, sailors wore high, flared-top boots. On returning from overseas trips, when they came ashore they smuggled in illicit goods tucked inside their ample boot legs. The practice came to be known as bootlegging. The term was revived during the Prohibition Era (1919–1933) and referred almost exclusively to smuggling hard liquor, or to domestic making and selling of it.

bootlicker. One who uses a fawning, servile manner to gain favor with someone else. The term originally applied to menial servants in manors and inns of 16th- and 17th-century England, whose job it was to keep the boots of masters and guests polished. Some servants over-extended their boot-polishing efforts to gain a word of praise and perhaps a small tip. They became known by their fellow bootmen as "bootlickers," referring to a groveling dog that licks its master's boots.

buck. Slang for a dollar. In American pioneer days deerskins were called bucks and had monetary value or barter worth among both the American settlers and Indians. Deerskins (or buckskins) ranged from 50 cents to several dollars, depending on size and condition. Thus the deerskin or buckskin became a form of currency called a "buck."

bunion. This, of course, is a sore and inflamed swelling of the big toe joint. It's from the French "buige," which means turnip, so that a foot bunion was a jocular term. However, a minority thinks the word is derived from the old Middle English word "boni," meaning a swelling or boil.

clodhopper. One of the meanings of "clod" is a dull, stupid fellow, a dolt. From this came our word "clodhopper" for a coarse, heavy shoe worn by plowmen with an awkward, rustic gait. The clodhopper made a clompy, thudding sound as if worn by an awkward, clumsy person. The shoe and the person became synonymous.

cop. A colloquialism for a police officer. The term came into our language around the turn of the century when policemen walked their beats wearing

169

boots with copper toe tips both as an offensive "weapon" and as protection for the toes of their boots. "Cop" became identified with copper toes.

flapper. The term originated in the early 1920s and referred to young, emancipated women breaking from the mold of convention with knee-high skirts, "bobbed" hair and rolled stockings. As part of this defiance of social convention they wore their overshoes unbuckled so that the buckles flapped loudly in walking. So was born the name "flapper."

foot. A measure of 12 inches. The reference to a measurement stems from the foot itself. King Edward II in the 14th century was the first to establish an "official" system of modern measurements. The length of an average man's foot was decreed to be 12 inches—which would have been a very large foot for foot sizes of that day. Nevertheless, that's how the designation for the measurement term "foot" came about. Our word "foot" is from the Old English "fot."

footloose and fancy free. It means a carefree attitude —free to go wherever one wants and do whatever one wishes. The expression is derived from the feudal Middle Ages when a large share of the people were serfs and not free to roam beyond the boundaries of the feudal lord's estate. The feudal lord acquired ownership of the serf with a simple legal gesture of placing his foot on that of the serf's, signifying that he had no rights of mobility or freedom. But the lord could also grant freedom by a reverse action—touching the serf's foot lightly and quickly removing it. This officially made the serf "foot loose and fancy free."

gams. Today it refers to a woman's legs ("she's got a great pair of gams"). This term is derived from the French word *gambe* for an animal's leg. From this also came old English words like gamashoes, gambages, gambadoes, gamashes, etc.—all meaning a tight-fitting, knee-high boot popular with upper-class women of the 16th and 17th centuries.

grieving widow. We apply this word to a saddened woman mourning the recent death of her husband. But the original meant something else. From ancient Etruscan times to the 18th century, soldiers wore protective leather or cloth leggings called "greaves." When soldiers died in battle, their widows back home then earned their living cutting and sewing greaves for other soldiers. They became known as "greaving widows," which evolved into "grieving widows."

gumshoe. Slang for a detective. In the latter part of the 19th century, many policemen and detectives wore rubber-sole shoes which were more comfortable for their weary feet. Their silent, soft-treading steps with gum-rubber shoe soles won them the label of "gumshoe," a term still occasionally used today.

heel. A despicable, unscrupulous person, a cad. This came into use in America in 1928. It refers, of course, to the heel of the shoe, the lowest part and associated with dirt and grime.

lacing. A thrashing, beating or lashing of a person with some kind of cord or strap. When the shoe lacing became popular with the introduction of the new oxford shoe style about 350 years ago, metal tips were attached to the ends. Imaginative jailers soon had very long rawhide lacings made. By bunching such laces together and using them as a lashing whip, the metal tips cut painfully into the flesh. Thus the early "lacings" were instruments of punishment and torture, as well as shoe fastenings.

oedema (or edema). The medical term for swelling. It is derived from Oedipus of Greek legend, a name given to him because he had swollen feet. The word is from the Greek "oidein," to swell, and "pous" for foot.

ped words. "Ped" is Latin for foot. Many English words are derived from this. Examples: pedal, peddle, peddler, pedastal, pedestrian, pedicure, pedometer, centipede, impede, impediment, etc. All involve some connection with the foot.

pod words. "Pod" and "pous" are Greek words for foot. From this are derived words like podiatry, podium, tripod, arthropod.

pecuniary. This is associated with money or things monetary. In ancient times, before minted currency, barter was the common manner of trade. For example, one traded an ox for silk or corn. But it became too cumbersome to bring along one's cattle for a trade. So a small piece of cowhide leather with a carved figure of an ox (*pecus* in Latin) served as currency. From the term "pecus" (ox or oxhide) came our word "pecuniary."

sabotage. Intentional and malicious destruction of property. We get this word from "sabot," the traditional wooden shoe worn by peasants and laborers in centuries past and even today. During the 19th century, Belgian and French textile mill workers protested against the new machinery that threatened their jobs. So they tossed their sabots into the machines to wreck them. Hence our word "sabotage." This idea, however, wasn't new. In earlier times, French peasants, protesting against their oppressively low wages, trampled the crops of the landlords with their sabots—another act of sabotage.

scruple. A feeling of doubt or uneasiness, a pricking of conscience. This is derived from the Latin "scrupulous," meaning a small stone or pebble. When Roman soldiers were on their long marches, sometimes small pebbles would become lodged inside their sandals, causing discomfort or unease. Our word "scruple" comes from this same awareness of something bothersome.

slipshod. Careless or slovenly in appearance or workmanship. This word dates back to the 15th century when shoes were worn with protective coverings called "slipshoes," worn in wet weather or on muddy ground. Some people began wearing the covers as loose slippers indoors and out. They were called "slipshod," meaning slovenly shod, hence untidy or shoddy.

spat. Referring to a quarrel or petty argument. This is taken from "spatterdash," a cloth knee-high or ankle-high covering used in the 19th century to protect shoes against splashings of water or mud. Thus a "spat" came to be known as an exchange of mild mud-slinging between two persons, usually spouses or lovers.

stogie. A long, coarse, strong, cheap cigar. In America, in the early 1800s, Southern plantation owners sent north to have cheap, coarse boots and shoes made for their slaves and servants. Foot lengths were measured by a broken length of stick. The sticks were bundled and shipped to a shoe factory up north where the boots and shoes were made to "stick length." Both the rough sticks and the sturdy boots were called "stogas." Later, the cigars came to be known as "stogies" because they resembled the rough sticks.

Uppity. Inclined to be haughty, snobbish, arrogant. This term came into the English language in the 17th century when an extremely high (8 to 26 inches) platform shoe called the "chopine" was popular with the aristocratic ladies. This style of shoe enabled them to "look down" on folks of lesser status, and for the latter to label the chopine wearers as "uppity."

upstart. A social imposter, or a person who has recently come into wealth or power and flaunts it with audacious behavior; a social climber. In 1509, a new kind of footwear called "startups" or "sturtops" became popular with the feudal aristocracy of Britain. It consisted of a legging that "started up" from the shoe. When some of the common folk adopted the fashion they were labeled "upstarts" for trying to emulate their social superiors.

well-heeled. Wealthy or well off or of upper social caste. When high heels were first introduced in the 16th century, they were eagerly adopted by the rich and the aristocrats. Later, some of the more socially ambitious commoners began to wear such heels. The aristocrats were indignant about what they considered an audacious invasion of their exclusive realm. So they had a law passed prohibiting anyone below certain ranks from wearing such heels. Hence our expression "well-heeled," signifying a person of wealth or high social status.

171